CAMBRIDGE NATIONAL LEVEL 1 / LEVEL

IT

Student Book

David Atkinson-Beaumont,
Alan Jarvis & Sarah Matthews

CAMBRIDGE
UNIVERSITY PRESS

University Printing House, Cambridge CB2 8BS, United Kingdom

One Liberty Plaza, 20th Floor, New York, NY 10006, USA

477 Williamstown Road, Port Melbourne, VIC 3207, Australia

314–321, 3rd Floor, Plot 3, Splendor Forum, Jasola District Centre, New Delhi – 110025, India

103 Penang Road, #05–06/07, Visioncrest Commercial, Singapore 23846

Cambridge University Press is part of the University of Cambridge.

It furthers the University's mission by disseminating knowledge in the pursuit of education, learning and research at the highest international levels of excellence.

www.cambridge.org
Information on this title: www.cambridge.org/9781009118064

© Cambridge University Press 2022

First published 2022

20 19 18 17 16 15 14 13 12 11 10 9 8 7 6 5 4 3 2 1

Printed in Italy by L.E.G.O. S.p.A.

A catalogue record for this publication is available from the British Library

ISBN 978-1-00911806-4 Paperback with Digital Access (2 Years)
ISBN 978-1-00911305-2 Digital Student Book (2 Years)
ISBN 978-1-00911304-5 1 Year site license

Additional resources for this publication at www.cambridge.org/9781009118064

Contents

Acknowledgements

The authors and publishers acknowledge the following sources of copyright material and are grateful for the permissions granted. While every effort has been made, it has not always been possible to identify the sources of all the material used, or to trace all copyright holders. If any omissions are brought to our notice, we will be happy to include the appropriate acknowledgements on reprinting.

Thanks to the following for permission to reproduce images:

Cover Maxiphoto/GI; Inside R050 Patrik Giardino/GI; Justin Paget/GI; chrisdorney/GI; Sergei Fadeichev/GI; Westend61/GI; SOPA Images/GI; PhonlamaiPhoto/GI; aydinmutlu/GI; Helen Camacaro/GI; James D. Morgan/GI; Jacobs Stock Photography Ltd/GI; SpiffyJ/GI; Jetta Productions Inc/GI; Monty Rakusen/GI; d3sign/GI; sestovic/GI; Tetra Images/GI; Peter Dazeley/GI; Dimitri Otis/GI; Catherine Falls Commercial/GI; Luis Alvarez/GI; Jasmin Merdan/GI; dowell/GI; NicoElNino/GI; Witthaya Prasongsin/GI; Figure 1.33 The Bluetooth® word mark and logos are registered trademarks owned by Bluetooth SIG, Inc. and any use of such marks by Cambridge University Press & Assessment is under license. Other trademarks and trade names are those of their respective owners; Luis Alvarez/GI; adamkaz/GI; Oscar Wong/GI; Cultura RM Exclusive/Leon Sosra/GI; R060 Weedezign/GI; RichVintage/GI; krisanapong detraphiphat/GI; SOPA Images/GI; Peter Cade/GI; andresr/GI; makaule/GI; Morsa Images/GI; Yuichiro Chino/GI; Marnie Burkhart/GI; SetsukoN/GI; Jose Luis Pelaez Inc/GI; R070 Coneyl Jay/GI; Bernhard Lang/GI; Georgijevic/GI; Coneyl Jay/GI; Oscar Wong/GI; Archive Farms/GI; Prostock-Studio/GI; evrim ertik/GI; Oscar Wong/GI; Pascal Deloche/Godong/GI; Coneyl Jay/GI; Monty Rakusen/GI; Qi Yang/GI; Coneyl Jay/GI; gorodenkoff/GI; JEAN-CHRISTOPHE VERHAEGEN/GI; Smith Collection/Gado/GI; Prasit photo/GI; David Malan/GI; porcorex/GI; Dean Mitchell/GI; Emma McIntyre/GI; Kyodo News/GI Coneyl Jay/GI; Figure 3.30 Image by David Atkinson-Beaumont featuring original AR creations by Oscar Whittle; gremlin/GI, Screenshots created using software by ARLOOPA

GI = Getty Images

About your IT Cambridge National course and qualification

The IT industry is fast-moving and varied: it includes careers within specialist technology and telecommunications organisations alongside IT roles in areas such as finance, health, retail and media. You might want to work in applications or game development, data analysis, or engineering, for example. Whatever you choose, you will benefit from having a wide range of IT technical, data and creative skills.

During your course, you will learn about how IT is used in an increasingly digital world (including the Internet of Everything), data manipulation and Augmented Reality. You'll have a chance to develop skills relevant for a range of roles while designing, creating, testing and reviewing IT solutions and products.

How you will be assessed

You have to complete three units.

Mandatory units:

- R050: IT in the digital world. You will take a written exam for this unit. The exam lasts for 1 hour 30 minutes, and is worth 70 marks. The exam is set and marked by OCR.

- R060: Data manipulation using spreadsheets. You will be given an assignment to complete for this unit, which is worth 60 marks. This set assignment contains three to five practical tasks.

- R070: Using Augmented Reality to present information. You will be given an assignment to complete for this unit, which is worth 60 marks. This set assignment contains three to five practical tasks.

How to use this book

Throughout this book, you will notice lots of different features that will help your learning. These are explained below.

These features at the start of each unit give you guidance on the topic area, what you will learn and how you will be assessed.

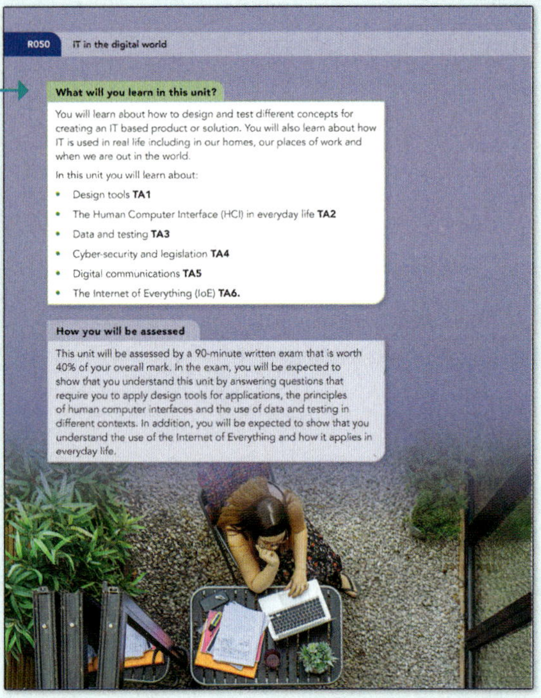

R050 IT in the digital world

What will you learn in this unit?

You will learn about how to design and test different concepts for creating an IT based product or solution. You will also learn about how IT is used in real life including in our homes, our places of work and when we are out in the world.

In this unit you will learn about:

* Design tools **TA1**
* The Human Computer Interface (HCI) in everyday life **TA2**
* Data and testing **TA3**
* Cyber-security and legislation **TA4**
* Digital communications **TA5**
* The Internet of Everything (IoE) **TA6**.

How you will be assessed

This unit will be assessed by a 90-minute written exam that is worth 40% of your overall mark. In the exam, you will be expected to show that you understand this unit by answering questions that require you to apply design tools for applications, the principles of human computer interfaces and the use of data and testing in different contexts. In addition, you will be expected to show that you understand the use of the Internet of Everything and how it applies in everyday life.

Thought-provoking questions at the start of units and topics will get you thinking about the subject.

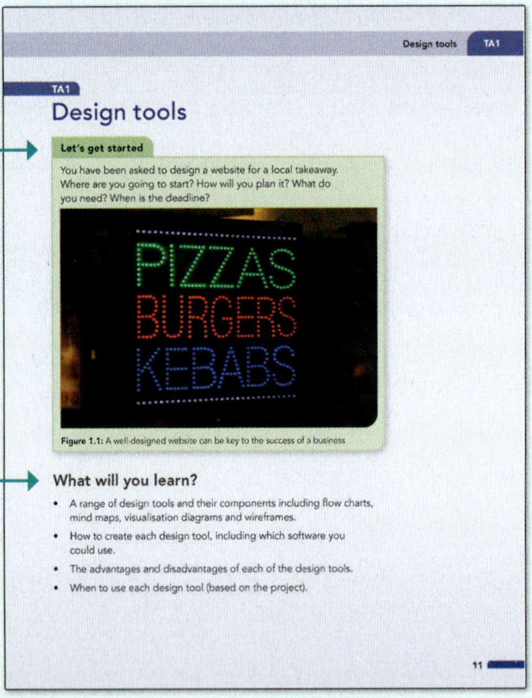

Design tools   TA1

TA1

Design tools

Let's get started

You have been asked to design a website for a local takeaway. Where are you going to start? How will you plan it? What do you need? When is the deadline?

Figure 1.1: A well-designed website can be key to the success of a business

What will you learn?

* A range of design tools and their components including flow charts, mind maps, visualisation diagrams and wireframes.
* How to create each design tool, including which software you could use.
* The advantages and disadvantages of each of the design tools.
* When to use each design tool (based on the project).

11

This section gives you information about what content is covered in the topic.

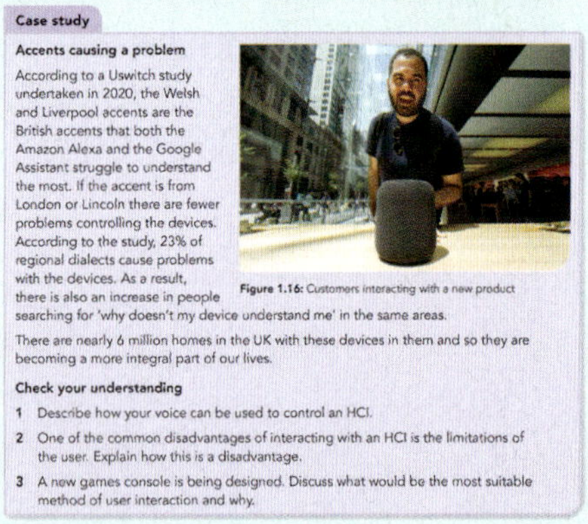

Case study

Accents causing a problem

According to a Uswitch study undertaken in 2020, the Welsh and Liverpool accents are the British accents that both the Amazon Alexa and the Google Assistant struggle to understand the most. If the accent is from London or Lincoln there are fewer problems controlling the devices. According to the study, 23% of regional dialects cause problems with the devices. As a result, there is also an increase in people searching for 'why doesn't my device understand me' in the same areas.

Figure 1.16: Customers interacting with a new product

There are nearly 6 million homes in the UK with these devices in them and so they are becoming a more integral part of our lives.

Check your understanding

1 Describe how your voice can be used to control an HCI.

2 One of the common disadvantages of interacting with an HCI is the limitations of the user. Explain how this is a disadvantage.

3 A new games console is being designed. Discuss what would be the most suitable method of user interaction and why.

Case studies based on real-life situations put key concepts and practices into context. The accompanying questions check your understanding and challenge you to take your learning further.

Key words are highlighted in the text and explained fully in the glossary, often using examples, to ensure you fully understand key terminology.

Practical activities that you can do on your own give you the opportunity to practise important skills and techniques, and to prepare for your assessments.

Over to you! activities let you apply your knowledge, and think more deeply about your course.

Stretch activities and questions give you the opportunity to try more challenging questions and to extend your knowledge.

These question boxes give you regular opportunities to test your knowledge so that you feel ready for your exam or assessment.

Summary sections help you review your learning, to check you understand key concepts and can apply your learning. They also show you where to look back for more information if you need to read it again.

Support for you

Our resources in this series are designed to work together to help you with your Cambridge National course.

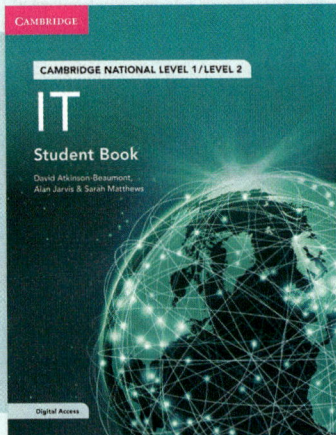

Your Student Book covers all the units and is where you will find the core information you need. This will help you with your knowledge and understanding of the subject. Information is arranged by Unit and then by Topic Area, so you can easily find what you're looking for. Questions and activities will help you to apply your knowledge and understanding and to develop practical skills. You can assess your progress with the Test your knowledge questions. When you've completed the quiz, check your answers in the digital edition.

Your Revision Guide and Workbook supports you with the externally assessed unit of your course. The exam preparation section offers advice to help you get ready for this assessment. The revision guide section provides concise outlines of the core knowledge you need. Each page focuses on a small piece of learning to help you break your revision up into manageable chunks. The workbook section brings your revision and learning together with practice questions. Digital quizzes help you to understand the language used in your assessment and to check your knowledge and understanding of key concepts. The Revision Guide and Workbook has not been through the OCR endorsement process.

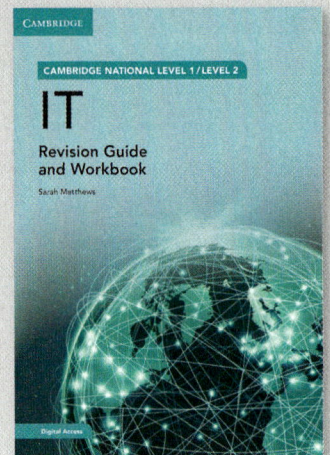

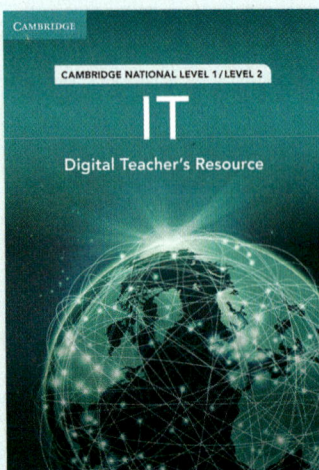

The Teacher's Resource covers all the mandatory and optional units and is a rich bank of ideas to help your teacher create engaging lessons to meet the needs of your class. It contains PowerPoint slides, worksheets and audio-visual material, in addition to activity and delivery ideas that can be personalised for your lessons. Digital quizzes help test understanding and unlock the language used in assessment.

IT in the digital world

Think about the device you last used. How do you think it was designed?
How did you interact with it? What data does it collect about you?
How is it secured? Does the device connect to other devices?

What will you learn in this unit?

You will learn about how to design and test different concepts for creating an IT based product or solution. You will also learn about how IT is used in real life including in our homes, our places of work and when we are out in the world.

In this unit you will learn about:

- Design tools **TA1**

- The Human Computer Interface (HCI) in everyday life **TA2**

- Data and testing **TA3**

- Cyber-security and legislation **TA4**

- Digital communications **TA5**

- The Internet of Everything (IoE) **TA6.**

How you will be assessed

This unit will be assessed by a 90-minute written exam that is worth 40% of your overall mark. In the exam, you will be expected to show that you understand this unit by answering questions that require you to apply design tools for applications, the principles of human computer interfaces and the use of data and testing in different contexts. In addition, you will be expected to show that you understand the use of the Internet of Everything and how it applies in everyday life.

Design tools

Let's get started

You have been asked to design a website for a local takeaway. Where are you going to start? How will you plan it? What do you need? When is the deadline?

Figure 1.1: A well-designed website can be key to the success of a business

What will you learn?

- A range of design tools and their components including flow charts, mind maps, visualisation diagrams and wireframes.

- How to create each design tool, including which software you could use.

- The advantages and disadvantages of each of the design tools.

- When to use each design tool (based on the project).

1.1 Types of design tools

When you start a project, it is a good idea to have a plan of what you are going to do. Design tools such as **flow charts**, **mind maps** and **visualisation diagrams** can help to plan your final product. They can also help you manage your time, gather resources and stay on schedule. You can use software or sketches.

Flow charts

A flow chart is a visual illustration which shows the order of something taking place. For example, you could have a flow chart which shows you the steps you need to take to create an animation.

Flow charts are good at showing a clear path of how you are going to achieve the intended product. They are very logical and help with organisation. They can help you see where there might be a problem.

However, they can end up looking complex and be difficult to understand if there are too many options. You need to completely redo the flow chart if you make a change. A person might not understand what the components mean and therefore can't understand the flow chart.

Table 1.1: Common parts of a flow chart

Flow chart component	What it does
Terminator	Shows the start and end of a flow chart.
Process	Shows that something (an action) is taking place.
Decision	Shows where you can make a choice within the flow chart.
Input/ Output	Allows you to add or remove **data** in the flow chart.
(arrow)	Arrows show the direction through the flow chart.

Creating a flow chart

You can use a variety of software to create a flow chart, ranging from dedicated flow chart software to using the tools built into standard **word processing** software.

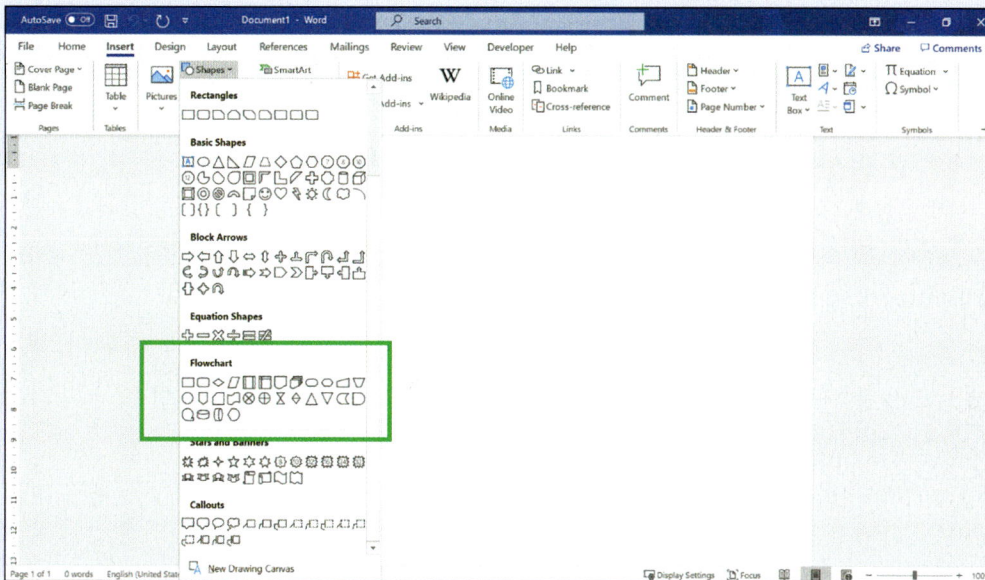

Figure 1.2: Microsoft Word includes shapes for flow charts

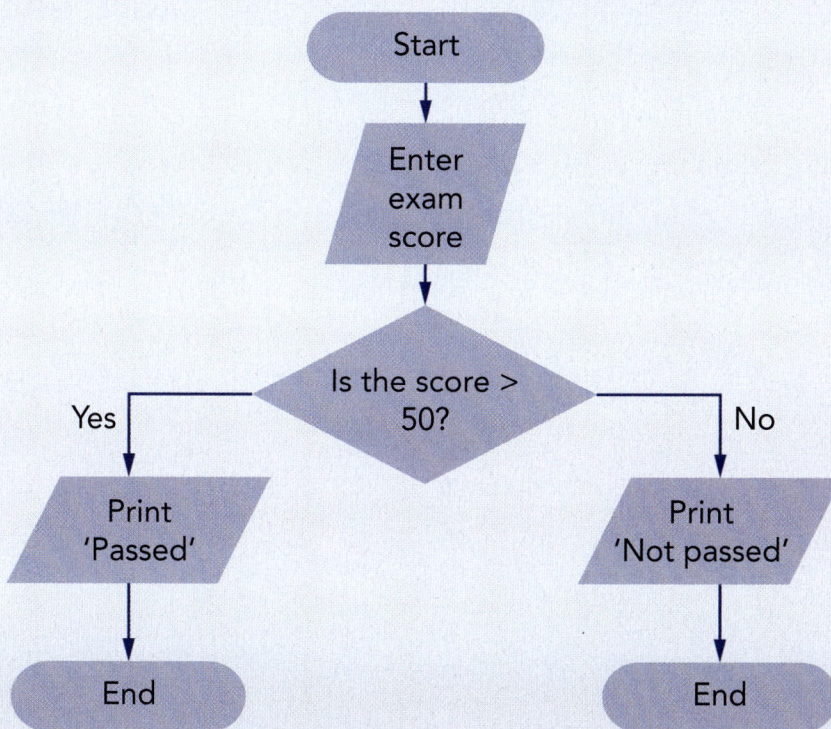

Figure 1.3: Can you relate the shapes in this flow chart back to those shown in the component parts? What happens if the score is 45?

Let's get digital!

Create a flow chart for the following problem:

A game shop wants to hire out games to its customers. Each game has an age classification, such as 12, 15 or 18. They need to check that customers are old enough to hire the game.

Mind maps

A mind map is a way of visually organising **information** that also shows the different relationships between the elements. There are three different kinds of mind maps that you need to know about.

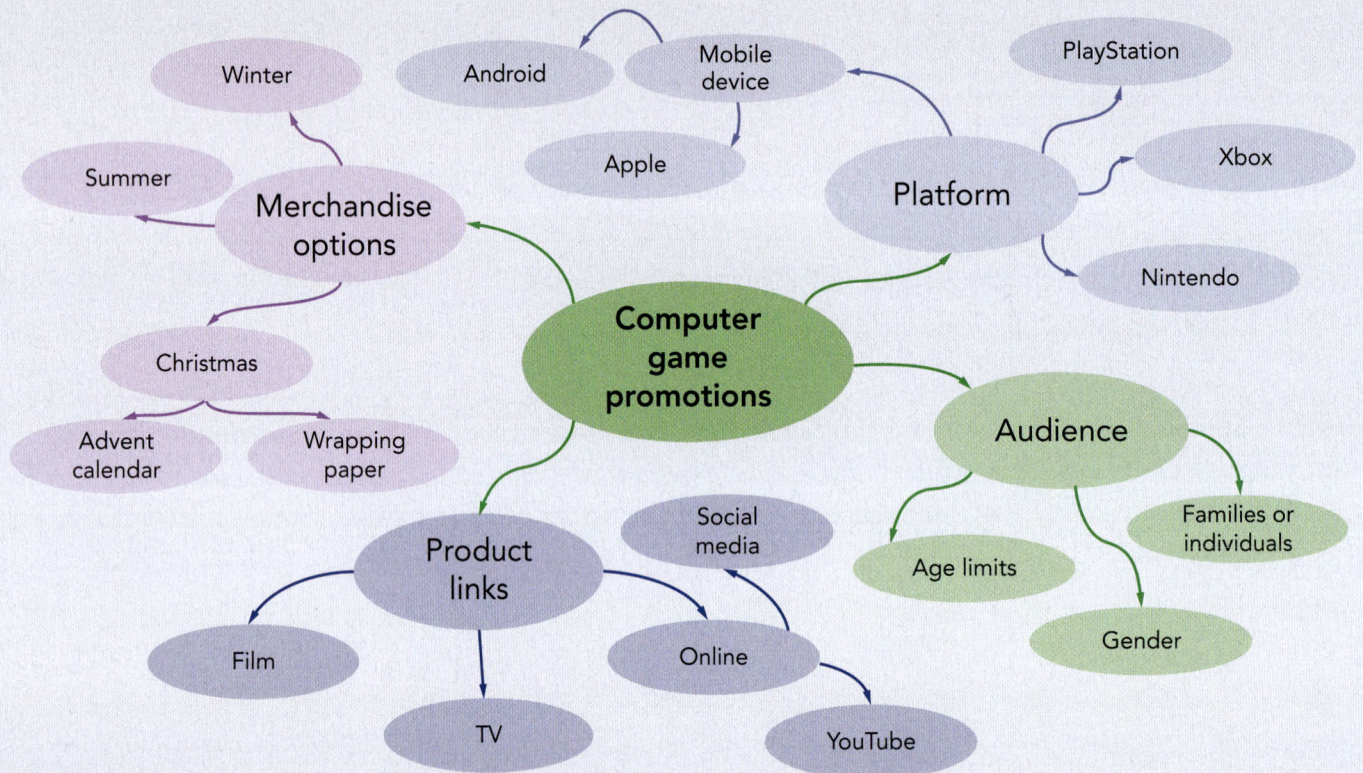

Figure 1.4: A library mind map, sometimes referred to as a reference map. These are used to organise information so that you can understand the topic better

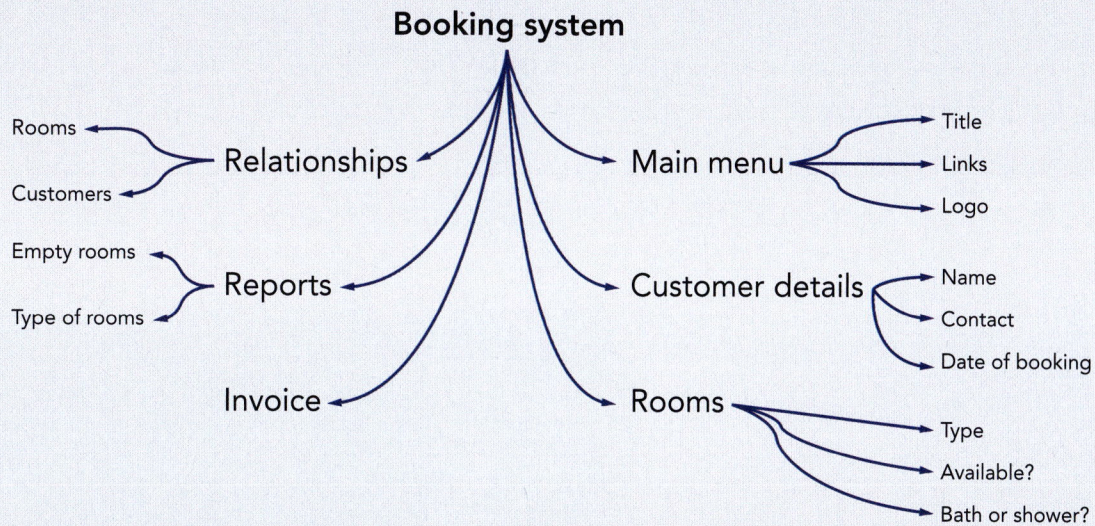

Figure 1.5: A tunnel timeline mind map, designed so that you can achieve a goal. It is used mainly for planning a project or solving a problem

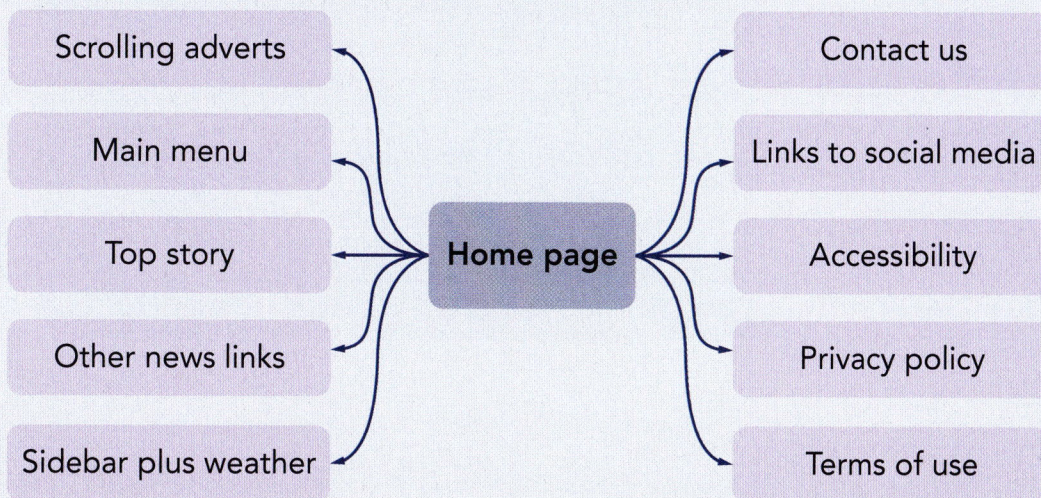

Figure 1.6: A presentation mind map, used to present an idea to a specific audience. The information is structured so the audience can understand it

When any mind map is created it has a central focus and all the related items are joined to it with connecting lines showing the relationship. A mind map ideally only uses single words rather than full sentences.

To create a mind map you would generally use specific mind map software, as it is easier to plan and organise. Mind maps can also be created on Office software such as PowerPoint.

Mind maps are easy to change and update. They make it easy to get people to focus on the central concept relationship between the ideas. Mind maps are concise in detail and so you can use them for summarising information into key points.

However, there is a limit to how much text you can include on a mind map. Detailed explanations are not suitable. A detailed mind map can take considerable time to create. It can be poorly structured and hard to understand when used for big projects.

Case study

Epic Games

Epic Games is a well-known video game and software company who are responsible for games such as Gears of War and Fortnite. It took over six years to design and create Fortnite. When they came up with the concept for the game, the designers might have used mind maps to plan out their ideas.

Games companies are always looking at what the next popular computer game could be. The designers will use different design tools to organise their ideas, plan different stages of the game as it develops and decide how the game will look.

Figure 1.7: A girl playing video games

Check your understanding

1   What type of mind map could Epic Games have used? Why?

2   Give an example of another design tool the designers could have used in planning one of their games and explain why you chose that one.

3   Discuss whether a flow chart would be a suitable tool for a game designer to use when planning a new game.

Visualisation diagrams

A visualisation diagram is a rough drawing or diagram of what a finished product might look like. It helps plan the visual **layout** (where things are). It is used for showing something that doesn't move such as a poster or a webpage. A visualisation diagram is also good for presenting data visually to help people understand it, for example, a chart or graph.

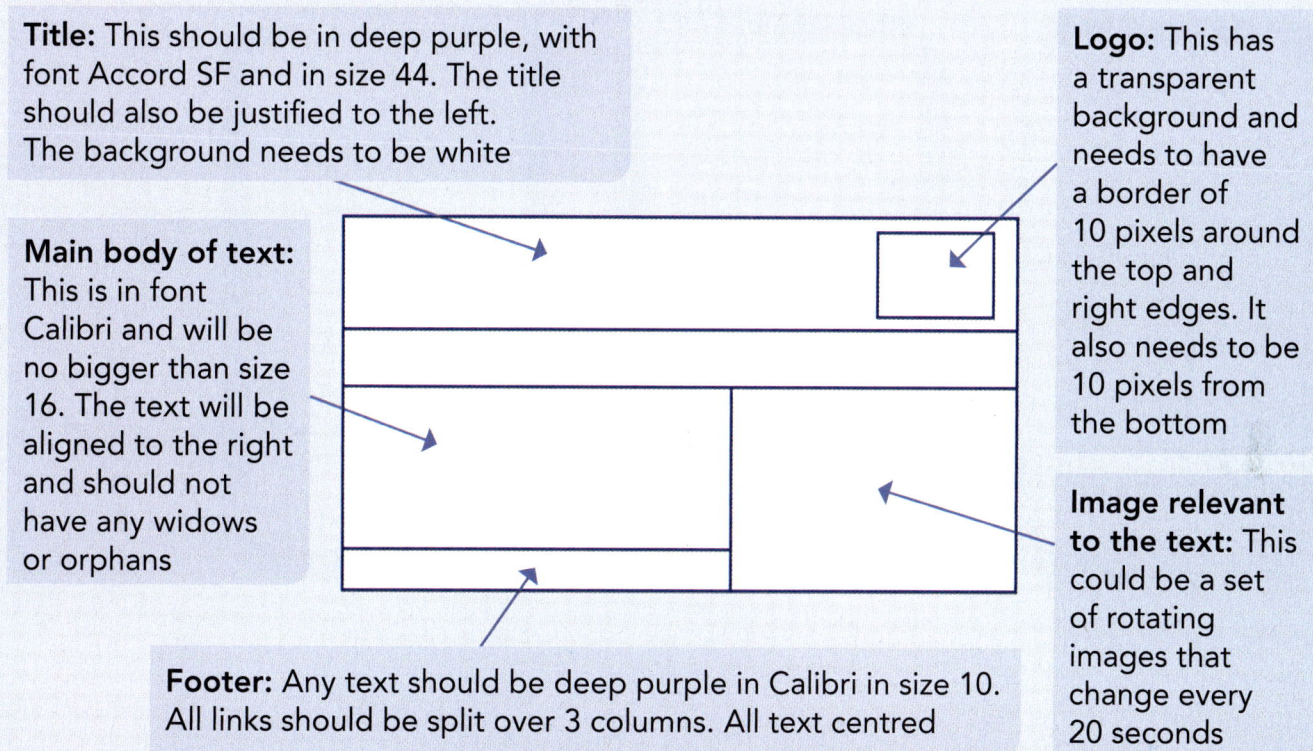

Title: This should be in deep purple, with font Accord SF and in size 44. The title should also be justified to the left. The background needs to be white

Logo: This has a transparent background and needs to have a border of 10 pixels around the top and right edges. It also needs to be 10 pixels from the bottom

Main body of text: This is in font Calibri and will be no bigger than size 16. The text will be aligned to the right and should not have any widows or orphans

Image relevant to the text: This could be a set of rotating images that change every 20 seconds

Footer: Any text should be deep purple in Calibri in size 10. All links should be split over 3 columns. All text centred

Figure 1.8: An example visualisation diagram showing where the text and images will go and what colours are to be used. The diagram is also annotated to add any further details

To create a visualisation diagram, you can use Microsoft Office software or image editing software. The focus is the basic plan and the **annotation** that supports it.

In visualisation diagrams, information and data can be easily and quickly understood. Patterns or trends can be quickly found. Anyone can understand the idea – they don't have to be a specialist.

However, they are not suitable for anything that involves a timeline, such as a video. Visualisation diagrams are open to interpretation – one person could see it differently to another. They are not always suitable for large or complex projects.

Wireframes

A **wireframe** is a plan for what something will look like and how the elements will work together. For example, when planning a website, a wireframe will show the style of the page as well as the planned interactivity (such as **buttons** or links).

Home screen   **Main page**   **Example**

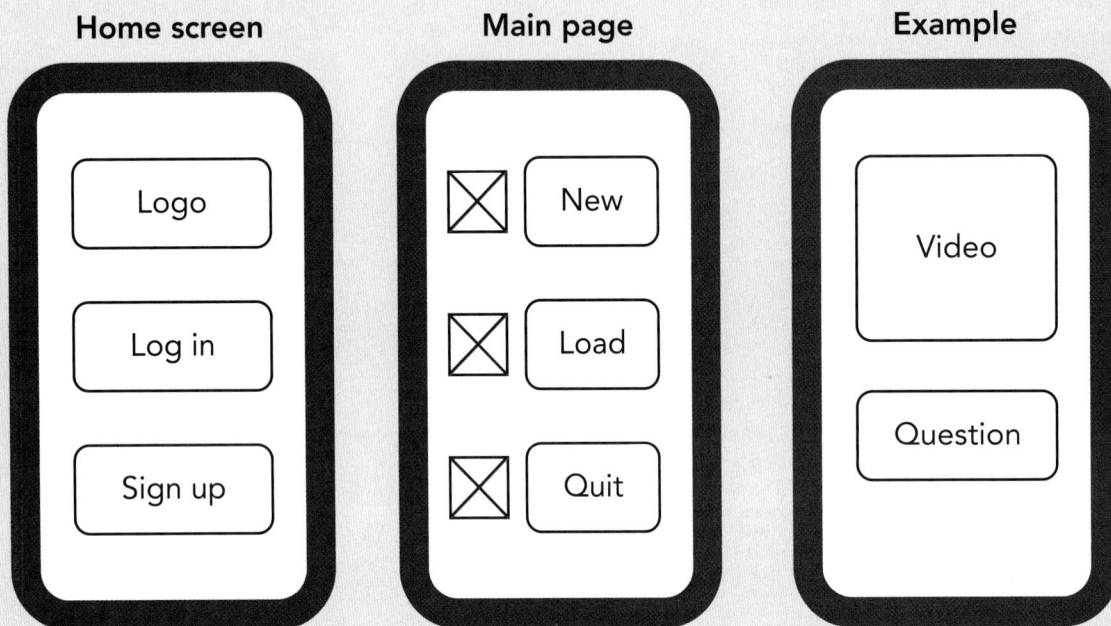

Figure 1.9: A simple example of a wireframe

A wireframe focuses on the structure of the product, such as layout and **navigation** rather than any other design features. It might have brief annotation, especially explaining the navigation.

You can use Microsoft Office software, image editing software or specialist wireframing software to create a wireframe.

A wireframe can help predict where there might be problems in the later design or creation stages. It is a clear way to see what needs to be created. It is quick and easy to make and edit, which is useful for getting feedback on early designs.

However, it can be easy to get caught up in the small details and to focus on them. Wireframes are not technical so what is planned may not work. It is easy to spend too much time on a wireframe and therefore it can become too heavily designed.

Over to you!

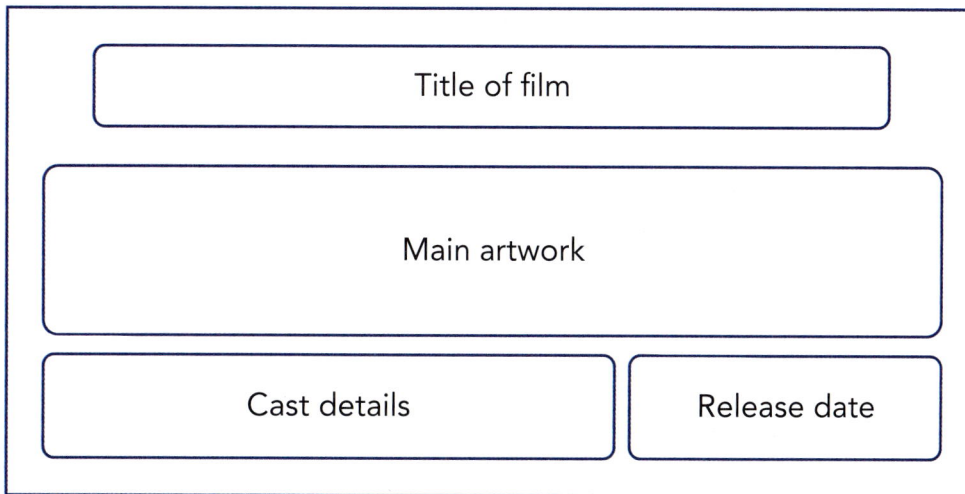

Figure 1.10: A wireframe that could have been used to design a billboard for the film *Thor: Love and Thunder*

1   Describe whether a wireframe was the most suitable design tool to use for this product. Why?

2   Explain what other design tool could have also been used and why it might not have been used.

Stretch

You have been asked to create a range of posters to advertise the opening of a new leisure centre in town.

1   Explain which design tools would be suitable to plan this project, including why you feel they would be suitable.

2   Use the design tool of your choice to plan one of the posters.

3   Justify why you have chosen the design tool you have used for 2 instead of the other design tools. First, you need to explain the advantages of your chosen tool. Following this, explain why the other design tools are not suitable – thinking about their disadvantages.

Review your learning

Test your knowledge

1 Which design tool might you use to plan out a leaflet? Why?

2 When designing a **database**, the designer might use a mind map as their initial choice of design tool. Why might they do this?

3 Give two examples of when you might use a tunnel mind map as a chosen design tool.

4 Why is a visualisation diagram not suitable for planning a video?

5 Before using a flow chart, what might you need to know?

6 A disadvantage of a wireframe is that it is not looking at the technical aspects of a product. Why might this be a problem?

7 If you are planning a webpage, which would be the best design tool to use and why?

What have you learnt?

	See section
• The different design tools available.	1.1
• The software you can use to create a design tool.	1.1
• The advantages and disadvantages of each design tool.	1.1
• How to create a suitable design using an appropriate design tool.	1.1
• How to justify whether the right design tool has been used for a given scenario.	1.1

Human Computer Interface (HCI) in everyday life

Let's get started

Think about the last time you went into your local high street.
How many times did you use a digital device? Where?
How did you use one?

What will you learn?

- The purpose of the **HCI**.

- How the HCI is used in a range of everyday areas, why this is important and its advantages and disadvantages.

- The different display types and sizes and their advantages and disadvantages.

- The impact of display and resources on the HCI.

- Software, the digital platforms used and their impacts on design.

- How the user interacts with the HCI and the limitations of each that might arise.

2.1 The purpose, importance and use of HCI in application areas

A **Human Computer Interface** (HCI) is about how a person uses or interacts with a computer in order to exchange information and instructions.

Software ⟷ HCI ⟷ Person

Figure 1.11: HCI is about how a person interacts with a computer

Different interfaces (ways to interact with software) are provided by the **operating system**. Some of the interfaces are entirely text-based whereas others use images to represent different commands.

Banking

You might naturally think of banking as using a cash machine to withdraw money or using a card reader to pay for an item. Cash machines use menus to display options about what service you need – withdrawing money or seeing your balance. Thanks to HCI, banking is more secure, quicker and there are fewer mistakes. However, the software and updates have a cost and the cash machines need maintenance as they are in constant use. There might also be accessibility issues for people who are hearing or sight impaired.

Embedded systems

An **embedded system** is a computer that is part of a larger system. It is there to allow the user to control the device that it is built into. An embedded system is not usually programmable and so cannot be easily updated.

Examples of devices with embedded systems are central heating systems, dishwashers, electronic calculators, engine management systems in vehicles and digital watches. Embedded systems are cheap to build, require less power to run (some run on batteries) and they don't need a lot of **processing power**.

Over to you!

Look around your home.

1   Identify a piece of equipment that you use frequently.

2   Think about the HCI for that piece of equipment. Create a mind map showing the different ways you can interact with it.

3   What limitations does the piece of equipment have?

For example, you might select your TV.

In the mind map, you would consider how you interact with the TV. This is not just using the remote control, but thinking about the different options you have with your TV, e.g. can you use voice control? What are the advantages of using voice control? What are the disadvantages of using voice control?

Entertainment

You access the content using simple menus online, through your **smart TV**, games console or mobile device. You can choose what you wish to watch or which game you would like to play without having to look through a very long list. HCI in entertainment can be customised to suit the user and is simple to update. It enables wider choice and quick, **portable** access to content. However, there is usually a cost to access the content and this technology is dependent on an **internet** connection for downloading and streaming.

Figure 1.12: These days we take access to a wide range of films and TV programmes through different streaming platforms for granted

Fitness

Many of us like to keep track of our fitness. This might involve keeping a log of how far you have run over a month or how many steps you walk in a day. Many of the HCIs we use when keeping fit are touchscreens or use **sensors** to track our progress. This is more convenient than pressing buttons during exercise and so these HCIs are easy to use in a variety of circumstances. They also often provide other information such as heart rate. A disadvantage is the cost of any subscription service.

Let's get digital!   1

Use a suitable design tool to design a new HCI for someone who likes to run and cycle. Think about how the user will access the software when they are in the middle of a workout.

Home appliances

We may not realise it, but our homes are filled with HCI devices, many of which make our lives easier. Think about how your evening meal was cooked last night – both the oven and the microwave are HCI devices. The boiler that heats your home and hot water is also an example of an HCI. You decide when the heating comes on and what temperature it heats up to simply by turning a dial or pressing a button. By using an HCI, you can safely control the device. HCIs make the use of home appliances and the troubleshooting of problems easy. However, appliances need to be replaced on a regular basis and when software is out of date it cannot be easily updated.

Let's get digital!   2

Look around your kitchen.

1   Identify an appliance that you use frequently.

2   Draw a flow chart showing the process of using the appliance, including the decisions you can make.

3   In looking at the flow chart you have created, and thinking about the decisions you can make, can you identify any problems with how you interact with the appliance?

Retail

Retail customers don't see the computer system that keeps track of all the stock (both on the shop floor and in storage). The software can be used to create reports for the business owner, such as which items are popular, what needs reordering or a summary of stock levels. HCI in retail allows direct ordering of stock, based on sales. It prevents staff from entering incorrect prices and provides an efficient system to track stock and sales. However, the HCI devices and software have a cost. It takes time to enter data into the system initially or update prices, and mistakes can be made in the set up.

Figure 1.13: An HCI can be used in retail to scan the barcodes of items at a till in order to calculate the total cost

2.2 Hardware considerations

An HCI can be a variety of sizes depending on what it is being used for and what it is being used on. Think about the fact that most computer monitors range from 19 to 34 inches (48–86 cm), measured diagonally from corner to corner, with most users happy with 22–24" (56–61 cm) screens. In comparison, the HCI on a washing machine is quite small, usually between 6 and 8 inches when compared to the HCI on a TV. Display size can impact on **functionality** and how a user accesses the HCI. The smaller a display, the more precise the user must be when selecting an option, especially buttons. It can take longer to select an item.

Figure 1.14: An example of a large screen being used in a shopping centre

Display screens commonly found with HCIs can be light and thin. They are usually either **LED** or **LCD**. HCIs are long lasting and reliable. HCI hardware can be expensive as the technology develops and updates.

The number of tasks an HCI needs to perform will determine the **memory** and processing power it needs. The more complex the tasks, the more processing power required. However, this is still a relatively low amount.

2.3 Software considerations

Operating system

The HCI will always have an operating system running the computer. The operating system will help deal with the instructions that the user gives and help with the security of the system. Often the operating system is the element that provides the interface for the user to access the software.

If you think about the most common platforms that users access, there are some noticeable differences in how you interact with them.

The Windows operating system (as an HCI) is a graphical system that allows users to select what they need from a variety of icons. This operating system (OS) cannot be adjusted by the user other than to change display settings. For example, you can make the icons larger or arrange the order they are viewed in. These limitations on the OS also limit the design of an HCI.

The iPhone Operating System (iOS) works in a similar way to the Windows OS in that the HCI is also a graphical system which is based on apps (or 'applications'). Like Windows, the iOS cannot be adjusted by the user other than to change the display settings. For example, you can arrange the way the apps are displayed or change the size of the text. However, what makes iOS different is that you can create your own app. This gives you more flexibility in an HCI design, but it must be approved by Apple before it can be used.

However, the Android operating system is very different to both Windows and iOS. This is because the OS is **open source**. This means that anyone can change the code in the operating system to make it do something they specifically want. This has a huge impact on the design of the HCI as you can design one that meets your needs. The Android OS can be adjusted to suit.

Digital platform

A digital platform is the system that runs the software, such as an operating system or even a web browser. The digital platform chosen will depend on how the HCI will be used. For example, if the HCI is being used in a factory as part of an automated process then the digital platform will need to reflect this. It will probably be a database rather than an app. This will also impact on the design for the HCI. For example, the design of an HCI in an automated factory will focus on users being able to select the commands efficiently rather than making it look appealing.

Database

A database is a collection of related tables that are used to store data. By using a database as the digital platform, you are often limited by the data you can enter and the format it takes. This will impact the design as it will be much more text-based or user-entry driven.

Mobile app

Using a mobile app as the digital platform allows more scope for creativity in the design of the HCI. The display size is limited but as it is more interactive there is a greater chance of the user spending time on it.

Spreadsheet

This is like using a database as the digital platform. You are often limited by the data that can be entered and how it will be displayed. There are limited ways in which the user can interact with a **spreadsheet** based HCI.

Figure 1.15: The small screen of a tablet or phone makes the digital platform more convenient to use

Website

This is similar to using a mobile app as the digital platform. There is more scope for creativity in the appearance of the HCI and you have more user interaction options. Unlike a mobile app, display size is not limited. As it is more interactive there is a greater chance of the user spending time on it.

Let's get digital!   3

Your local takeaway would like its customers to order via their app rather than using a website.

1   How will the design of the app be different when compared to the design of the website?

2   Using an appropriate tool, create a design for the app.

2.4 User interaction methods

Table 1.2: HCI user interaction methods

Method	Explanation	Advantage(s)	Disadvantage(s)
Gesture	Where a body motion is used for communication, for example, a hand gesture is used to close apps on a **smartphone**.	• Gestures feel natural and therefore the user is more comfortable using them.	• Users might not be able to be perform the gesture. • Not appropriate for all audiences
Keyboard	The users manually input the instructions using a keyboard – either on screen or attached.	• Users have more freedom in what they can enter (free text). • Users might be more confident in using the HCI as they will be familiar with a keyboard. • Shortcuts can be used to make movement around the HCI simpler.	• Could be time consuming to enter the information. • Users may find it difficult to use a keyboard due to limited use of their wrist / fingers.
Mouse	Small handheld device which is moved across a surface to move the cursor on a computer screen.	• Can accurately select an object. • Users can perform lots of functions quickly.	• Reliant on a secondary device (the mouse).
Touch	Users can select the icons by touching areas of the screen.	• Quicker than using a mouse / keyboard. • A screen is straightforward to use and is easy to clean.	• Cost. • Accuracy can be an issue. • Sensitivity of screen. • Screen size needs to be appropriate.
Voice	Users can give the computer a command rather than having to manually enter or select the commands.	• Quicker than having to manually type or select. • Users don't have to be physically next to the device (hands-free).	• Varieties of language and pronunciation mean that the command is not always understood. • Background noise might interfere with the HCI understanding the command.

Case study

Accents causing a problem

According to a Uswitch study undertaken in 2020, the Welsh and Liverpool accents are the British accents that both the Amazon Alexa and the Google Assistant struggle to understand the most. If the accent is from London or Lincoln there are fewer problems controlling the devices. According to the study, 23% of regional dialects cause problems with the devices. As a result, there is also an increase in people searching for 'why doesn't my device understand me' in the same areas.

Figure 1.16: Customers interacting with a new product

There are nearly 6 million homes in the UK with these devices in them and so they are becoming a more integral part of our lives.

Check your understanding

1   Describe how your voice can be used to control an HCI.

2   One of the common disadvantages of interacting with an HCI is the limitations of the user. Explain how this is a disadvantage.

3   A new games console is being designed. Discuss what would be the most suitable method of user interaction and why.

Stretch

Think about your living room and the HCIs that you have there.

1   List the devices that are there.

2   For each device, describe the user interaction methods.

3   For each device, explain why that specific interaction was chosen.

4   Pick one device. How could the device be changed to include an alternative interaction method? Use an appropriate design tool and plan it out. Also justify your choice of additional interaction method.

Review your learning

Test your knowledge

1 Define the term 'HCI'.

2 Describe the purpose of an HCI.

3 Describe how an HCI could be used with a gaming console.

4 Explain how the display size can impact the use of an HCI.

5 Describe the issues surrounding an HCI when using gestures to interact.

6 Explain the term, 'embedded system'.

7 Discuss the benefits and issues of using an HCI if you are blind.

What have you learnt?

	See section
• The purpose of the HCI.	2.1
• How the HCI is used in a range of everyday areas, why this is important and its advantages and disadvantages.	2.1
• The different display types and sizes that an HCI can be used on and their advantages and disadvantages.	2.2
• The impact of display and resources on the HCI.	2.2
• How the software and digital platform that the HCI uses will impact on the design.	2.3
• How a user will interact with the HCI and the advantages and disadvantages of each?	2.4

Data and testing

What will you learn?

- The relationship between data and information.

- The use of data types.

- How data is validated and verified and the differences between the two terms.

- How data is collected and stored.

- Why testing is needed, including the implications of a product not being tested.

- The types of testing that can be done on a product.

- The types of data that can be used during testing.

3.1 Information and data

What is 'data'?

In its basic form, data is just facts and figures that have no meaning or links. For example: 45, 89, 103 and 179. These numbers could be ages, test scores or bus route numbers. As we have no context or background about the numbers, they can be called data.

Case study

Supermarkets

When we go shopping at the supermarket, data is collected about what we have bought. On average 25 000 people a week will visit one supermarket chain so a massive amount of data is being collected.

Supermarkets use the collected data in a variety of ways:

Figure 1.17: A shopping trolley in a supermarket aisle

- To target offers based on shopping habits
- To arrange key products in store in a way that will gain attention
- To change stock levels in stores based on popularity of items
- To make decisions about holding events such as 'Cleaning Week'.

The data can also be made available to individual brands, who in return can use it to monitor customer preferences. For example, a new chocolate brand could work with a supermarket to use the sales data to launch a new chocolate bar.

Check your understanding

1   Other than collecting data about what you have bought, what other data could the supermarket be collecting when you shop?

2   Why do supermarkets want to collect all this data about shopping habits?

3   'People are getting fooled into buying more because shops know too much about us.' To what extent do you agree with this statement?

In your answer consider the data that shops can collect about their customers and how this can be used. Your answer should consider both points of view.

What is 'information'?

The relationship between information and data is that data has been given a meaning to turn it into information. It is put into context and given a structure. There is a **formula** for turning data into information:

> **Information = data + [structure] + [context]**

By using this formula, we are turning meaningless data into something useful – information. When data is processed into information it is formatted and this provides the structure. For example, one structure of a postcode is LLNN NLL where L represents a letter and N represents a number. When data is processed into information, it is given a meaning. This means that we can make sense of what it is.

Over to you!   1

1   Explain the difference between data and information.

2   Why would information be more valuable than raw data to a company?

3   Explain the impact there might be of selling information to other companies. In your answer consider how the sold information can be used and the impact this has.

3.2 Data use

Use of data types in different contexts

Before data can be processed, it needs to be stored. When data is stored, this is done by using a data type.

Table 1.3: The data type used depends on what the data is and how it is going to be stored

Data type	Explanation	Example
Text	This will store any type of character.	Name
Alphanumeric	This will store any combination of letters and numbers only.	Postcode
Numeric	This will store integers, real numbers, currency, percentages, fractions and decimals.	Salary
Date / Time	This will store a range of date and time formats.	Date of Birth
Logical / Boolean	This stores data in two ways – either Yes / No or True / False.	Have you any allergies?

When applying a data type to a set of data, it is important to think about what the data is and how you are going to use it.

Over to you!   2

Flipflop is a new shoe shop in Kendal. In preparation for opening, they did a survey of potential customers. The manager wants to work out the best way to store the answers to each question.

Copy and complete Table 1.4.

Table 1.4: Flipflop survey

Questions	Data type	Example answer	Justification of choice
Do you live in Kendal?			
What is your postcode?			
How many times a month do you shop in Kendal?			
When you are looking for a new pair of casual shoes, what is the most important factor in your decision?			
On average, how much do you pay for a pair of casual shoes?			
Would you want to shop online or just in store?			

Data validation

Data **validation** is making sure that data entered is sensible and reasonable. For example, data validation could be applied to the date / time data type so that the user must select a date in the future. Validation does not make sure that the data is correct. All validation does is return an error if the data entered fails the check.

Data validation tools

There are a number of checks that can be made to validate data.

Table 1.5: Types of data validation checks

Method	Description
Data Type Check	This checks the data that is entered against the data type. This is usually employed when using dates or numbers.
Format Check	This checks that the data being entered is in the expected format. For example, it is currency when entering a price.
Input Mask	This controls how you input the data and is commonly used for items such as postcode. It is usually set up as a series of hashtags for example, ### ###
Length Check	This checks that the data is the correct length as it is entered. An example would be making sure a password is at least eight characters long.

Table 1.5: Continued

Method	Description
Limited Choice	This is where the user can only select from a range of options. This could be in a drop-down list, a tick list or selecting radio buttons.
Lookup	This checks the data entered against a list of acceptable values.
Presence Check	This checks that data has been entered, in other words, it is not left blank.
Range Check	This checks that the data entered is within a specific range, for example, a number is between one and ten.

Data verification tools

Data **verification** is used to check that the data that has been entered matches the original data. For example, when setting a password a user might be asked to enter it twice to make sure it matches. This is called double entry. Another method is manual checking. This is when the data entered is checked by an individual. Comparing the entered data to the original reduces the possibility of errors being made. Verification does not check that the data is correct.

3.3 Methods of data collection

There are different ways in which you can collect data and information. You will choose your method depending on what data and information is to be collected, where it is from and how you will process and store it.

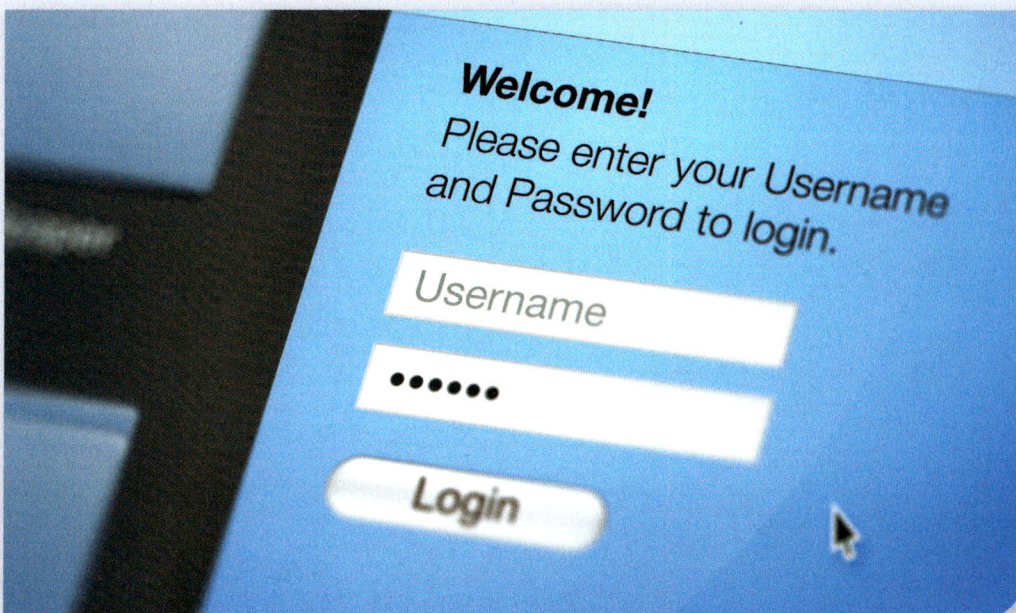

Figure 1.18: When you set a password you are often asked to verify it by entering it twice

Primary methods

Table 1.6: Ways to collect data and information yourself, which is known as primary data collection

Method	Purpose	Advantages	Disadvantages
Email	Through including an interactive form or a link to an online survey, email has become a useful tool to collect data and information.	• No limit on how many people the email can be sent to. • As it is electronic, results can be collected automatically and so the chance of human error is low.	• Can be sent to the wrong recipient or can end up being diverted to the Junk folder. • Not everyone has an email address or checks it frequently.
Interview	Takes place between two individuals, where the questions are planned in advance and asked face to face. The questions will generally be **open questions**.	• The relationship between the **interviewer** and the **interviewee** can help with the questions being answered more honestly. • The interviewer can adapt their questions to previous answers or ask further questions to clarify responses.	• Interviewing people is costly and can take time. • Not a convenient method if you need to interview a large number of people. • A poor interview can lead to poor data being collected.
Online questionnaire or survey	This contains a specific set of questions that are designed to collect data and information from the individuals completing the questionnaire or survey.	• No limit on how many people can be asked to fill in the questionnaire or survey. • Can be cheaper to conduct than other primary methods. • Can be simple to analyse the results, especially where **closed** or **ranking** question types are used.	• Not everyone has access to the internet. • Results might be inaccurate if the people completing the survey are not the intended audience. • If questions are not correctly designed the results might not be accurate or in the required format.

Let's get digital!

A local holiday firm would like to expand the range of weekend getaways that they offer.

1 Create a suitable mind map that could be used to design a survey. This would be emailed to all local residents to find out what they would look for when considering a weekend getaway.

2 Using your mind map, create a template for the survey that the company could use.

Secondary methods

Table 1.7: Data and information that has been already collected, known as secondary data

Method	Purpose	Advantages	Disadvantages
Books	Written by a specialist, a book contains data and information already collected by the author on a specific topic.	• Generally written by someone who is knowledgeable on the topic. • Will contain references to where the data and information came from or how it was collected.	• Data and information might not be up to date. • Author could be **biased**.
Government statistics	Data and information collected from the population and analysed and broken down by different demographics.	• Data and information will come from a large sample. • Will be presented in an unbiased way.	• Data and information might cover a large area rather than a specific area. • It might not have been updated for some time.
Magazines	Written by a range of authors on specific topics. The data and information will relate to the topic of the magazine.	• Generally written by someone who is knowledgeable on the topic. • Data and information will be updated regularly.	• Data and information could be presented in a biased way.
Websites	Contain data and information on a specific topic and published online.	• Data and information can be updated quickly and frequently. • Simple and quick way to search for the information and data.	• May not be clear who the author is. • May not be obvious where the data and information came from or how old it is.

Over to you!   3

The tourist board in your town would like to research public opinion about the local area. Select and explain which methods of data collection you might use. Justify your choice.

3.4 Storage of collected data

As data and information is collected, it will need to be stored before it can be processed and analysed. You can store data and information in a variety of ways.

Logical methods

Table 1.8: Logical methods to store data

Name	Description	Advantages	Disadvantages
The cloud	General term for storage that can be remotely accessed through the internet. Location of the data is not important but rather that the data is stored on a server that is connected to the internet.	• Can access the files from any device and any location providing you have an internet connection. • Can share data with other users easily so they can access the data at the same time. • Data is usually stored securely on your behalf. • Data you store is usually backed up for you, reducing your need to do so. • Not limited to how much you can store as you can pay to increase your limit.	• Need to have an internet connection to access your data. • Owners of the servers have access to your data. • No guarantee that your data is being backed up and secure – you are relying on other people. • If you have access to your data from any location, then potentially so can a hacker.

Figure 1.19: A server room at one of the cloud bases might look like this

Physical methods

Table 1.9: Types of physical storage

Type	Advantages	Disadvantages
Internal storage device	• You have primary control over who has access to the storage. • Easy to back up.	• Easily damaged when moved. • Reliant on being kept cool. • Noisy.
External storage device	• All options are easily portable. • All can be used as a back-up option for primary storage.	• Needs additional security as the devices (and therefore contents) can be physically stolen. • Reliant on power sources in most cases.

Table 1.10: Physical methods to store data

Physical location	Name	Description	Advantages	Disadvantages
Internal storage device	Primary hard drive	Most computers have some form of internal storage such as a hard disk drive. The storage device is built into the computer and generally only the user can access the data and information. As the user, you can create, edit and delete files.	• You can store a large amount of data and information. • It is a fairly cheap method of storing data. • You are not relying on any form of connection to access your data. • Access to data and information is limited to the users of the computer it is stored on.	• The data and information can only be accessed using this device. • There is a limited amount of storage for your data. • You are responsible for security and backups of your data and information. • If your computer breaks, you might lose your data and information.
Internal storage device	Network drive	This is where data and information are stored on servers located within the building you are working in. You can access the files that you need whenever you are at that specific location.	• The company knows exactly where the data and information is stored. • The company can allow other people to access the files when you are not working on them. • Some network drives allow you to have remote access to them through a secure internet connection. • The company is in control of the security of your data and information and how frequently it is backed up.	• You are limited as to when and where you can access your data and information. • There is a responsibility to ensure the data is secure, which can be costly. • Hackers can still access the data and information if it is not secure. • Setting up and running a network can be costly. • The company will need to have suitable knowledge to run a network or pay someone to do so.

Table 1.10: Continued

Physical location	Name	Description	Advantages	Disadvantages
External storage device	Portable external hard drive disk (HDD)	This works just like a primary hard drive with the key difference being that it is housed in its own casing and is connected to the computer through a USB port.	• It increases the storage capacity of your device. • It can be used as a back-up drive, as it can be removed and stored securely. • It can improve the performance of a computer as it can be used as the main drive when starting up the computer.	• It is easily broken, especially if dropped, with minimal chance of recovering the data stored. • At risk of damage through natural means such as sunlight, heat and dust. • Devices are not automatically password-protected so if you misplace your device anyone can access it unless you add your own security.
External storage device	Portable solid-state drive (SSD)	This works just like a portable hard drive with the key difference being that it has no moving parts and as a result gives faster access times.	• The data is transferred faster between the device and the SSD as there are no moving parts. • An SSD is more convenient to move as it is lighter than a portable HDD. • As they have no movable parts, the devices are more robust, make no noise and use less power.	• A portable SSD is one of the most expensive ways of storing data externally. • If you accidently delete a file from an SSD, it is nearly impossible to retrieve the data. The same applies if the device is damaged.
External storage device	Network-attached storage (NAS) device	This is an external device that is connected to a network. It acts as a central location for all the network users to store and retrieve data.	• The contents of an NAS can also be accessed remotely by the network users, allowing flexibility. • You can set up user permissions, so that only specific people have access to a folder or file. • You do not need a specialist to set up and install an NAS.	• If there are too many users trying to access an NAS at the same time, this can slow down the network. • If there is a problem with the NAS, then you often need to hire a specialist to help try to recover the data. • As the data is stored on-site with an NAS, you would still need a back-up in case there was an on-site problem such as a fire.

Table 1.10: Continued

Physical location	Name	Description	Advantages	Disadvantages
External storage device	Portable USB flash drive	This is an external storage device that plugs into a USB port on your computer.	• You know exactly where the data and information is stored. • You can allow other people to access the files when you are not working on them. • Some network drives allow you to have remote access to them through a secure internet connection if plugged into a computer. • You are usually in control of the security of your data and information and how frequently it is backed up.	• You have a limited amount of storage for your data. • Due to their size, it can be easy to lose these storage devices. • If the drive is misplaced, any user can access the data and information unless you have put additional security in place such as adding a password to the device.
External storage device	Portable wireless drive	This is a hard drive that uses either **Bluetooth technology** or Wi-Fi to allow most mobile devices to access the files stored on it. Wireless drives are particularly useful for devices like smartphones or tablets as they don't have USB ports.	• These devices are very useful to back up any files or images from mobile devices, especially if you are not near a secure internet connection. • Unlike other storage devices, these are battery powered, meaning you are not reliant on an external power source to use them.	• These devices can have limited security, especially if they are connected via Bluetooth technology. • The physical size of the storage device is often small, and therefore it can easily be misplaced and lost.

3.5 Application of testing to a range of contexts

The importance and purpose of testing

No client will want to have a final product that doesn't work properly. To ensure this, it will need to have been tested. Through testing, the developer will be able to make sure that the final product is as expected and that there are no errors. How you are going to test the product should therefore be considered during the design phase.

Testing ensures that any problems are found early in development and that the client will be more confident with the final product.

Testing properly will ensure that every element of the product is checked thoroughly. However, it takes time to test and it must be done in a consistent way.

Testing data

Testing ensures that the finished product works as intended. Testing as you are developing a product can save time and money as any problems are resolved earlier rather than having to go back and fix them at the end. This also ensures that the finished product meets the needs of the user.

Testing can take considerable time and you must be clear what it is you want to test and what you expect to happen.

When testing, you often need to enter some example data. To ensure the product is working as expected, you need to use three types of data.

Valid data is data that should be acceptable to the product and, assuming the product is working correctly, should give an appropriate output. This would show that the product is working correctly.

Invalid (or erroneous) data is data that the tester knows is incorrect and should not be acceptable to the product. The product should automatically reject the data if it is working correctly.

Extreme data is data that is on the boundary between being valid and invalid. When entered into the product, it should be accepted as valid.

Over to you!   4

A game has been designed to test how quickly a user can do basic mathematics. The user can enter any two numbers between 1 and 20, and then has to quickly answer the question that appears on the screen using the numbers entered.

1   State two **inputs** that could be used as valid data when testing.

2   State two inputs that could be used as invalid data when testing.

3   State two inputs that could be extreme data when testing.

Types of testing

User testing

User testing is when the product is tested from the point of view of the final user. Can the user complete the task? How long does the task take? User opinions can be given and any errors reported either in person or by using additional software. This has advantages in that you can see how long it takes to complete specific tasks and how happy users are with the product. You don't need a specific workspace to complete the testing. Disadvantages are that it can take time to run the tests with a range of different users and it can cost money not only to run the tests but also to pay the users for their time. User testing focuses on the quality of the product more than technical errors.

Figure 1.20: An engineer carries out user testing with robotic production simulators in a robotic research facility

Technical testing

Technical testing is where the product is tested to make sure there are no errors and it meets the specifications of the client. Does the product work? Does each command work? Does the 'Save' button work?

Advantages of doing technical testing are that you can spot any errors early in development. It helps you measure progress easily and identify any risks and deal with them as a priority. Technical testing also has some disadvantages. It is time consuming and any problems can delay the completion of the product.

Stretch

Nana K's Nursery is setting up an app so that parents can book nursery sessions for their child, receive updates from the nursery and see upcoming events.

Using an appropriate design tool, plan the home screen and one other page of the app.

1 Describe three different user tests that the company could do when the app has been initially created.

2 Describe three different technical tests the company could do when the app is in development.

3 Explain what digital platform the app might use and justify your choice.

Review your learning

Test your knowledge

1 Describe the relationship between data and information.

2 Describe why a user might prefer to use alphanumeric as a data type rather than text to store the number plate of a car.

3 Explain the difference between validation and verification.

4 Explain what types of validation a user could apply to a password entry box.

5 Describe the drawbacks to using manual checking as a method of verification.

6 Explain the disadvantages of using a questionnaire for collecting customer opinions rather than using an interview.

7 Describe the benefits of using Government statistics as a secondary method of collecting data rather than using a book.

8 Describe the term 'The Cloud'.

9 Identify and explain the different types of testing data that could be used and give a relevant example of each.

What have you learnt?

	See section
• The terms data and information and the relationship between them.	3.1
• How to choose different data types, depending on their context.	3.2
• Validation and verification and the differences between them.	3.2
• The purpose of each method of data collection and their advantages and disadvantages.	3.3
• The characteristics of each method of data storage and their advantages and disadvantages.	3.4
• Why a product needs to be tested and the possible outcome of not testing a product.	3.5
• The different types of test data that can be used and the role of that data.	3.5
• The different types of testing and the advantages and disadvantages of each.	3.5

TA4

Cyber-security and legislation

Let's get started

'The most secure device is one that is kept in a locked room and not connected to the internet.'

What risks do devices connected to the internet present?
How can risks be reduced?

What will you learn?

- The different types of threats used by attackers.

- Why each threat is used by attackers.

- How each threat can occur and how to mitigate against them.

- What the impacts are of a cyber-security attack.

- The different prevention methods for a cyber-security attack.

- The purpose of each piece of legislation related to the use of IT systems.

Given the increased use of smart devices, we need to keep our data and information secure. **Cyber-security** is the combination of using policies, procedures and technology to keep our devices secure from internal and external threats to data and information.

There are a variety of reasons why individuals or organisations want to try and attack our devices. This might be to cause a disruption, to steal data or information, for financial gain, for fun or even to spy on competitors.

4.1 Threats used in a cyber attack

There are a wide range of threats that can be used in a cyber attack. Each one has a different purpose and can be used in different ways. All cyber attacks are best prevented by ensuring that your **anti-virus software** is up to date and scans your device regularly. You should also never click on files or links from an unknown source.

Denial of service (DoS) attack

This form of attack is where the attacker tries to make a computer or network (collection of connected computers) unavailable to its users by disrupting its services. They do this by flooding the targeted computer with too many requests and so overloading the system.

This is a popular method of attack for taking down websites or preventing user access to a specific network, especially by activists trying to make a point. To prevent a DoS attack, a **firewall** can be used to prevent large amounts of traffic.

Hacking

This form of attack is where an individual looks for weaknesses in a computer system and tries to exploit them. For example, getting past the network security and acquiring information that doesn't belong to the hacker. A hacker can try to access a system at any point they wish. Whilst **hacking** in general is illegal as it breaches the Computer Misuse Act, there are different types:

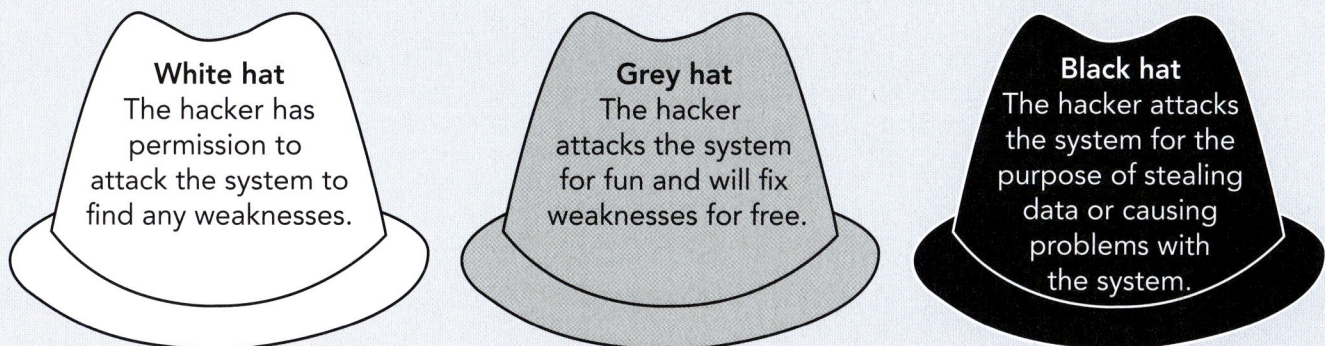

White hat
The hacker has permission to attack the system to find any weaknesses.

Grey hat
The hacker attacks the system for fun and will fix weaknesses for free.

Black hat
The hacker attacks the system for the purpose of stealing data or causing problems with the system.

Figure 1.21: Types of hacking

One of the best ways of reducing the risk of hacking is to keep any security you have up to date. You can also make sure that your passwords are strong and that you don't use public networks when you are accessing personal or financial data.

Malware

This is a type of software that has been created purposely to cause a security risk on a device or computer network.

Table 1.11: There is a wide variety of **malware** that can be used, each with its own purpose.

Malware type	Description	Purpose/threat	How it is installed	How it is prevented
Adware	This is software that shows an advert to the user.	By showing the advert the creator gains a fee. Fairly harmless as it is just annoying to the user. Can be made malicious by including **spyware**.	Often as a pop-up on a webpage or on an installation screen in software.	Anti-virus software, firewalls and by not clicking on any adverts that pop up.
Botnet	A group of internet connected devices which are running a **bot**.	A bot is a piece of software that does a specific task. Can have some benefits, as it can be faster than humans at repetitive tasks. It can be also used for cyber attacks.	Often as part of a piece of software that you have downloaded and installed.	Anti-virus software, firewalls.
Ransomware	This is a unique piece of malware that **encrypts** all the files on a device, preventing you from accessing them unless you pay the attacker for the password.	If you try to **decrypt** the files without paying the ransom you risk losing them.	Often through attachments in emails, which activate when you download and open the attachment.	Anti-virus software, firewalls. Have anti-virus software installed on your device so that it can be detected as soon as it tries to encrypt files.
Spyware	This is a piece of software that is designed to monitor and collect information about what you are doing on a device.	It can monitor which websites you have visited and what files you have created or edited, for example, a **keylogger**. This keeps track of every key you press and so will know all your login details and passwords.	Often as part of a piece of software that you have downloaded and installed.	Anti-virus software, firewalls.
Trojan Horse	This is a piece of software that looks like it is valid, but in reality is a malicious piece of software that allows another computer to take control of your device.	Named after the Greek myth, a **Trojan Horse** is hidden within a piece of useful software and when installed it will make copies of itself.	Often as part of a piece of software that you have downloaded and installed.	Anti-virus software, firewalls. Check the source of any files and software that you download and install.
Virus	This is a simple program which makes copies of itself by attaching itself to another program.	Can badly affect the performance of a device and can change and destroy files. If a device is part of a network, the **virus** can easily spread to other devices causing further problems.	Often as part of a piece of software that you have downloaded and installed or through the attachment in an email.	Anti-virus software, firewalls.

Table 1.11: Continued

Malware type	Description	Purpose/threat	How it is installed	How it is prevented
Worm	Like a virus in that the program makes copies of itself and spreads through the device's system.	Depending on how it has been programmed, a **worm** can do all sorts of damage to a device such as deleting files or accessing the users' contacts and sending messages.	Often as part of a piece of software that you have downloaded and installed or through the attachment in an email.	Anti-virus software, firewalls.

Over to you!   1

1 Describe how malware can cause problems for a user.

2 Explain how a user can prevent or remove malware.

Case study

Ransomware

The clothing company FatFace is yet another example of a business that has been the victim of a ransomware attack. In recent years hackers have been using ransomware as their main way to gain money. FatFace paid a ransom of US$2 million. A further example was when the NHS was infected and the cybercriminals wanted US$300 for each infected computer. There were over 70,000 infected devices.

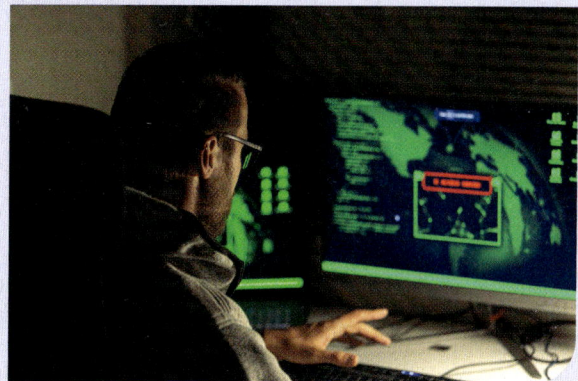

Figure 1.22: A computer hacker in action

There are, on average, 200 million ransomware attacks each year. It started out as just targeting individuals but hackers have discovered that there is much to be made from attacking organisations. Today, it is not just big organisations that are attacked but hackers will target anyone who has potential to pay, including schools and charities.

Check your understanding

1 Describe what happens in a ransomware attack.

2 Explain how you can prevent a ransomware attack.

3 Discuss the impact that a ransomware attack could have on a well-known business.

Social engineering

Social engineering is the art of manipulating people to get them to reveal confidential information. It influences a person to do something that might not be in their best interests. Social engineering can take many forms, and usually looks very innocent.

Baiting

Baiting is where the victim is offered something appealing in exchange for information, such as login details.

Over to you!   2

1   Explain how baiting is a form of social engineering.

2   Describe how a potential victim could spot that they are being baited.

3   Research conducted by the University of Illinois in the USA shows that curiosity is a natural human reaction. Discuss how an individual can prevent curiosity causing them to be a victim of baiting.

In your answer consider the options you have when receiving something that looks like baiting and how you prevent yourself from just responding.

Phishing

Phishing is using a copy of a website that looks real (most commonly a bank's) and sending people a link to the fake site with the hope that they will enter their details.

Pretexting

Pretexting is where someone tries to convince someone to give them information or access to a service or system by pretending they need to confirm the individual's identity. For example, someone claiming to be from the bank could call on the telephone and ask questions in order to steal login details.

Quid pro quo

Quid pro quo means 'something for something'. When used in the context of social engineering, it is like baiting. Quid pro quo is used by individuals to call random numbers pretending to offer help that is usually in the form of IT support. They will then 'help' fix the problem but at the same time will install malware or gain the user's password.

Scareware

Scareware builds on the user's worry about malware and convinces them to download or buy malicious software. A common example is convincing people to install fake anti-virus software. There is usually an increase in this type of social engineering being used when there has been a high-profile example of malware in the news.

Shoulder surfing

Shoulder surfing is a type of social engineering that involves an individual looking over your shoulder as you are using a device in public. For example, using a laptop at a coffee shop or entering your PIN code at a cash machine. Whilst this can be done close to the victim, it can also occur using a pair of binoculars from a greater distance.

4.2 The impact of a cyber-security attack

Naturally, for every cyber-security attack that takes place there is going to be an impact on individuals and organisations. This can also include not just the business but also the customers.

Impact of an attack

Table 1.12: Impacts of a cyber-security attack

Impact	Description
Data destruction	The data is destroyed by the attacker.
Data manipulation	The data is changed by the attacker but it is usually spotted quickly.
Data modification	The data is changed by the attacker but for a different purpose to data manipulation.
Data theft	The data is stolen with the aim of revealing confidential or private information.
Denial of service to authorised users	Any authorised users will not be able to access their system during or after the attack.
Identity theft	This is where personal details are stolen and then used to commit fraud.

Each of these impacts has an effect. Whilst losing data can be frustrating, it is good practice for individuals and organisations to regularly backup their data. Where there is a regular backup, the only loss is the data that is not yet saved on a backup.

Financial impact

When data is lost or modified, an organisation or individual can also lose money. The lost data could be a list of money owed or an organisation might have to pay compensation to its customers if their data has been lost. An organisation might also now need to pay to increase or replace the security of its computer system.

An individual who is the victim of a cyber attack could also have financial problems. By taking their data, the attacker could take out loans or credit cards in their name.

Reputational impact

When an organisation suffers a cyber attack, there might be an issue with how its customers view the business and its security. This has an impact on finances if customers leave and impacts productivity. When thinking about how an individual's reputation suffers, a good example is **identity theft**. When someone steals your information, it can have an impact on how other people and companies view you even though it was not your fault.

Safety impact

Any IT systems that are related to our immediate safety are heavily protected against a cyber-security attack but there is also a risk that they could become targeted. Given our everyday use of and reliance on IT systems, any cyber-security attack could compromise our safety if aimed at Government systems. For example, if an attack targeted the traffic system, it could cause a series of traffic accidents simply by controlling the traffic lights changing.

A cyber attack could also compromise the safety of workers in other types of organisations, such as factories if it targeted production lines.

4.3 Prevention measures

Physical methods

Biometric devices

These measure some feature of a person such as their fingerprint or voice in order to identify them and allow them access to a computer system. The system compares the feature to the version it has on the system. Only individuals who have their **biometric** features saved within the system can have access, thus keeping the data secure as the features are unique to just one person.

Firewalls

This software that is installed on a device controls the data that can and cannot pass through it. When you set up a firewall you tell it what is allowed to have access to your device. Based on these rules the firewall will either allow connections or not (a bit like a gate keeper). A firewall will reduce risks as it limits what data is allowed into the device, therefore stopping any potentially malicious connections that might cause a problem.

Keypads

We commonly see a keypad being used when we want to pay for an item. A keypad is also used as a method of entry to a room instead of a key. Using a PIN (personal identification number) as an additional method of security adds a further layer of protection. The user sets up a PIN on the keypad to allow entry. If the wrong pin is entered then entry is denied. This keeps the data or devices secure, just like on your mobile phone.

Radio-frequency identification (RFID)

This is a wireless system used to identify things or people. There is a tag containing a code that is attached to an item or individual. A reader sends a radio signal to the tag asking for its code. The code is used by the reader for identification. This can be used to prevent theft. For example, if the tag leaves an area, then an alarm will sound. If an RFID tag is used to enter a secure area then the presence of the tag could unlock a door.

Secure backups

These provide a separate copy of the data on a device or system in case any of the original data is lost or destroyed. It is good practice to keep the backup (copies of files) in a separate location. This is in case there is an issue with the building where the original data is stored such as a flood or a fire.

Logical methods

Figure 1.23: Backup data is sometimes saved on a USB stick

There are a range of logical methods that can also be used. Both firewalls and secure backups are not only physical methods of security but are also logical methods of prevention.

Access rights and permissions

A network should be set up so that different users have access to specific folders or files. This helps to protect the data by limiting who can access it. For example, in a business a manager may have access to additional folders that a worker may not. In limiting who has access to the data you can track what happens to it if there is an issue. The same is true for permissions. You can set who has permission to edit a document and who can just view a document. Doing this helps limit who has access to important data.

Anti-virus software

Anti-virus software is designed to look through the files on a device with the aim of finding malware. When you download and/or open a file, the anti-virus software scans the file to make sure it doesn't include any malicious code. If it does, the anti-virus software quarantines the file to stop it doing any damage to the device.

Two-factor authentication

This is an additional layer of security where a user provides two examples of evidence to allow them access to a website or system.

For example, when entering a username and password to access online banking, users are also often asked for a memorable word or are sent a unique code that they then need to enter. If they cannot provide the code or word then they cannot have access. This keeps the data secure as it could easily be someone with your details who is trying to access it.

Encryption

Encryption is a good way of protecting data as it encodes the information so that it is unreadable unless you know the decryption code to unscramble the data. You can encrypt any file or folder with a password. Anyone who tries to access the file/folder will not be able to read the data as it will look like gibberish. It is only when you decrypt the file/folder that the data makes sense. If someone steals the encrypted data it can take a long time to break the code, even if they are using very powerful computers.

Usernames and passwords

It can be useful to those running a network to make sure they know who is accessing it. This involves giving everyone their own username so they can identify who is on the network and what they are accessing. Combining this with passwords provides additional security as only a user should know their password.

Over to you! 3

Go to the website, 'How secure is my password'.

Enter an example of a password you use. How long would it take to break your password? Try a different example. Does it make any difference?

Secure data destruction

Data erasure

This is where software is used to overwrite the existing data on the device with a series of 0s and 1s. This can easily be done by saving new files on the existing device, thus replacing the old files. By doing this, the original data cannot be recovered.

Data sanitisation

Data sanitisation masks data as a user enters it. For example, on some websites as you enter your password it appears as a series of * rather than the characters that you actually enter. This prevents anyone watching from seeing what was entered and therefore keeps the data secure. Some sanitisation will even add extras *s so that you cannot even see the true length of the password.

Magnetic wipe

Many storage devices contain magnets as they control the method by which data is read and stored on the device. By removing the magnetic field of a storage device, any data that is stored on it will become unreadable and so protect the data. However, in doing this you are also making the storage device unusable as you are removing the instructions that make the device work.

Physical destruction

This is where you literally destroy the device the data is stored on – fire or a large hammer will do the trick. By breaking up the device into pieces, the data cannot be recovered. You need to make sure that the device is broken up into lots of pieces otherwise it can be put back together and the data restored.

Stretch

You have been asked to review the different methods of keeping data secure for a well-known business that employs 50 people.

Write a report for the business using the following questions to help with the structure:

a   What are the different methods that a business could use to keep data secure?

b   How effective is each method at keeping data secure?

c   Which method would you recommend to the business to use? Why?

4.4 Legislation related to IT systems

The increased use of IT and the increase in cyber attacks have led to the introduction of some laws to protect both individuals and organisations.

Computer Misuse Act

It is against the law to gain unauthorised access to computer material, gain unauthorised access to a system with the intent to commit a crime or to change/modify data or a system with the intent to cause damage. A business or organisation will have policies in place that inform staff that they also cannot do this. It is usually part of the Network User Agreement. If anyone is caught, they can receive a lengthy prison term and/or a fine.

Data Protection Act

This gives individuals the right to see what data a business holds about them whilst at the same time restricting what data is collected, how long it is stored and who can access it.

A business or organisation needs to consider the data it collects from individuals, how it is stored and how long it is stored for.

If any data that is stored does not meet any part of the Act, the business can be heavily fined. Given that a cyber-security attack can steal data from a company, it is crucial that the data is not only secure but that only a limited amount is kept.

Figure 1.24: The Data Protection Act protects both individuals and businesses in how your data is collected, stored and viewed

Copyright, Designs and Patents Act

This makes it illegal for someone to copy your work without permission. This could be a file, an image or sound. The Act gives individuals and organisations the means to prosecute someone if it can be proved that they have copied work. You need to be aware of what you are using or if someone is using something you have created and if it breaks the Copyright, Designs and Patents Act. This is particularly relevant today when one of the most copied items is software. If you are using an illegal copy of a piece of software, there is a chance that there could also be malware attached to it that will make you vulnerable to a security attack or data leak.

Freedom of Information Act

The Government and other organisations hold a great deal of information about their activities. This act gives the right to ask to see information about these activities. For example, the police could be asked how much it costs to police football games and how much the football club contributes. Any individual or organisation can make a Freedom of Information request.

An organisation must ensure that its information records are up to date and accurate as it can take considerable time and effort to respond to any reasonable requests. A business may decide that a request about its network security is unreasonable. This might be because if they answered such a request they might be providing too much information about how their network is secured and therefore provide any potential attackers with a way to attack them.

Health and Safety at Work Act

This act ensures that both workers and employers work safely without the risk of individuals acting recklessly or acting in a way that endangers others. The act ensures individuals feel safe whilst at work and organisations know that their workers are safe. For organisations there is often a cost implication to ensuring safety. A cyber-security attack could impact some of the systems such as heating or safety systems that are in place to protect individuals.

Review your learning

Test your knowledge

1 Define the term 'malware'.

2 Identify and explain the difference between the different types of hacking.

3 Discuss the reasons why malware might be used by an attacker.

4 Describe how a firewall can prevent malware.

5 Explain why social engineering is becoming a more serious threat.

6 Identity theft is now a common breach of cyber-security. What is the impact on an individual of identity theft?

7 Describe the benefits of using biometrics as a security method.

8 Discuss why a Freedom of Information request might not be granted when it relates to a cyber attack.

What have you learnt?

	See section
• The threats used by cyber attackers.	4.1
• Why the threats are used, how threats occur, how they work and how to defend against them.	4.1
• The impacts of a cyber-security attack on individuals and organisations.	4.2
• The prevention measures used to keep data and devices secure.	4.3
• The purpose of each legislation related to the use of IT systems.	4.4

TA5

Digital communications

Let's get started

Think about your friends and family. List the ways you communicate with them. Is there any common method? Is there a method you don't use with some people?

Figure 1.25: Digital communication has fast become the easiest and quickest way to talk to others

What will you learn?

- The purpose of different digital communication methods.
- The characteristics of different software used to create digital communication.
- The characteristics of different digital devices.
- The characteristics of different distribution channels.
- The characteristics of different connectivity methods.
- The impact of audience demographics when selecting a digital distribution channel.

5.1 Types of communication

In the 21st century we use different ways to communicate with each other. This includes instant global communication, and with the International Space Station, we can now communicate beyond our planet.

Audio

One of the most common methods of communication is the telephone. 95% of the UK population has a mobile phone.

Audio communication also includes **podcasts**, which are an effective method of communication as they are easily copied, you can communicate with many people at once and share **information** instantly. However, they are not interactive, some people prefer images and the quality of the audio depends on the equipment used.

Collaboration tools

These allow two or more people to work towards the same goal using software that allows multiple people to access and work on the same document at the same time. By using such tools, you are often saving people travel time and costs as well as increasing productivity. However, many of the tools are reliant on the internet and reduce in-person contact.

Figure 1.26: Collaboration tools are useful in work and social situations

Leaflets

A leaflet is a great way of promoting something by providing both written and visual information. Leaflets are often used by local companies to advertise their services or products. A leaflet can be visually pleasing and can be cost-effective to create and distribute. It can contain as much information as you need and can be tailored towards your intended audience. Unfortunately, poor quality leaflets are easily ignored and can be easily disposed of once people have read them.

Infographics

An **infographic** is simply a collection of images, **charts** and minimal text that gives an easy to view understanding of a topic. Infographics include relevant data, presented clearly and simply. They are good for catching the attention of the reader and can be created to suit your audience. You are not limited to a specific format or layout and they can easily be shared. However, an infographic can take time to create and the information misinterpreted. Not all infographics are easily accessible to their intended audience.

Let's get digital!

There are 18 species of penguin in the world, some of which are more well-known than others.

Create an infographic that provides key facts and figures about penguins which is aimed at 8 to 12-year-olds. Unit R060 Data manipulation using spreadsheets (TA1) includes creating charts, which may be useful.

Newsletters

This is an update that is sent out periodically to people who have an interest in a particular topic. Newsletters can be printed or sent electronically. The intended audience are usually interested in the content and newsletters are cheap to make. They can usually be adapted to address any accessibility issues. However, creating a good newsletter can take time. Not all are read, especially if someone receives many newsletters from different sources.

Presentations

A presentation is a clear, visual way of giving information to a large audience. Generally, a presentation contains minimal information and visual prompts, which are added to by the presenter. The contents of a

Figure 1.27: Live streaming is popular presentation method that can reach widespread audiences

presentation can be tailored to suit the audience. However, location can be a limiting factor unless it is recorded or **live-streamed**.

One advantage is the ability to interact with your audience. You can watch their reactions and adjust your presentation accordingly. In addition, you can emphasise any key points of information. There are downsides to a presentation as it is only as effective as the presenter. Also, not everyone might be able to attend and would therefore miss the information.

Reports

A report is generally a text-based format of communication. Reports are usually used to provide an account of something that the author has seen or researched. Whilst a report can be tailored to suit any specific audience, it generally has minimal visual content. A report is an effective way of communicating detailed data. It should be easily understood, especially if you are a specialist in the topic.

Social media

The purpose of social media is to share ideas, thoughts and information through a virtual network and online community. You can also use social media as a way of documenting memories and forming friendships. Social media audiences can vary in age depending on the media used.

One of the key advantages of using social media as a communication method is that not only can you reach a large audience, but you can have direct contact with them. Social media is usually free to use and can be accessed on any device if you have internet access. Drawbacks include the possibility of trolling, false information and online bullying.

Video

Video provides both verbal and nonverbal communication. Video relies on images and motion, and can be combined with sound and other communication tools, including infographics. Using a video can quickly engage and be adapted to suit any audience. It can be shared easily with others and enhance social communication through software such as FaceTime or Skype. However, it is easy to edit a video to alter the intention and it can lack a personal touch.

Voice-over Internet Protocol (VoIP)

VoIP is simply a set of rules that makes it possible to use the internet for telephone or video conferencing. An advantage is that by using the internet you do not have to pay any additional costs. This can make global communication much cheaper or even free. You can also have group conversations or video calls. However, the person you are communicating with must be using the same software as you and you are reliant on the quality of your internet connection.

Websites

Websites are a useful tool in communicating information to a wide audience. Anyone with an internet connection is able to view it. A website can contain a combination of text, images and other multimedia which make it adaptable and accessible to all. It can be used to share information and opinions about every topic imaginable such as through **forums** and **chat rooms**.

A key advantage is that any website has the potential to have a global audience. However, given that anyone can create a website the reader has to be aware of the bias and validity of the information being provided. A website can also be out of date and not overly secure.

Over to you!   1

You have recently set up a shop selling trainers. Choose an appropriate type of digital communication, set up a marketing plan for your shop.

a   Justify the use of each communication type.

b   Describe the audience you are targeting for each type including age, gender and location.

c   Explain how you will adapt your communications for customers with audio/visual and physical needs.

5.2 Software

When creating any form of digital communication, there is a range of software that can be used. These software applications can be used on PCs, Macs or mobile devices. The software is configured to be user-friendly on this wide range of devices.

Desktop publishing (DTP)

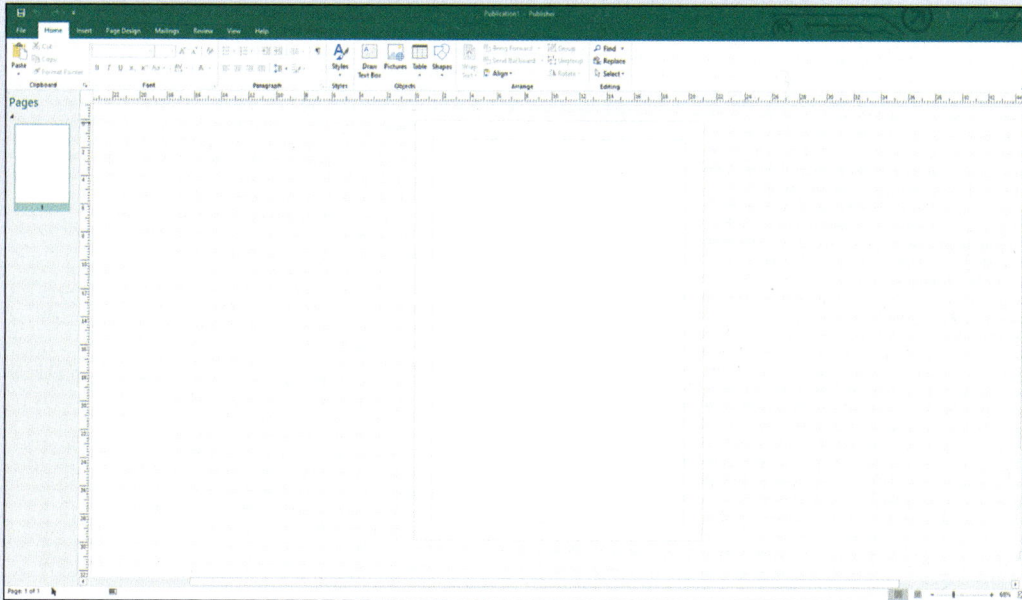

Figure 1.28: Desktop publishing software

Desktop publishing (also known as **DTP**) is a useful piece of software when designing digital communications. In addition to having a range of available templates that the user can apply, there are built-in styles and fonts. To help create any communications, there are additional features to apply character and line spacing. You can also use the design setup screens to support the creation of any specific publication. To help get the layout you require, you can use grid lines and placeholder text to save time before filling the publication with your information. DTP is beneficial, in its adaptability for your audience, as it is simple to change a publication based on their needs.

Standard office applications

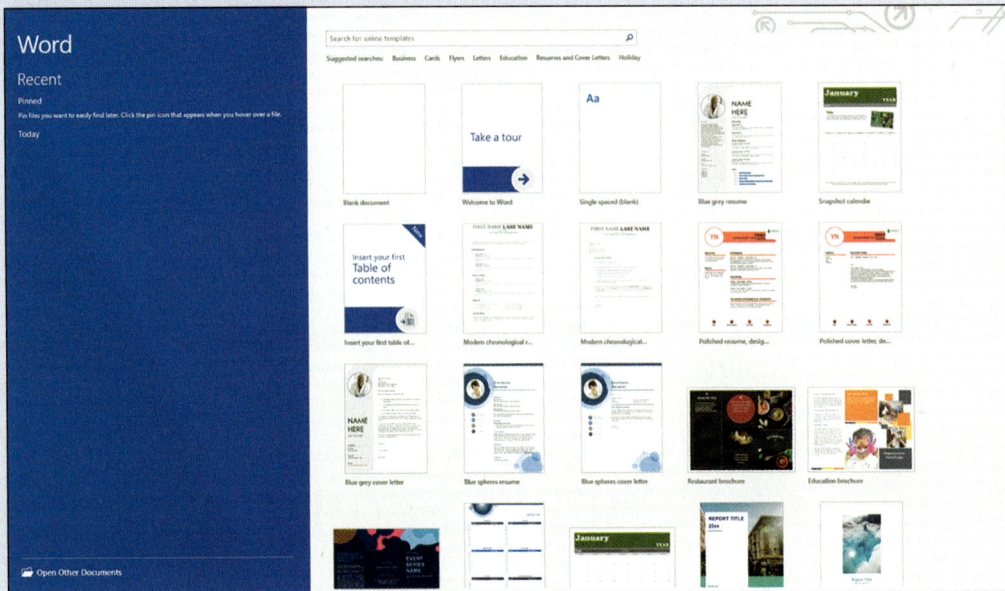

Figure 1.29: Word processing software

Word processing is software that is used to create digital communications. Whilst similar to DTP in that it has a range of templates that you can use, you are more limited in how you can arrange your information. Word processing is of benefit when you need more control over the format, such as typographical details. Any document created using word processing is generally aimed at a more adult audience as it is good for creating reports and newsletters.

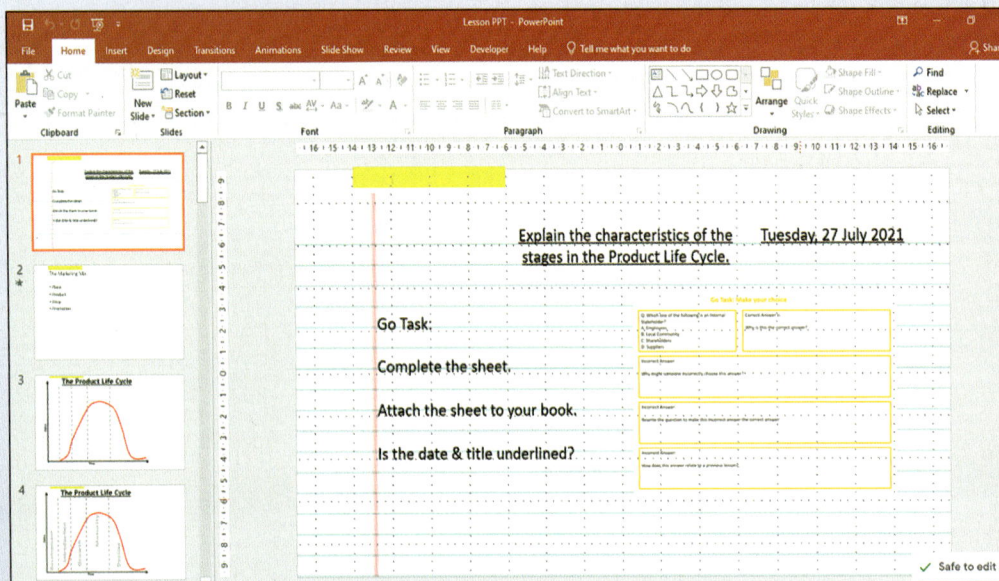

Figure 1.30: Presentation software

Presentation software has one main use in creating digital communications and that is for making presentations. It is already set up with slides for the content, and the author can add appropriate layouts and **formatting**. There is a bank of designs that can be added to a presentation, along with slide transitions and animations. You can also embed video and other multimedia into the slides.

Over to you!   2

Using the marketing plan you created in Over to you! 1, suggest at least one suitable piece of software that you could use to create one element of your marketing campaign.

Over to you!   3

1   Describe how a presentation can be used as a digital communication tool.

2   Explain how a presentation can be adapted to suit the intended audience.

3   A presentation can often be a distraction from the information it is meant to be giving. Explain how this can be prevented by the author.

4   A charity wishes to update its publicity material. Describe which software it might choose and justify your answer.

5.3 Digital devices

Today we are surrounded by a wide range of different digital devices, many of which we take for granted as we interact with them daily.

Smartphone

A smartphone has an instant connection to the internet, often through a mobile browser. Through this connection, you can have access to email accounts as well as other communication tools such as social media and video conferencing. Other features include a digital camera, typically with video capability, and **GPS**. To keep a smartphone simple, it has a touchscreen and a software-based on-screen keyboard.

Smart TV

Like a smartphone, a smart TV has a connection to the internet that gives you access to additional services as compared to a traditional TV. Using the internet connection you can browse the internet, access video services such as YouTube or video conferencing, play games and connect to social media.

PC/laptop

We are all familiar with using a PC or laptop, however we don't always consider the features of one. You can connect a range of **peripheral devices**, including adding additional displays. You can access the internet, through a **wired** or wireless connection, and have increased storage, both internally and externally. In addition, a PC/laptop can be enhanced through adding accessories as well as improving existing elements such as the graphics card.

Tablet

A **tablet** device is often seen as a happy medium between having a smartphone and having a laptop, and as such it shares similar features. Tablets have on-screen keyboards or you can attach a small keyboard to them. Like both smartphones and laptops, they have an instant internet connection and camera and the features that come with this.

Smartboard

We often see **smartboards** in the classroom or similar educational spaces. A smartboard has plenty of features that enhance a presentation. In addition to having an internet connection, when giving a presentation you can write notes on the slides to support what you are saying. There is also the opportunity to record your presentation and share it, including any notes. A smartboard generally has an on-screen keyboard and handwriting recognition software which converts it to text.

Figure 1.31: A tablet will have a larger touchscreen than a smartphone

Stretch

1. When choosing a smart device to use for an elderly person, what do you need to consider?

2. When wishing to work remotely, what device would be the most suitable? Why?

3. Teachers often view a smartboard as a waste of money. Discuss why they might have this point of view.

4. A sales manager travels around the UK on a regular basis, checking on each sales office. Explain what digital device would be suitable for them to use. Justify your choice.

5.4 Distribution channels

Types of distribution channel

A **distribution channel** is the method whereby the communication is delivered to the intended audience. There are a variety of methods that could be used.

Cloud

As described in TA3, the cloud is a general term for (mostly) free storage that can be remotely accessed through the internet. All the different communication tools can be created, edited and stored in the cloud and accessed via an internet connection.

As it is internet-based, it can be accessed from any location by multiple people at once and there is a lot of support available for users. However, cloud storage is reliant on having a connection to the internet and it is not easily usable on all devices.

Email

An email is an electronic message that can be sent to multiple individuals and to which the recipients can reply. In the email, sender (and recipients) can attach files and other multimedia elements. In addition, you can apply formatting to the message, such as setting elements in bold. You can also automatically reply to emails (for example, telling people you are out of office) as well as forward them to others.

Email can also be sent and received instantly from a wide range of devices, including smart TVs and games consoles with an internet connection. Email accounts are free to set up and are environmentally friendly by using no paper. However, email can be used to spread computer malware and there is no guarantee that the recipient has read the email.

Messaging

This uses technology to be able to send instant messages using an internet connection. The messages are sent and received by the recipient instantly. Most messages are text-based but you can also send images, video and audio files.

Any device with an internet connection can be used to send messages. Furthermore, you are not limited to just sending a message to one person, but you can send messages to a group. One key drawback to messaging is the security risks as some messaging services are a target for black hat hackers. Equally, some of the multimedia messages that can be sent can contain malware.

Mobile apps

A mobile app (or mobile application) is a computer program that is designed to run on a mobile device, such as a smartphone or tablet. Its main purpose is to provide the user with a service or experience. This could be work-based such as a calendar or email or it could be for entertainment such as a game.

There is a large selection of apps to choose from, some of which are free and some of which have a cost. Creating a basic mobile app doesn't take long and they are usually quick to download and updated regularly.

One of the downsides is that not all mobile apps are secure and can cause security risks to your device. Some free apps can also have a lot of advertisements included. Using lots of apps can cause issues with how you manage your time and your health.

Multimedia

Multimedia is an excellent form of communication that provides content by combining text, audio, images, animation and/or video into a single presentation. This makes it easy to adapt the content for any audience, regardless of their age, gender or location.

Using multimedia gives the author the opportunity to be creative and provide variety. It can make a topic seem incredibly realistic. However, to share any multimedia, you need to be able to access the content, including the file format. It can be costly to create multimedia, as well as taking time and needing the appropriate skills and knowledge.

VoIP

VoIP is an excellent method of distribution when you have a reliable internet connection. This is because VoIP can be used to share a variety of media without the need for specific software or hardware. You can share audio. VoIP relies on the internet so it is a low-cost method that can be used to connect multiple global users at once. However, you can experience problems if your internet connection is not strong enough.

Websites

Creating and using a website as a distribution channel has many advantages. It can be used to share most digital communications such as video, audio, infographics and leaflets. Hosting and creating a website can be low-cost (even free). You need to make sure your website is secure so that no one can change the content. You also need to make sure you are following any laws such as the Copyright, Designs and Patents Act. Having a website gives you a global audience for your digital communications. There are freely available templates so you do not need to have much experience to create one.

Case study

Flappy Bird

Creating a mobile app is not as tricky as you might think. It takes a good idea and some time to create it using any of the free pieces of software available. Publishing a completed app to either the Apple App Store or the Google Play Store can be a little difficult. You must meet specific criteria and you have to pay a fee.

However, having a successful app is often down to luck – there are over 25,000 new apps being released each month. It took over eight months for Flappy Bird to get noticed. At the height of its success, the app was making its developer $50,000 a day and it had been downloaded more than 50 million times.

Figure 1.32: A player playing an action game on a mobile

Unlike other free apps, there was no in-app purchasing. The profits were being made from the adverts that were on the bottom of the screen. The simplicity of the game made it incredibly popular and, to some users, very addictive. Following messages on social media the developer took the game down. Today there are many apps that have copied the original Flappy Bird idea to try to be as successful.

Check your understanding

1   Explain how a mobile app can be adapted to suit its audience.

2   Which other distribution channels could the game have used? Justify your choice.

3   'Playing games on a smartphone is natural; there are no issues.' Discuss the advantages and disadvantages of using a smartphone as a communication tool.

Distribution channel connectivity

So far, we have looked at the different channels of communication, and one of the most common features or characteristics has been that the majority rely on an internet connection – but how can you connect to the internet?

4G/5G

This stands for 4th generation and 5th generation mobile phone technology. It provides faster speeds of internet connection, allowing the user to access a wider range of media more quickly than the previous versions (3G and 2G). A device can access the internet without the need for a Wi-Fi **router**, as the data is transmitted through the phone network instead of through the broadband (internet) network.

The biggest advantage is that it provides the user with an internet connection on the move and the ability to transfer data fairly quickly. Unfortunately, it can be expensive to download data in this way and not all areas have 4G or 5G connections.

Bluetooth® wireless technology

This is a wireless method for exchanging data over short distances. It uses a special radio frequency to transmit the data. It is frequently used for wireless communication between devices and some peripherals, such as hands-free sets. When using Bluetooth technology, there is generally no interference from other devices and it has a low power consumption. In addition, it is very cheap and has no additional costs. However, Bluetooth technology is not overly secure as it can be hacked. It can also lose connection depending on the conditions, especially as it only has a short range.

Figure 1.33: The recognisable Bluetooth symbol

Mobile Wi-Fi hotspots

These are portable mobile routers that you can use to set up an internet connection using 3G and 4G signals from local network providers. You often find them in public places like shopping centres or hotels and coffee shops. You can also use your smartphone as a **hotspot**.

Using a hotspot is fantastic if you are on the move and need internet access. By combining a hotspot with your laptop or tablet, you can work anywhere. However, depending on what you are doing, the speed of the hotspot might be slow and you might have a limit on how much data you can use without paying for more. Public hotspots are also notoriously insecure so not recommended for confidential work.

Wi-Fi

Wi-Fi is the ability to connect to the internet without the need for cables. Wi-Fi signals use radio frequencies to connect to a wireless access point or a router. The router allows the device to access the internet.

A Wi-Fi network can easily be created and extended and the users can move around the area whilst still staying connected. However, there is still a limited range with Wi-Fi and you can experience interference which will reduce the speed of your connection. Wi-Fi can be made secure with the addition of a password or other security methods, but it is not perfectly secure as it can still be hacked.

Wired

A wired connection allows internet access directly from an access point to a device via an ethernet cable. In using a wired connection, the data is transferred much more quickly than using a wireless connection, and without any interference.

One of the biggest advantages is that it is one of the most secure methods as no one can hack into the data as it is being transferred along the cable. However, the cost of the cable can be expensive, it is not always convenient since you are limiting your movement and not all devices, such as tablets or smartphones, allow a wired connection.

Over to you!   4

A local youth club is being renovated and the staff have been given a choice about how their digital devices will be connected to each other and the network.

The staff generally use their devices to take a register for who is attending a session and for checking emails.

Write an email to the youth club co-ordinator explaining which methods of connectivity are available and which one would be suitable for the needs of the staff. Make sure you justify your choice.

5.5 Audience demographics

When considering digital communications as well as the distribution channel, you obviously need to consider who is the intended audience. This is known as audience demographics.

The key areas to consider are:

Accessibility: How easy is the method to use and approach, especially if the user has any disabilities? For example, if a user has a visual impairment, can the digital communication be zoomed in?

Age: Whilst you naturally might think about users being too young for the content of a digital communication, you also need to consider the age of a user for which the distribution channel is suitable as some users might not be comfortable connecting with Bluetooth technology, for example.

Gender: This is a tricky issue as at times some individuals still hold the traditional view that digital communications can be tailored to suit specific genders, for example, pinks for girls and blues for boys.

Location: Currently there is still the issue of digital connectivity in some areas of the UK (and beyond) where some methods of digital connectivity are more effective than others. Equally, a user might wish to consider the cyber-security risks of using some of the connectivity methods, depending on their location (public or private).

Review your learning

Test your knowledge

1   Define the term 'VoIP'.

2   What method of communication would be suitable for sharing news and information with your local community? Why?

3   Explain how DTP can be used to create digital communications.

4   Describe the characteristics of a tablet.

5   Explain the benefits of using email to communicate with others.

6   Describe the differences between a 4G and a Bluetooth technology connection.

7   What method would you use to share a multimedia presentation with a colleague? Why?

What have you learnt?

	See section
• The purpose of a range of digital communications and their advantages and disadvantages.	5.1
• The characteristics of the software used to create digital communications.	5.2
• The characteristics of a range of digital devices.	5.3
• The characteristics of each type of distribution channel and its advantages and disadvantages.	5.4
• The characteristics of different methods of connectivity and their advantages and disadvantages.	5.4
• The suitability of different digital communications linked to specific audience demographics.	5.5

Internet of Everything (IoE)

Let's get started

Think about your home. How many devices do you have connected to the internet? Make a list of the devices you have.

Figure 1.34: Many forms of home entertainment depend on the internet

What will you learn?

- What is meant by the IoE.

- How the World Wide Web (WWW) and the internet are used in the use of the IoE.

- The four pillars and how they interact.

- The advantages and disadvantages of the IoE.

- Digital interactivity and how devices can be tailored to meet the needs of the end users.

- How the IoE can be used in everyday life.

6.1 Use of IoE

What is the Internet of Everything (IoE)?

The **Internet of Things** is a general term that refers to devices being connected to the internet and therefore sharing data. It is based on the concept that an internet connection doesn't have to be limited to a laptop or a tablet, but rather any device can be connected in order to support our lives and do more tasks automatically. The **Internet of Everything** builds on this to use people, processes and data to make everyone's lives better.

Figure 1.35: Any device can be connected to support our lives

The internet versus the World Wide Web (WWW)

The internet is an ever-growing network of devices that are connected using standard protocols (communication rules), whereas the **World Wide Web** is a collection of files such as webpages and other documents linked together. The IoE uses the internet to share data between devices, such as requesting a light to be switched on.

The four pillars of the IoE

People: Nowadays, people can connect with others using smart devices. We are wearing more technology, such as smart watches. Designers are incorporating technology into clothing. This is just the start of how people are connecting with technology.

Data: As devices are used, a large amount of data is gathered and analysed. The results can then be shared so that the technology can be improved.

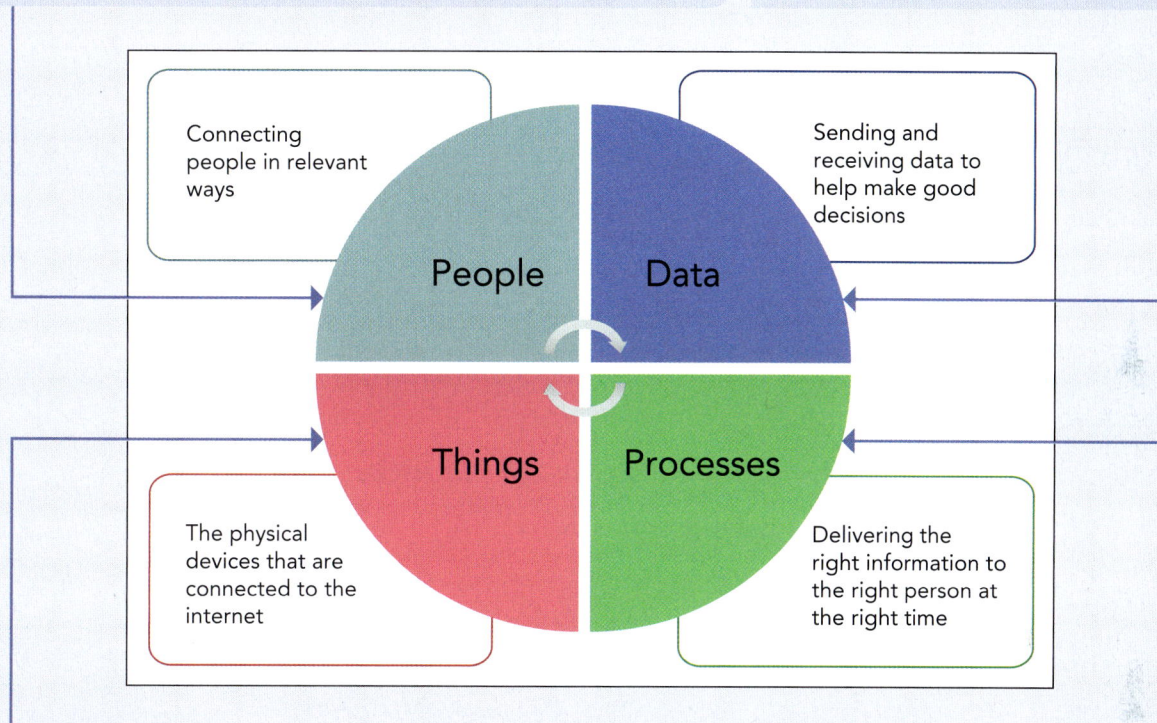

Connecting people in relevant ways

Sending and receiving data to help make good decisions

People

Data

Things

Processes

The physical devices that are connected to the internet

Delivering the right information to the right person at the right time

Things: These are the physical devices that are connected to the internet and to each other. This is the foundation of the IoE. Smart devices are capable of sensing, recording and gathering data.

Process: This pillar focuses on delivering the right information to the right person or device, at the right time.

Figure 1.36: The four pillars of the IoE

The interactivity between the four pillars

As these four pillars work together, they become more powerful in terms of when or how they are used. No single pillar can be used in isolation, they are dependent on each other. For example, if **people** were not accessing the devices, then data would not be generated. Alternatively, if it was not for **things**, then there would be no devices for **people** to use and no data that needed processing.

We can easily access data and information wherever we are, in real time. This is possible because of the network of devices.

We can access any information from anywhere in the world. There is better communication because a network of connected devices can work together. Through the IoE, tasks can be done automatically which saves time and can be cost-effective. The biggest issue surrounding the IoE is that data might not be secure and confidential information might not be safe. As we become more dependent on technology, if something goes wrong, we might not be able to do that task ourselves. As tasks become automated, there will be less need for people to do those jobs. This will have an impact on employment.

Over to you!

1   Describe how the internet and the WWW are different.

2   Discuss why some people might have concerns over privacy and security when using the IoE.

3   Choose two of the pillars and think of three tasks that would need both pillars to interact in order to complete the tasks.

4   Discuss what kind of technology you would like to see added to items of clothing.

IoE digital interactivity

As we have previously covered in TA2: Human Computer Interface (HCI) in everyday life, there are a range of ways in which the user can interact with a digital device. However, the IoE takes this further as the device is tailored to meet the users' needs.

Device to device

As part of a network, smart devices often communicate with each other, especially for automatic tasks. For example, a smart thermostat could be connected to the smart valve on a radiator. When the temperature drops below a set value the thermostat could send a message to the valves to heat up the radiators.

Human to device

When considering the Internet of Everything, human to device is the element that we are the most familiar with. Humans (users) give commands to devices, such as to turn on a light or to play some music.

Sometimes, the user isn't giving a physical demand but rather is connected to a device. An example is when you wear a smart watch that monitors your heart rate.

How digital devices can be tailored to meet the needs of the user

Most devices that are part of the IoE have been designed to consider what users want or need. If they didn't, there would be minimal interest in and use of the devices.

For example, Amazon have designed a range of devices that are part of the IoE. These include the Kindle, the Echo and the Ring Video Doorbells and Security systems. These devices have all been carefully designed to address the wants and needs of the user. They have considered how and where the user will access the device and how it looks. Equally, a device can be adjusted for individuals. For example, an Amazon device doesn't have to be called Alexa and a Ring Video doorbell can have a personalised sound such as an animal noise or a favourite song.

As the IoE develops, so does the technology such as smart fabric and smart cars. It is worth keeping a watch on what is new.

Case study

e-Readers will destroy book shops

It has been over 12 years since the Kindle was first released. At the time, experts confidently said that by 2020 print books would be largely decorative and we would all have a personal pocket electronic library.

In fact, e-books account for around 20% of book sales, the rest being traditional print. A decade ago, we'd have expected those numbers to be the other way around by now. So, what happened? It all comes down to two factors, consumer habits and money.

Figure 1.37: A man and his daughter using a tablet

Most people now spend a large quantity of their time in front of a screen. Using an e-reader is popular amongst certain groups of people, but the majority still prefer an actual book to read.

Continued

The cost of e-books is also still high. When combined with the initial cost of an e-reader, it is still cheaper to buy the physical book unless you are buying all books digitally in future.

Check your understanding

1   Describe how an e-reader is part of the IoE.

2   Explain what concerns a user of an e-reader might have about being part of the IoE.

3   'The IoE will never be as fully utilised as it could be.' Discuss this statement and explain why the IoE might not be fully used by an individual.

   In your answer consider a range of concerns that an individual might have about the IoE. Then to balance your answer, consider how some of the concerns could be resolved.

6.2 Application areas in everyday life

Table 1.13: Application areas of the IoE in everyday life

Application area	Description	Security risk	Advantages	Disadvantages
Energy management	We use the IoE in our homes to monitor our usage of gas and electricity through smart meters. In 2020 there were 21.5 million homes and small businesses that had a smart meter installed. This number is expected to rise over the coming years, especially with all the new homes being built. Energy firms are also using a 'smart-grid' to monitor how much energy an area is using. Using this with weather forecasts, traffic flows and other 'live' data they can predict how much energy they will need to supply and when demand will be at its highest.	Risk from black hat hackers. They target the smart grid and attempt to take it offline. This would leave users in the area with no power.	• Users know exactly how much energy they have used and therefore what their energy bill will be. • Data can be monitored closely to meet environmental targets. • Users no longer need to send off their meter reading. The company don't have to send someone to read the meters when users don't respond.	• A smart meter is not always easy to read or use, especially for elderly people. • People who rent homes cannot install a smart meter. • Switching energy suppliers is difficult as they all use different smart meters.

Table 1.13: Continued

Application area	Description	Security risk	Advantages	Disadvantages
Health	Patients can be monitored remotely for symptoms rather than needing frequent checks by doctors. For example, a diabetic patient can monitor their sugar levels easily and send the results of the tests automatically to their doctor. They do not need to record them on paper and take them to the doctors every few weeks. By collecting results automatically, the doctor can be alerted if there is a sudden issue, potentially saving the individual's life.	One concern about using the IoE with our healthcare is privacy and security. Who has access to our medical records? How secure are they?	• Real-time remote monitoring through connected devices and smart alerts can diagnose illnesses, treat diseases and save lives in case of an emergency. • Smart sensors can review health conditions and make recommendations. This will reduce the occurrence of diseases and other health issues. • By using the IoE there can be a reduction in how frequently individuals need to see a doctor or visit the hospital. This will save money.	• If the equipment doesn't work, the individual's life is at risk. • Not all medical suppliers use the same equipment or software so it might not work together. • It can cost quite a lot for the right equipment and to make sure it is connected to the IoE.
Manufacturing	It is expected that the IoE will continue to transform the manufacturing world. The IoE will make a lot of the processes automatic, and they will be controlled from one main machine.	Risk of industrial spying. Competitors might try to access systems to find out what a business is doing and steal its ideas.	• Equipment can be monitored to ensure that maintenance schedules are based on actual wear. • Keeps workers safe. Prevents accidents from happening by analysing live data from factories. • Makes it simpler to track products and the progress of them being made.	• Not all equipment can be converted and added to the IoE. It may be unique. • Some roles in manufacturing still require a human operator.
Military/ Emergency Services (Police, Fire Service, Ambulance, Coast Guard, Mountain Rescue, Army, Navy, Air Force)	The IoE has made it easier to find and respond to emergency situations. For example, if someone is injured when climbing a mountain, the walker can use the GPS on their smartphone to notify Mountain Rescue of their exact location.	Risks to confidentiality of information. In the military and police there will be data that needs to be kept secret.	• Allows a more prompt and appropriate response to an emergency. • More lives can be saved by using a range of data sources rather than just relying on a phone call.	• The source of the data can be manipulated, putting lives at risk. • The equipment can be a security risk, not just the data that is being shared.

Table 1.13: Continued

Application area	Description	Security risk	Advantages	Disadvantages
Smart devices (in the home, and in personal and business contexts)	We all have a range of smart devices in our lives. As a result, some big businesses are gaining a lot of data about how we spend our time and our money, either personally or as an organisation.	Risk to information – either your personal information or corporate information. A smart device is considered to always be 'on' so in our homes, on our person or in our office it can be listening to everything we say – but what happens to those recordings?	• Gives the user the convenience of using it hands-free. • The user can save time by using it for automatic tasks such as turning on the lights at dusk. • It can make the user more time efficient, especially with their daily routine.	• Smart devices can be expensive, especially if you have them throughout the home or office. • They can react to what is being said around them rather than directed at them. • Most are voice controlled, which can be an issue for someone who has a hearing impairment.
Transport	The IoE is becoming key to ensuring that journeys take place on time and without any hold-ups. An example of this is smart motorways. In manufacturing the IoE helps to ensure that products arrive or depart on time for the customer.	Risk is focused on people and ensuring that no harm comes to individuals on journeys. With essential goods, such as medicine or food, it is vital that they reach their destinations on time.	• Modes of transport can be tracked in 'real-time'. Users can monitor if there is a problem. • Efficient travelling times can be calculated and used. • Where there is an issue, such as a breakdown, other modes of transport can be redirected via another route.	• Dependent on having a suitable infrastructure to make it work effectively. • Not all modes of transport are capable of being adapted to joining the IoE.

Stretch

1   Describe five ways in which smart devices can help a user at home.

2   Explain the privacy concerns an individual might have about using a smart device in the home.

3   Discuss whether the benefits outweigh the concerns about using a smart device at work.

4   Research new ways the healthcare profession is using the IoE to help people. Pick one of the new methods and explain why you think this will be successful.

Let's get digital!

Go to the FlightRadar24 website.

Using some suitable software, create a leaflet that discusses the suitability of using the Internet of Everything in the aviation industry. Include its advantages and disadvantages.

Review your learning

Test your knowledge

1   Define the term 'Internet of Everything'.

2   Describe the difference between the Internet of Things and the Internet of Everything.

3   The four pillars interact with each other. Explain how this interaction occurs.

4   Explain the role of the internet in the IoE.

5   Explain how the coastguard might use the IoE.

6   Discuss the security risks that motorways face when connecting to the IoE.

7   Discuss the pros and cons a car factory might be evaluating regarding connecting to the IoE.

What have you learnt?

	See section
• What is meant by the IoE.	6.1
• How the World Wide Web (WWW) and the internet are used in the use of the IoE.	6.1
• The four pillars and the interaction between them.	6.1
• The advantages and disadvantages of the IoE.	6.1
• The term 'digital interactivity' and how devices can be tailored to meet the needs of end users.	6.1
• The purpose, security issues and advantages and disadvantages of the IoE when applied to a range of areas in everyday life.	6.2

Let's get started

Can you think of a situation where it is useful to sort information into a particular order (such as prices of phones you are interested in, from high to low) or to categorise it (such as certain phone features)? Why might you want to use sorting or categorising?

What will you learn in this unit?

Spreadsheets are powerful tools which allow businesses to collect, analyse and present data. They can range from a simple spreadsheet which adds up the sales to a sophisticated mini application created by IT professionals which can be used by businesses' employees to support them in their job roles.

In this unit you will learn about:

- Planning and designing the spreadsheet solution **TA1**

- Creating the spreadsheet solution **TA2**

- Testing the spreadsheet solution **TA3**

- Evaluating the spreadsheet solution **TA4**.

How you will be assessed

This unit is assessed by an assignment set by OCR (the exam board). The assignment will be marked by your teacher and is worth 60 marks. The assignment will include a client scenario, with practical tasks for you to complete. For example:

- planning a spreadsheet solution for the brief in the assignment

- creating your spreadsheet solution

- testing and reviewing your spreadsheet against the brief.

TA1

Planning and designing the spreadsheet solution

Let's get started

Why do you think the design stage is important for creating a spreadsheet? What might happen if the design stage is not completed properly? Look back at Unit R050 IT in the digital world (TA1) and note down three key points about design.

What will you learn?

- Design tools you can use.

- How to design the **functionality** of the solution including calculations and user aids.

- How to design **outputs** for the solution such as **charts** and reports.

- How to design the way in which the user will navigate around the solution.

1.1 Design tools

Within organisations, an IT professional will often create a **spreadsheet** solution to meet the requirements of a user who might not be an IT expert. In this situation the IT professional must understand what the user needs the spreadsheet to do and make it easy to use. A design is also important if you are working in a team and other people need to work on parts of the solution.

Figure 2.1: The user will need a spreadsheet solution including graphs and charts

The design needs to cover several things:

- **Functionality** – what the spreadsheet solution will actually do. For example, it might do calculations automatically or print out reports.

- **Navigation** systems – how the user will move around the parts of spreadsheet they need to use. How users will input any required **data** and choose different options.

- Outputs – how the spreadsheet will present results to the user such as **graphs** or charts.

You can choose various different tools to design the spreadsheet solution. Different tools are better suited to designing different parts of it. **Flow charts** can be used to design the way a user might work through the spreadsheet or how calculations might be done. **Mind maps** are best for exploring initial ideas and aspects of the solution that need to be considered.

All the examples in this unit use Microsoft Excel. Other spreadsheet software such as Google Sheets can be used and many of the features are similar to those found in Excel.

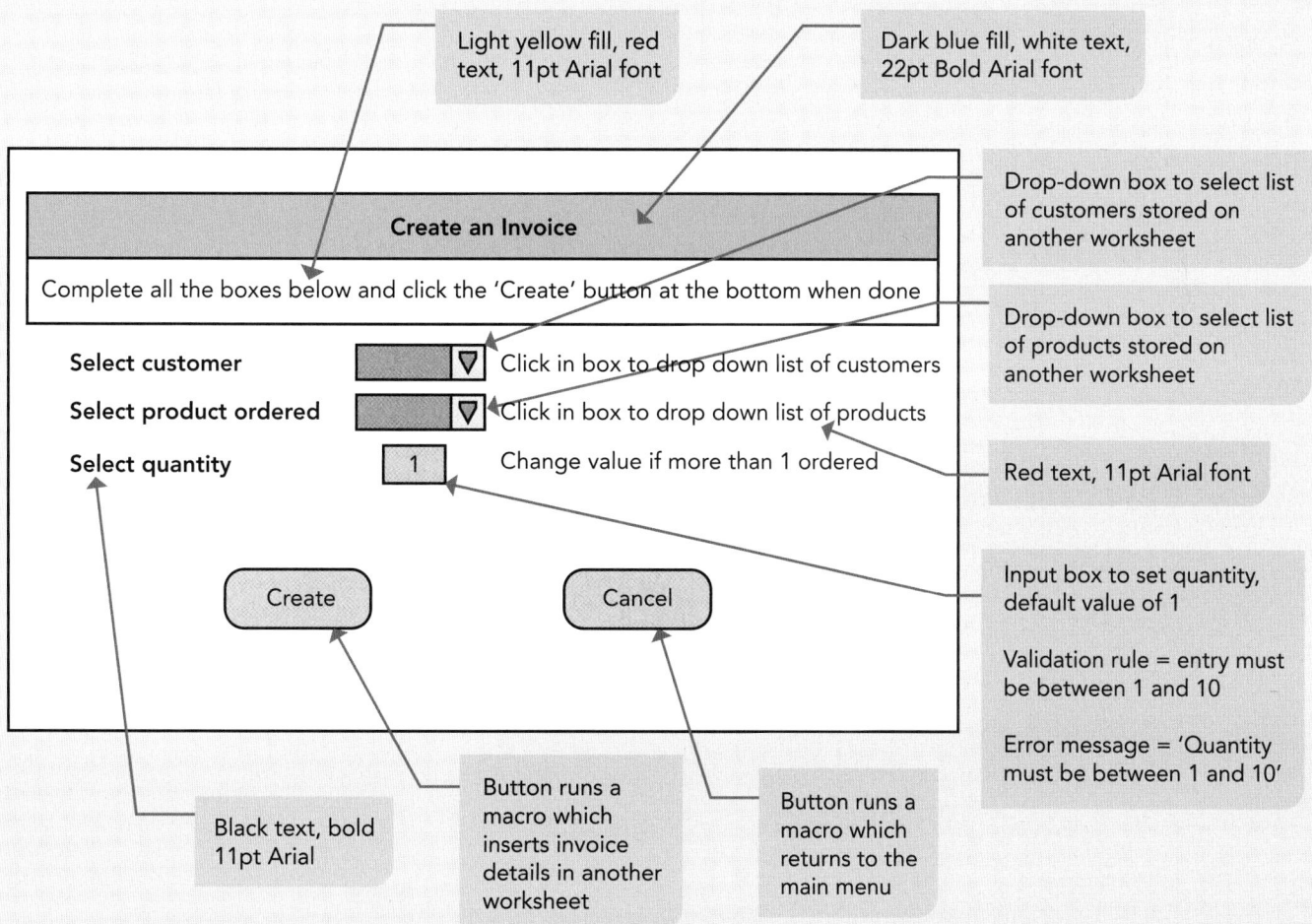

Figure 2.2: An example of a **wireframe** design for an input screen for a spreadsheet solution

Visual design tools

There are also several different tools that can help you design how a spreadsheet solution will look if it contains forms or navigation. You will also use these design tools where features like charts, graphs and reports for printing are included in the spreadsheet. You might not need to use them all. The tools include:

- **Visualisation diagram** – good for outlining initial ideas of how the solution will look to a user

- Storyboard – used to design the way a user would work through a solution step by step, telling a 'story' of what they would see

- Wireframe – used for designing the way a solution will look and provide more detail than the visualisation diagram.

- Mind maps – also good for initial development of ideas for the solution including all the aspects which need to be considered and they are related.

You can draw these diagrams by hand or use software tools such as Microsoft Word drawing tools, Draw.io or Microsoft Visio.

1.2 Human computer interface (HCI) design conventions and principles

The **HCI (Human Computer Interface)** for the spreadsheet solution is important because this is the part that users will see and interact with. Your spreadsheet solution should be intuitive, meaning it should be clear and easy to use. For example, in a typical spreadsheet you would give your columns meaningful and descriptive names.

Functionality

Designing what the spreadsheet solution will actually do is an important part of the design. The functionality of the solution includes a number of things.

Calculations

Typically, a spreadsheet solution will involve inputting some data (usually numbers) and carrying out a calculation using the data that has been input. Flow charts are a good way of designing calculations that involve

Case study

Flow chart for a spreadsheet solution

Dal is a self-employed painter and decorator. He needs to produce estimates to paint rooms for customers. Instead of manually calculating how much paint he will need he asks his daughter to create a spreadsheet solution which will do the estimation for him. She draws a flow chart to help her work out how the calculation can be done. This is shown here.

Check your understanding

1   Can you explain the meaning of the different types of flow chart boxes used in the diagram?

2   What other **information** do you think Dal will need (not included in the flow chart) to produce the final estimate?

3   Along with the flow chart, what other tools can be used to complete the design?

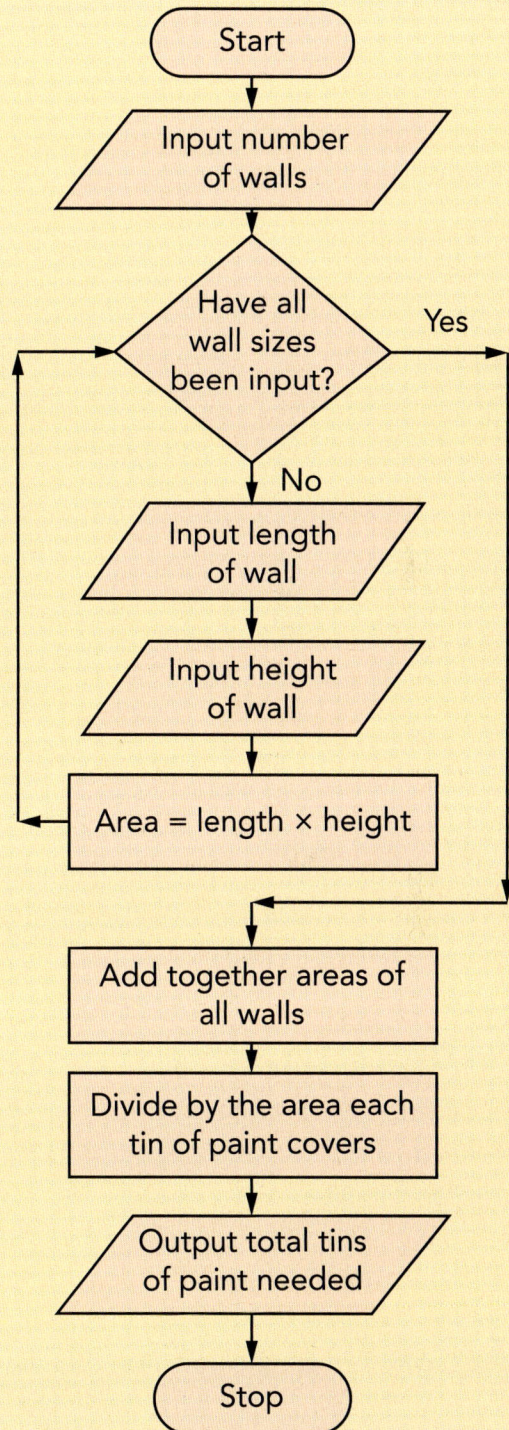

Figure 2.3: A flow chart for a spreadsheet solution

multiple steps. At the design stage calculations do not need to include actual spreadsheet **cell references**.

Sorting

If a spreadsheet solution outputs a long list of data it might be helpful to have sorted it into a particular order.

For example, imagine a list of companies that owe you money.

- Having the company that owes you the most money at the top and the company that owes you the least at the bottom might be a good idea. This is known as sorting in descending order

- Text data such as people's names can be sorted into alphabetical order

- Information about whether data should be sorted should be included in the design. This could be an **annotation** on the wireframe design.

Sorting is discussed further in TA2: Creating the spreadsheet solution.

Filtering

Filtering can be applied if the spreadsheet solution outputs a long list of data. This removes the results in the data that do not match certain criteria. For example, you could filter out data less than a particular value. This can also be indicated on design documents using an annotation. Filtering is discussed further in TA2 Creating the spreadsheet solution.

User aids

These are features in the spreadsheet that help users understand what they need to do to use the system and what they can and cannot do. Examples include:

- **Data entry messages.** These are text labels on the spreadsheet which indicate to the user what data they are expected to enter. These would be included on the wireframe design.

- Data **validation** is used to make sure the data that the user **inputs** are of the correct type. For example, if a calculation in the solution requires a numerical input from the user and they input a text value, this will cause problems with the calculation. Validating the input to make sure it is numeric before it is used in the calculation is therefore a good idea.

If the input fails the validation test then a meaningful error message should be output so the user knows where they are going wrong.

The design for the user aids and meaningful error messages should be included in the **storyboards** or wireframe diagrams for the solution.

> ### Let's get digital!
>
> Create a wireframe diagram for Dal's room painting estimator from the earlier case study. What data validation should be applied to the inputs on the painting estimator? Add the error messages to be displayed if validation fails as annotations to the wireframe diagram.

Types of outputs that clearly present information for an organisation

For any spreadsheet solution it is important that the output produced is clear and meets the needs of the users. It needs to provide meaningful information that can be easily understood. There are several ways information can be presented.

Charts

Charts can be every effective in summarising large amounts of information. They can also make it easy to compare sets of data (for example, the amount of rainfall in summer compared to winter) and spot trends (for example, are sales increasing or decreasing over time?). There are many different types of charts but the main ones are:

- **Pie charts** – can only represent a single data series and are best when you want to show how a total amount is divided up by different categories, so for example, you could use a pie chart to show the different methods of transport children use to get to school.

- **Bar charts** – can represent multiple data series and show changes over time. So, a business that has three different shops could show how sales in each shop have changed over three months using a bar chart.

- **Line charts** – are used to show how values change over time and are useful for spotting trends. A line chart could be used, for example, to show the average temperatures in several different cities over a year.

Which charts you plan to use, their **formatting** and labels should be considered.

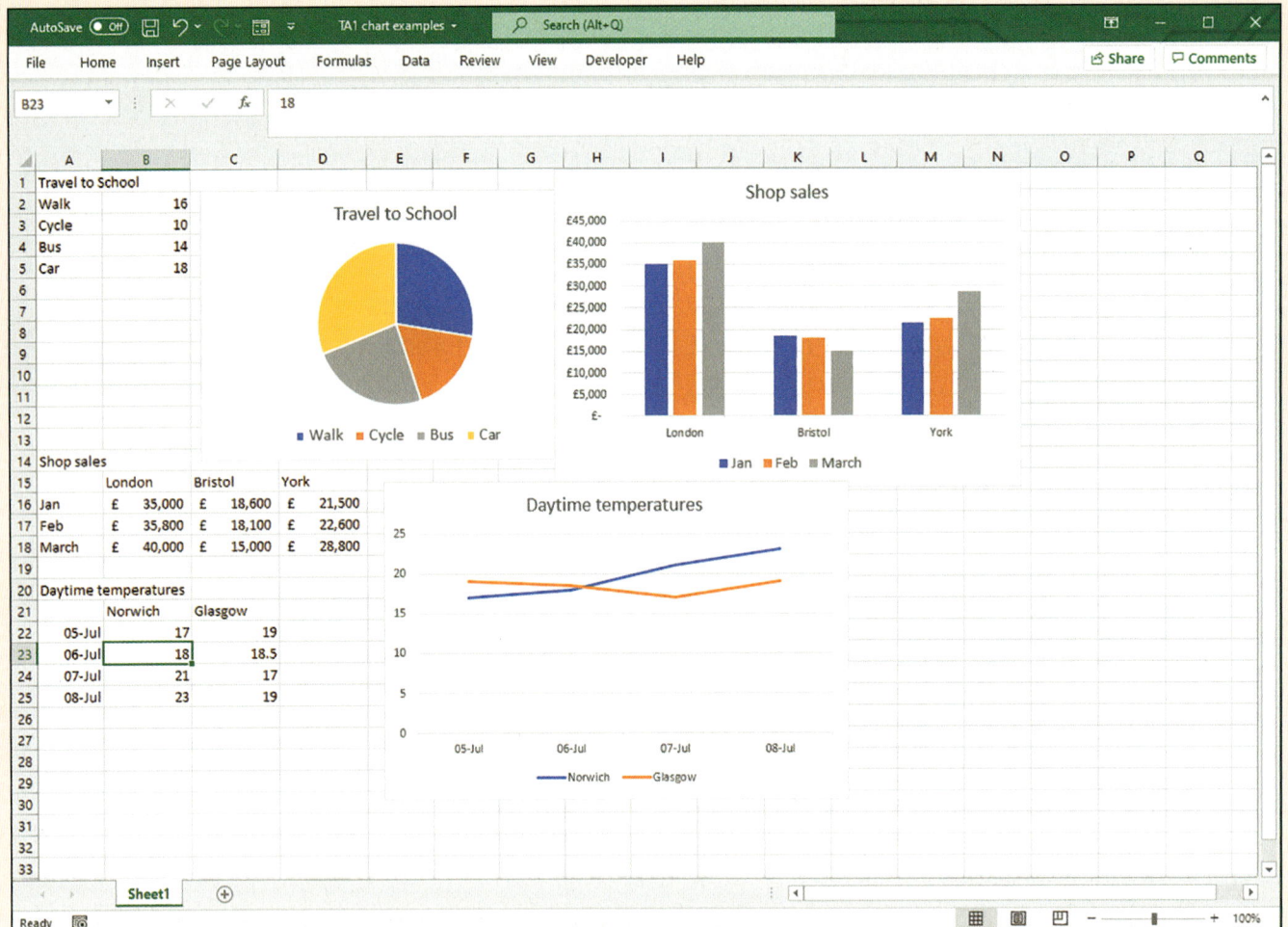

Figure 2.4: You need to decide what charts would be useful for the users and where in the worksheets of the solution the charts will be displayed

You might need to format the charts using a **house style**, which is discussed later in this section. You should also consider whether the chart will be printed and how this should look.

Lists

Lists of data can be difficult to read if they are long. However, lists might suit some types of data, such as the names and addresses of people or companies. It is often a good idea to sort lists or filter them to make sure only relevant data is shown. If you plan to use a list in your spreadsheet solution you need to design what data will be included in the list and where in the worksheets of the solution the list will be shown.

Invoices and reports

Reports are a type of list that is formatted in a more user-friendly way. For example, it may show groupings, subtotal and totals. So, you could produce a report on unpaid invoices grouped and totalled by company and with an overall total. Invoices are a particular kind of report that a spreadsheet solution might be developed to produce. It is a document that one company sends to another requesting payment for goods or services provided.

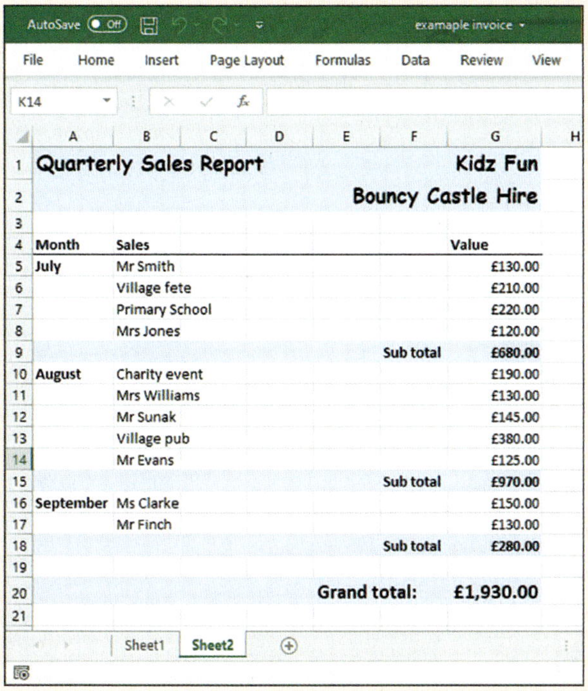

Quarterly Sales Report			Kidz Fun
			Bouncy Castle Hire
Month	Sales		Value
July	Mr Smith		£130.00
	Village fete		£210.00
	Primary School		£220.00
	Mrs Jones		£120.00
		Sub total	£680.00
August	Charity event		£190.00
	Mrs Williams		£130.00
	Mr Sunak		£145.00
	Village pub		£380.00
	Mr Evans		£125.00
		Sub total	£970.00
September	Ms Clarke		£150.00
	Mr Finch		£130.00
		Sub total	£280.00
		Grand total:	£1,930.00

Figure 2.5: Spreadsheet report example

When creating your design, you will need to consider where the data to create the report is going to come from. For example, the data might exist within the spreadsheet on another worksheet.

Worksheets

Spreadsheets can consist of multiple worksheets, and you can use these in your solution for a number of purposes. Different worksheets can be used to provide a structure that the users can work through such as a main menu and sub menus. They can also be used to form a simple 'front end' that the user can interact with while the main workings of the spreadsheet are held on another worksheet. Therefore, in your design for the spreadsheet solution you need to think about how many different worksheets will be needed and what they are used for.

Printing

Any of these outputs (or parts of them, such as charts) may need to be printed. How the output will look when printed can be set from the page **layout** menu. Will you use margins, scaling or print guidelines? Will you need to set a print area? Features such as headers and footers (content at the top and bottom and repeated on each page) may also need to be added. How your output will look when printed should be considered.

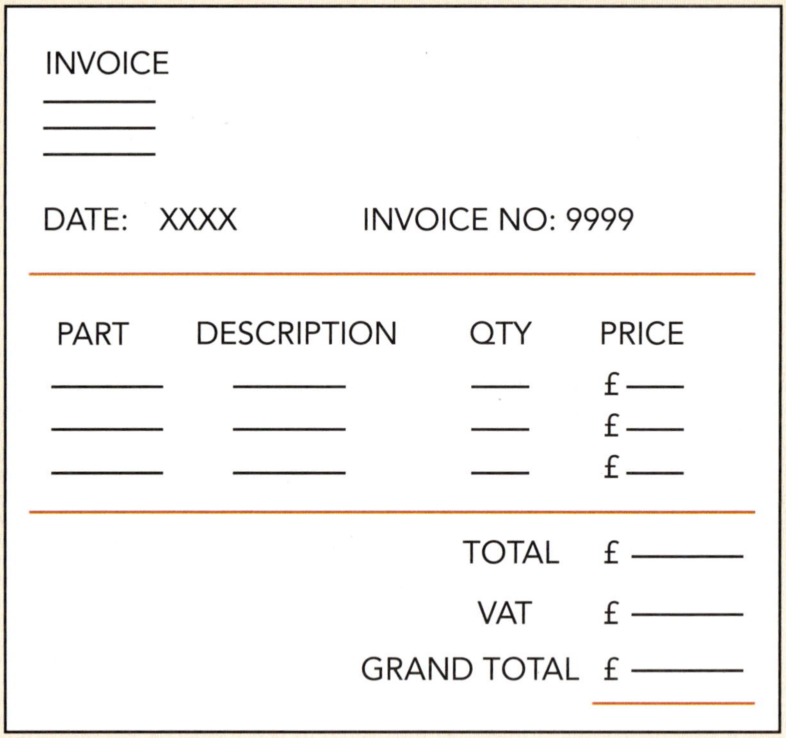

INVOICE
DATE: XXXX
INVOICE NO: 9999
PART
DESCRIPTION
QTY
PRICE
£
£
£
TOTAL £
VAT £
GRAND TOTAL £

Figure 2.6: Example visualisation diagram for an invoice

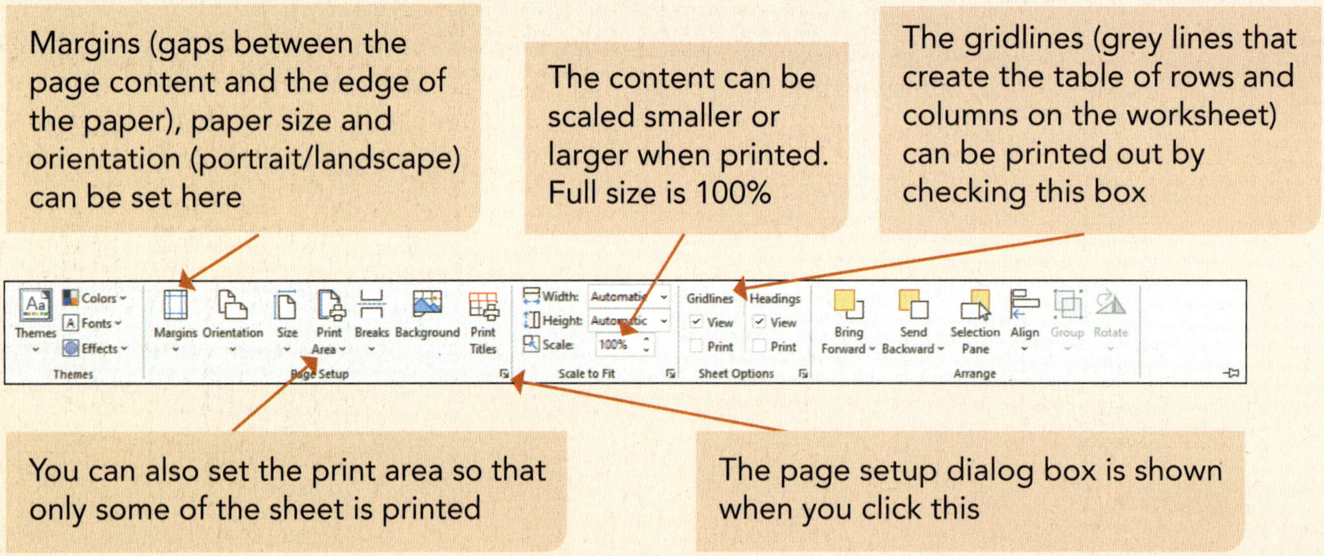

Margins (gaps between the page content and the edge of the paper), paper size and orientation (portrait/landscape) can be set here
The content can be scaled smaller or larger when printed. Full size is 100%
The gridlines (grey lines that create the table of rows and columns on the worksheet) can be printed out by checking this box
Themes
Margins
Orientation
Size
Print Area
Breaks
Background
Print Titles
Page Setup
Width:
Height:
Scale:
100%
Scale to Fit
Gridlines
Headings
View
Print
Sheet Options
Bring Forward
Send Backward
Selection Pane
Align
Group
Rotate
Arrange
You can also set the print area so that only some of the sheet is printed
The page setup dialog box is shown when you click this

Figure 2.7: Page layout options

House style, formatting and branding

You might need to think of using a company or organisation house style across all parts of the spreadsheet solution. Using this is important for many companies. A house style is the colours, text fonts, branding and logos that a company uses. For example, the London Underground uses specific colours in its branding and logo. The text used to create a station sign uses the same font, font size and alignment across the network. Alignment is whether text is lined up on the left, the centre or the right. If you don't need to follow a house style, you will still want to think about how your output will look.

Figure 2.8: The London Underground has a distinctive house style

Human computer interface (HCI)

Navigation

The way a user can navigate around the spreadsheet solution and the way the individual menus, input and output screens are designed are important in making the solution easy to use. The navigation system of the interface should be logical and allow the user to return to the main menu at any point. The process a user follows to do this is something that should be designed using visualisation diagrams and/or wireframes.

There are several things to think about which can have an impact on how easy an interface is for users.

Accessibility

Accessibility is about making the solution usable by as wide a range of people as possible, including those who might have disabilities and impairments. Users with visual impairments can struggle to see things on the screen if they are too small or if there is insufficient contrast between light and dark areas. Screen tips (messages that pop up when the mouse hovers over certain areas) might also be useful along with meaningful titles and messages. Guidance on creating interfaces for use with people who have visual impairments can be found on the RNIB website.

Colour

When you are designing your screens that will give choices or convey information it is very important to think about the following considerations:

- Are you using colours to group ideas or information?
- Are you using colours to help make choices?
- Are you using colour to draw attention to certain areas of the screen?

You should use colour carefully to group ideas together so that the user will be able to remember which colours are associated with which information.

Layout

There are several things to consider about the layout of the interface. The navigation should be clear. The actions and flow through the system should be obvious, including returning to the main menu.

Most interfaces will produce messages to inform the user. For example, if an input is validated and the validation fails (such as if a text rather than a numeric value is entered in the quantity box) a message needs to be displayed to tell the user why it failed

Colours can be used to divide up sections of the interface. Colours like yellow or red can be used to indicate things which are important. Colours used should be subtle and complementary and not too bright and garish

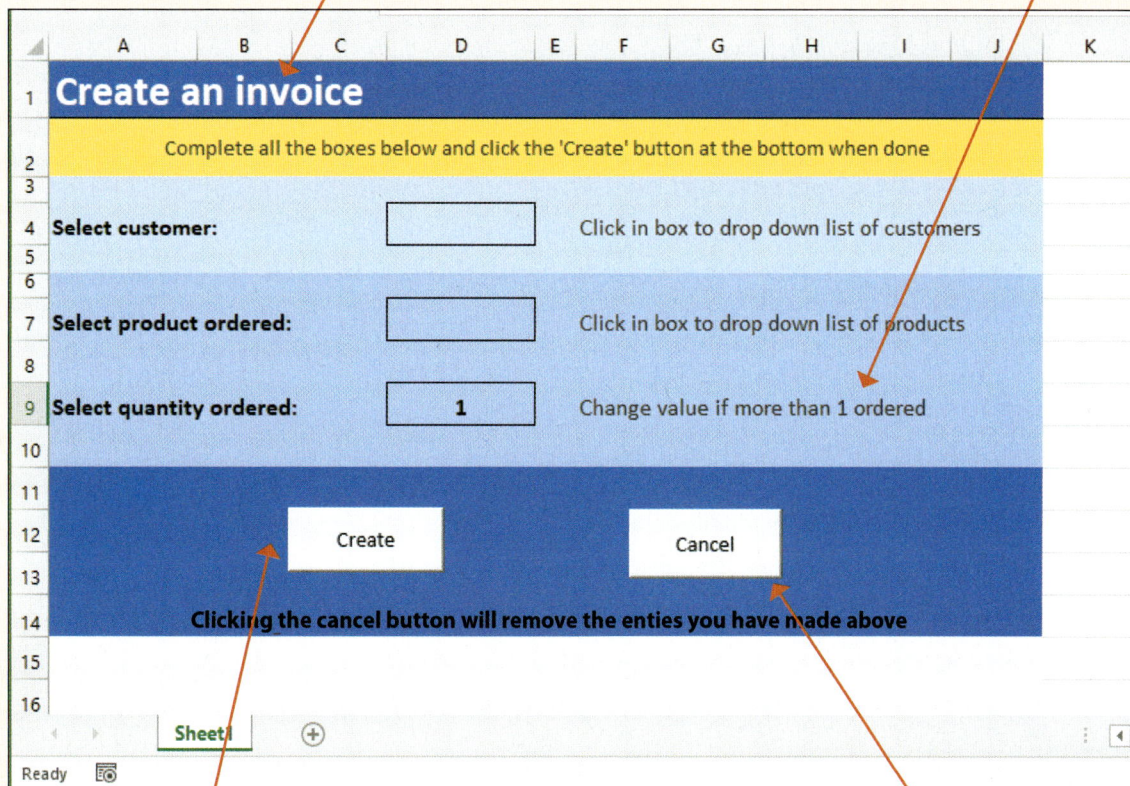

The purpose of the interface must be clear and the user must know what it is used for. This can be made clear using titles and instructions

Include a design which has sufficient 'white' space around the objects in the interface so they are not crowded together. Make sure similar objects are aligned to each other. Place buttons (which complete or cancel the data entry) logically. This is usually at the bottom

Figure 2.9: An example of an interface

Learnability and memorability

The interface should be easy to learn and remember, even if you don't use it very often. Ideally it should be obvious how to use it. For example, some interfaces use icons to represent various option choices rather than words. For this to be effective the icons must clearly represent the action that they perform. **Internet** browsers sometimes have a house icon, which when clicked takes the user to their home page. This is effective because most people relate an icon of a house with returning home. It is therefore easy to initially **learn** the meaning of the icon and to **remember** its meaning when you next use the internet.

Messages

There will be times when messages need to be sent to the user. These might be instructions, questions or messages telling them that they have made an invalid entry. These messages need to be concise and easy to understand. Ideally, the message should be sufficient to solve any problem on its own. If the message is ambiguous and the user is forced to refer to the manual or to the frequently asked questions then their user experience will be poor and they will not be satisfied with your solution.

Purpose

You are designing a solution to serve a particular purpose. The purpose has been carefully specified in the design brief. You should analyse each part of your solution to be able to identify what role it plays in achieving the intended purpose of your interface.

User perceptions

What does a user see and feel when they use an interface? If the interface is messy with bright, clashing colours, has confusing titles for input boxes, incomprehensible messages and misaligned buttons they are likely to perceive the interface as poor quality and difficult to use. In contrast a well-designed interface is likely to be perceived as high quality and easy to use.

Review your learning

Test your knowledge

1 What does 'intuitive' mean? How can you make a spreadsheet solution intuitive?

2 What is the purpose of validation and when should it be used?

3 What is a house style and why is it important?

4 When designing the calculations that your spreadsheet solution will use what design technique should you use?

What have you learnt?

	See section
• The different design tools.	1.1
• How to design the functionality of a solution.	1.1
• How to design the outputs of a solution.	1.1
• How to design the navigation features of a solution.	1.1

TA2

Creating the spreadsheet solution

Let's get started

What spreadsheet software have you used before?

What spreadsheet features do you find easy to use? Which ones do you find more difficult?

What will you learn?

- Spreadsheet formulae and functions.
- Formatting cells.
- Validating data input.
- Sorting and filtering data.
- Creating outputs.
- Creating **user interfaces**.

2.1 Use spreadsheet tools and techniques to create the solution

Spreadsheets are used to store and process numerical data, which is why they are widely used for carrying out calculations. However, they can also be used to manipulate data to model different scenarios, create charts and graphs to present information clearly and manage accounts. In this section, you will focus on data handling and manipulation **functions** that will help you to create spreadsheet solutions that are fit for purpose and that present information clearly to the end user.

Follow the examples from Mo, a personal trainer, as he builds a spreadsheet to keep track of his business's finances. Mo delivers training sessions to his clients. He wants to keep track of the sessions he has delivered and create invoices using a spreadsheet.

Creating a spreadsheet

A single spreadsheet file typically consists of one or more worksheets, which are a bit like very large pages. Each worksheet is divided into multiple rows and columns, creating a table like format.

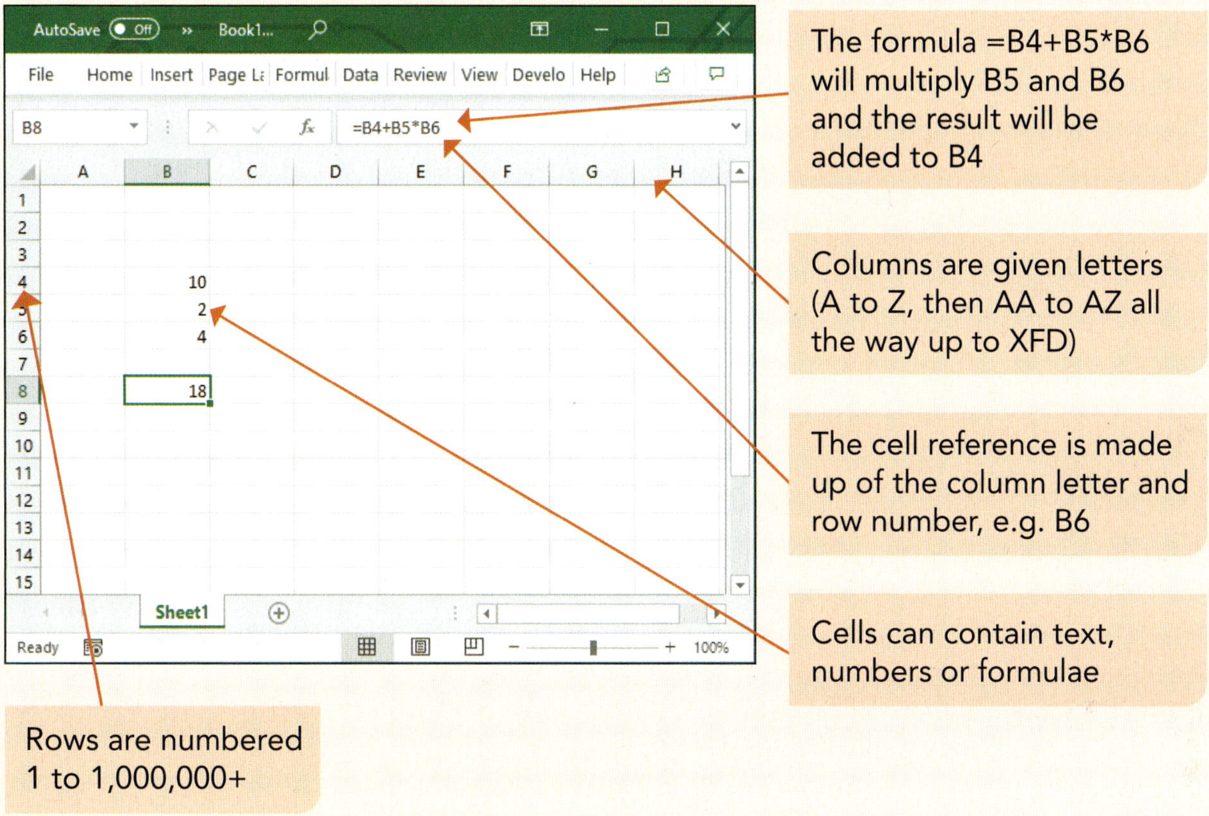

AutoSave Off Book1...
File Home Insert Page La Formul Data Review View Develo Help
B8
=B4+B5*B6
A B C D E F G H
10
2
4
18
Sheet1
Ready
100%
The formula =B4+B5*B6 will multiply B5 and B6 and the result will be added to B4
Columns are given letters (A to Z, then AA to AZ all the way up to XFD)
The cell reference is made up of the column letter and row number, e.g. B6
Cells can contain text, numbers or formulae
Rows are numbered 1 to 1,000,000+

Figure 2.10: The real power of spreadsheets is their ability to do calculations based on the values in other cells

Data handling and manipulation

Formulae

Formulae (the plural of formula) always start with an equals sign (=). Add, subtract, multiply and divide are simple **arithmetic operators**. Spreadsheet formulae use * for multiple and / for divide.

Using multiple operators and parentheses

It is important to understand that when formulae include multiple operators, the calculation is done in a specific order. Multiplication and division are done first, followed by addition and subtraction.

You might have learnt the order of operations, BIDMAS (Brackets, Indices, Division, Multiplication, Addition and Subtraction) from your lessons in Mathematics. Brackets are sometimes called **parentheses** (this is the plural of parenthesis) and can be used to modify calculations.

Over to you!　　**1**

Look at the spreadsheet shown in Figure 2.10

1　Explain why the sum in cell B8 is 18.

2　Add brackets to the formula so that the total remains 18.

3　Add brackets to the formula so that the total becomes 48.

Cell references

Having created a formula in a cell you might want to copy that formula to other cells, for example, to add up total month's expenditure.

Relative referencing

When you copy formulae, the cell references change to reflect the row or columns that you copy the formulae to. This is called **relative referencing** (as the cell reference changes relative to where it is copied).

Absolute referencing

There are some situations where you don't want a cell reference to be changed when it is copied. For example, if you are multiplying the cell contents with a fixed value in a single cell (such as a discount or percentage). When you copy this type of formula, you don't want the cell reference of the fixed value to change. To fix cell references, you need to include a dollar sign ($) in front of the column letter and row number, such as B4. This type of cell reference is called an absolute cell reference.

Stretch   1

Mo wants to work out how much he should charge each of his customers. He enters a formula in cell E4 to multiply the number of hours in cell D4 by the hourly rate he charges, see Figure 2.11.

He now copies this formula down through cells E5 to E17. The cell reference D4 changes as it is copied down the rows to D5, D6, D7, and so on, so that the calculation is correct in each cell.

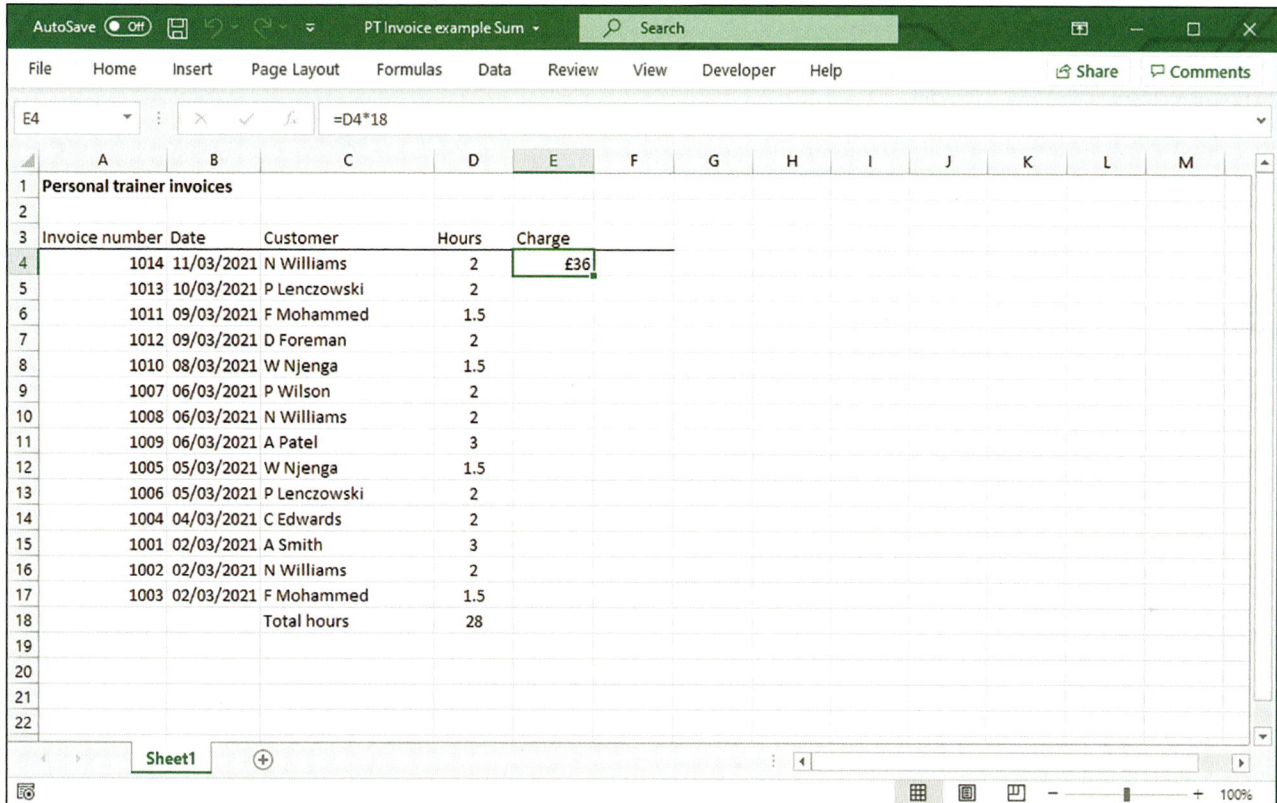

	A	B	C	D	E
1	Personal trainer invoices				
2					
3	Invoice number	Date	Customer	Hours	Charge
4	1014	11/03/2021	N Williams	2	£36
5	1013	10/03/2021	P Lenczowski	2	
6	1011	09/03/2021	F Mohammed	1.5	
7	1012	09/03/2021	D Foreman	2	
8	1010	08/03/2021	W Njenga	1.5	
9	1007	06/03/2021	P Wilson	2	
10	1008	06/03/2021	N Williams	2	
11	1009	06/03/2021	A Patel	3	
12	1005	05/03/2021	W Njenga	1.5	
13	1006	05/03/2021	P Lenczowski	2	
14	1004	04/03/2021	C Edwards	2	
15	1001	02/03/2021	A Smith	3	
16	1002	02/03/2021	N Williams	2	
17	1003	02/03/2021	F Mohammed	1.5	
18			Total hours	28	

Cell E4 formula: =D4*18

Figure 2.11: Copying a formula

Now create your own spreadsheet solution with two columns. In column A add the first ten digits (1 to10) to the first ten cells down the column (A1 to A10). In column B, multiply the contents of the first column by 20. You can do this by completing the first cell and dragging the cell contents down through the column. You should see the first 10 multiples of 20. Don't forget to save your work.

Stretch   2

Mo has added the rate he charges per hour to cell E3, see Figure 2.12. He now wants to calculate the charge per session.

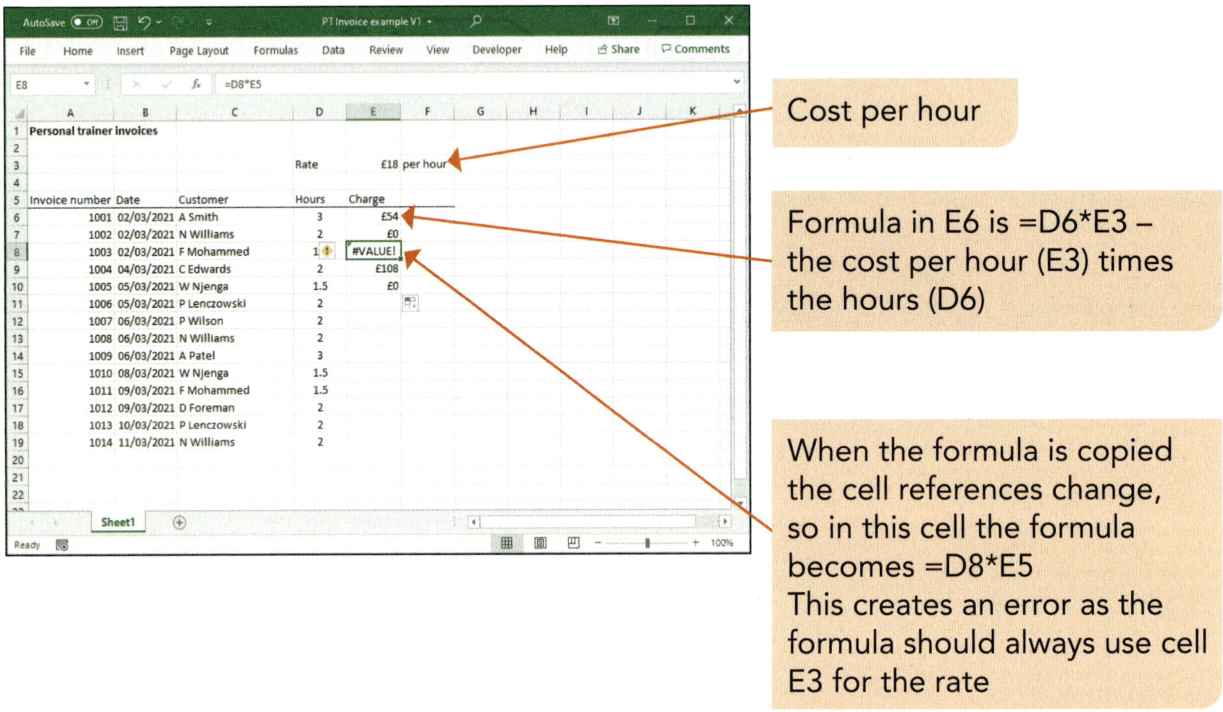

Cost per hour

Formula in E6 is =D6*E3 – the cost per hour (E3) times the hours (D6)

When the formula is copied the cell references change, so in this cell the formula becomes =D8*E5
This creates an error as the formula should always use cell E3 for the rate

Figure 2.12: Problem with copying cell references

If the formula is changed to =D6*E3 then the E3 cell reference will not change as it is now an **absolute reference**.

Using your spreadsheet from Stretch 1, add the multiple used (in this case '20') to cell D1. Now change the formulas in column B to use an absolute reference to this cell. This way you can change the value in D1 to any number you like and see the multiples in cells B1 to B10. Don't forget to save your work.

Multi-sheet referencing

To start with, a spreadsheet just contains one worksheet called 'Sheet 1'. You can add others by clicking the plus icon next to the worksheet name (shown on the tab at the bottom). You can rename them by double clicking 'Sheet1' and typing a more meaningful name.

In a formula, you can also use values from cells in a different worksheet. You include the sheet name followed by an exclamation mark before the cell reference. For example, the formula '=Sheet2!B6' is equal to the value in cell B6 in the worksheet called 'Sheet2'.

Functions

Being able to use formulae to carry out basic arithmetic such as adding or multiplying values is a useful spreadsheet feature, but there are also a wide range of spreadsheet functions that carry out more complex mathematical tasks. A function is a way to calculate a formula more quickly and easily. Each function performs a specific type of calculation.

Some examples of commonly used functions are shown in Table 2.1 but there are many more, including advanced engineering and statistical functions.

Table 2.1: Common functions used in spreadsheets

Function	What it does
SUM	Adds up a **range** of cells
MIN and MAX	Display the minimum or maximum value within a range of values
AVERAGE	Displays the arithmetic mean of the values in a range of cells
COUNT	Counts how many cells in a range contain numbers
COUNTIF	Counts only the cells in a range which meet a given criterion

Stretch 3

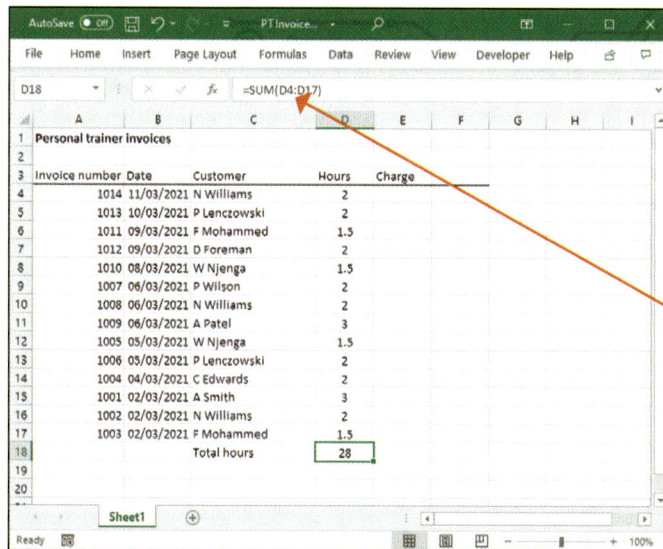

A colon, ':', is used to show a range of values. Think of it as the word 'between'. The SUM function adds everything between cells D4 and D17. The result of the formula is shown in cell D18

Figure 2.13: The SUM function is used in the formula in cell D18 and adds all the values between D4 and D17

Mo wants to calculate the hours he has worked. Using your spreadsheet from Stretch 1, add up the multiples in the second column using the SUM function. Your total should be 1100 if you left the multiplier in D1 as 20. Don't forget to save your work.

Stretch   4

Mo wants to understand better what he is charging for his sessions, so he uses the AVERAGE, COUNT, MIN and MAX functions in his spreadsheet.

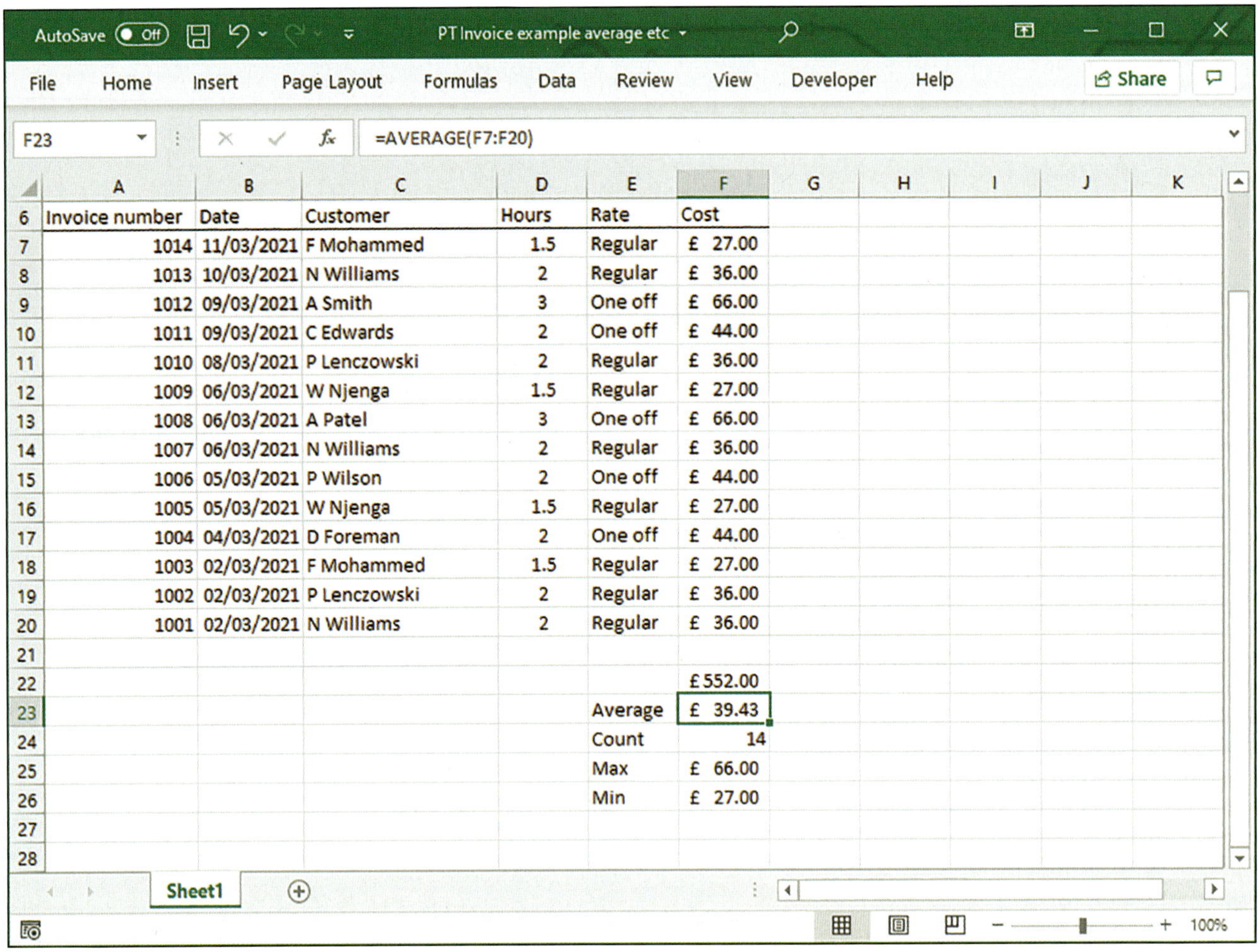

	A	B	C	D	E	F
6	Invoice number	Date	Customer	Hours	Rate	Cost
7	1014	11/03/2021	F Mohammed	1.5	Regular	£ 27.00
8	1013	10/03/2021	N Williams	2	Regular	£ 36.00
9	1012	09/03/2021	A Smith	3	One off	£ 66.00
10	1011	09/03/2021	C Edwards	2	One off	£ 44.00
11	1010	08/03/2021	P Lenczowski	2	Regular	£ 36.00
12	1009	06/03/2021	W Njenga	1.5	Regular	£ 27.00
13	1008	06/03/2021	A Patel	3	One off	£ 66.00
14	1007	06/03/2021	N Williams	2	Regular	£ 36.00
15	1006	05/03/2021	P Wilson	2	One off	£ 44.00
16	1005	05/03/2021	W Njenga	1.5	Regular	£ 27.00
17	1004	04/03/2021	D Foreman	2	One off	£ 44.00
18	1003	02/03/2021	F Mohammed	1.5	Regular	£ 27.00
19	1002	02/03/2021	P Lenczowski	2	Regular	£ 36.00
20	1001	02/03/2021	N Williams	2	Regular	£ 36.00
21						
22						£ 552.00
23					Average	£ 39.43
24					Count	14
25					Max	£ 66.00
26					Min	£ 27.00

Cell F23: =AVERAGE(F7:F20)

Figure 2.14: The AVERAGE function across the cell range F7:F20

Write the formulae for each of these functions for Mo. The first is shown here. Don't forget to save your work.

IF

The IF function carries out different actions depending on the results of a test. The test can be as simple as checking a value in a cell. If the cell contains the value the function does one action and if it doesn't then the function does a different action.

Suppose a teacher had a list of students marks in cells B2:B15. Students are awarded a merit if their marks are 70 or above, otherwise they are awarded a pass. The teacher enters an formula using the IF function to display the word 'Merit' next to their marks in cells C2:C15. The formula in C2 would look like this:

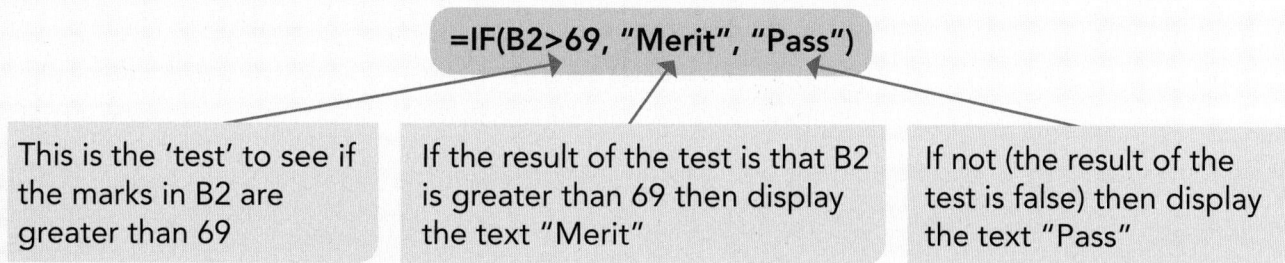

=IF(B2>69, "Merit", "Pass")

This is the 'test' to see if the marks in B2 are greater than 69	If the result of the test is that B2 is greater than 69 then display the text "Merit"	If not (the result of the test is false) then display the text "Pass"

Figure 2.15: In this example the test used in the IF function uses the greater than(>) comparison operator

As well as displaying text, formulas can be used to carry out different calculations depending on the result of the test.

Other comparison operators can be used if the test involves a number.

COUNTIF

COUNTIF counts the number of times a test is passed within a range. So, it will look like this in a formula: =COUNTIF(range, criteria). The criteria use logical operators such as >, <, <> and =. The symbol <> represents 'not equal to'.

Here's an example: =COUNTIF(D1:D50, '<' & B1). This counts the number of cells in the range D1 to D50 that are less than the value in cell B1. '&' is used to add cell references to the criteria.

SUMIF

SUMIF is a combination of the IF and SUM functions. While the SUM function will add up all the cells in a range, the SUMIF function only adds the cells in a range if they pass a given test =SUMIF(range, criteria, [sum_range]).

The [sum_range] is in square brackets because it is optional and so could be left out. If we leave it out then the values in the range given at the start of the formula are added up. The range and criteria use the same language as the COUNTIF function. Here's an example: =SUMIF(D1:D50, '>100'). This adds up the cells greater than 100 in the range D1 to D50.

You can also create more complex tests using the Boolean operators AND and OR.

Stretch 5

Mo wants to offer a 10% discount to customers if the cost of the session is more than £60. He could do this with a formula in G6 like this:

=IF(F6>60, F6*0.9, F6)

The test should be to see if the value in F6 is greater than 60 and if it is, display a value discounted by 10%, otherwise the value in F6 remains unchanged.

Suppose Mo wanted to see if he could sign up one-off clients for regular sessions if they had a session with him lasting two hours or more. To find those customers Mo should do two tests:

- Does column E equal 'One off'

- Is column D greater than or equal to 2.

What formula could Mo use?

Tip: *Try writing each test first. If both tests are true Mo wants to add the text 'Sign up', otherwise it should be left blank. To use both tests at once, your formula should start IF(AND(…*

G6 fx =IF(AND(D6>=2, E6="One off"), "Sign up", "")

	Invoice number	Date	Customer	Hours	Rate	Cost	
1	Personal trainer invoices						
2							
3				Rates	Regular	£18 per hour	
4					One off	£22 per hour	
5	Invoice number	Date	Customer	Hours	Rate	Cost	
6	1014	11/03/2021	N Williams	2	Regular	£ 36.00	
7	1013	10/03/2021	P Lenczowski	2	Regular	£ 36.00	
8	1012	09/03/2021	F Mohammed	1.5	Regular	£ 27.00	
9	1011	09/03/2021	D Foreman	2	One off	£ 44.00	Sign up
10	1010	08/03/2021	W Njenga	1.5	Regular	£ 27.00	
11	1009	06/03/2021	P Wilson	2	One off	£ 44.00	Sign up
12	1008	06/03/2021	N Williams	2	Regular	£ 36.00	
13	1007	06/03/2021	A Patel	3	One off	£ 66.00	Sign up
14	1006	05/03/2021	W Njenga	1.5	Regular	£ 27.00	
15	1005	05/03/2021	P Lenczowski	2	Regular	£ 36.00	
16	1004	04/03/2021	C Edwards	2	One off	£ 44.00	Sign up
17	1003	02/03/2021	A Smith	3	One off	£ 66.00	Sign up
18	1002	02/03/2021	N Williams	2	Regular	£ 36.00	
19	1001	02/03/2021	F Mohammed	1.5	Regular	£ 27.00	
20							

Figure 2.16: Using operators and functions

Can you write the formula to find the total amount of 'Regular' sessions? Don't forget to save your work.

Lookup functions

LOOKUP is a function that will find a value from a row in a table of cells by searching for a given value in another row within the table. (The LOOKUP function has been replaced by VLOOKUP and Microsoft doesn't recommend its use.)

VLOOKUP looks for a value in a table and then returns the corresponding value from a specified column. HLOOKUP searches horizontally across the columns in a table of data rather than vertically down the rows.

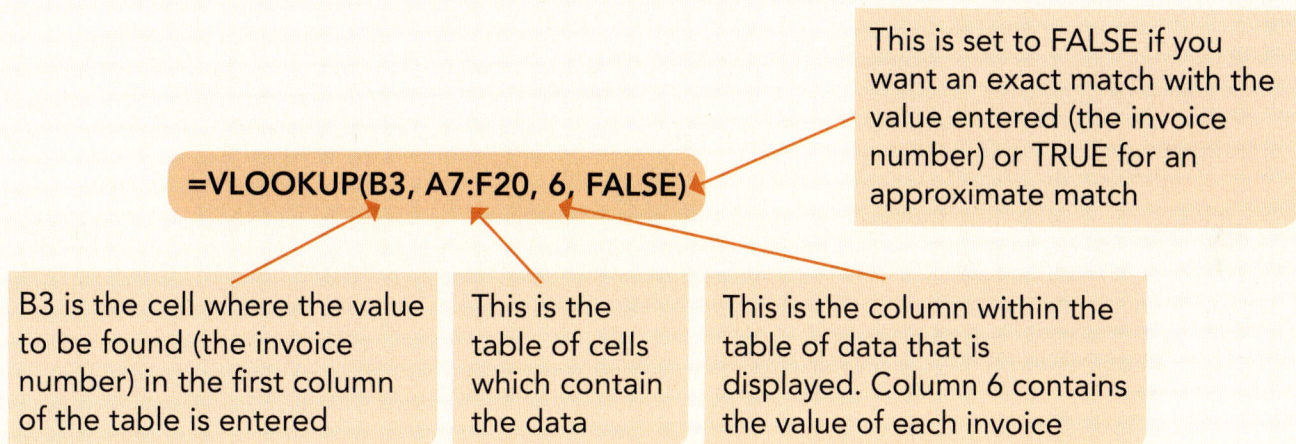

=VLOOKUP(B3, A7:F20, 6, FALSE)

This is set to FALSE if you want an exact match with the value entered (the invoice number) or TRUE for an approximate match

B3 is the cell where the value to be found (the invoice number) in the first column of the table is entered

This is the table of cells which contain the data

This is the column within the table of data that is displayed. Column 6 contains the value of each invoice

Figure 2.17: The VLOOKUP functions uses 4 parameters to work

Stretch   6

Finding an invoice

Mo wants to be able to find the value of a particular invoice number with a VLOOKUP function. The invoice number is entered in cell B3 and the function looks up that invoice number in the table of data and picks out the value of that invoice.

Continued

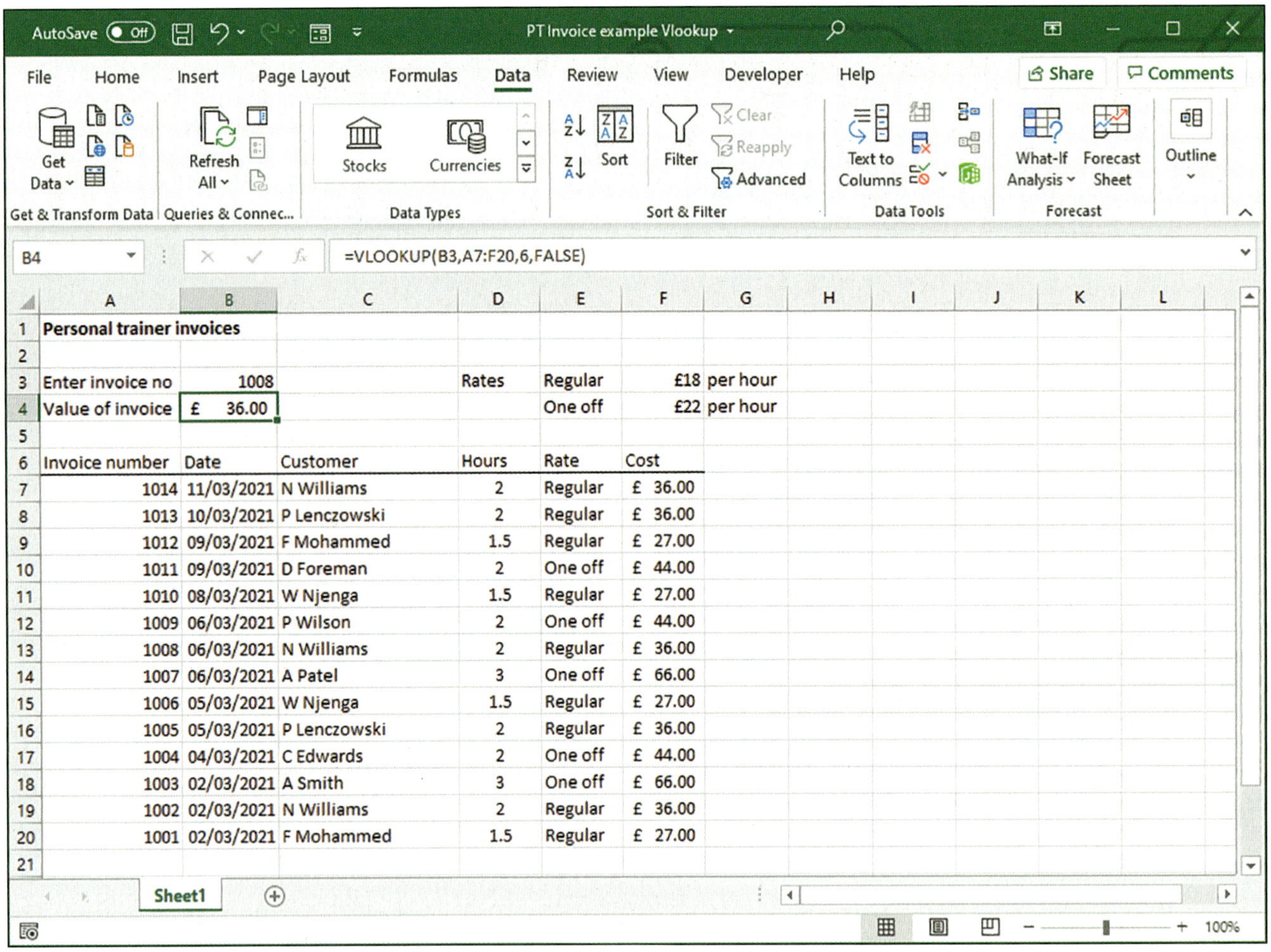

	A	B	C	D	E	F	G
1	Personal trainer invoices						
2							
3	Enter invoice no	1008		Rates	Regular	£18	per hour
4	Value of invoice	£ 36.00			One off	£22	per hour
5							
6	Invoice number	Date	Customer	Hours	Rate	Cost	
7	1014	11/03/2021	N Williams	2	Regular	£ 36.00	
8	1013	10/03/2021	P Lenczowski	2	Regular	£ 36.00	
9	1012	09/03/2021	F Mohammed	1.5	Regular	£ 27.00	
10	1011	09/03/2021	D Foreman	2	One off	£ 44.00	
11	1010	08/03/2021	W Njenga	1.5	Regular	£ 27.00	
12	1009	06/03/2021	P Wilson	2	One off	£ 44.00	
13	1008	06/03/2021	N Williams	2	Regular	£ 36.00	
14	1007	06/03/2021	A Patel	3	One off	£ 66.00	
15	1006	05/03/2021	W Njenga	1.5	Regular	£ 27.00	
16	1005	05/03/2021	P Lenczowski	2	Regular	£ 36.00	
17	1004	04/03/2021	C Edwards	2	One off	£ 44.00	
18	1003	02/03/2021	A Smith	3	One off	£ 66.00	
19	1002	02/03/2021	N Williams	2	Regular	£ 36.00	
20	1001	02/03/2021	F Mohammed	1.5	Regular	£ 27.00	
21							

Figure 2.18: Using the VLOOKUP function

Use your spreadsheet from Stretch 1. Add cells for the multiple of a number from column B and use the VLOOKUP function to find the number from column A. Can you change the function to work the other way round? Don't forget to save your work.

DATE and TODAY

These are useful when you need to work with dates. The TODAY function displays the current date in a cell. You can do calculations with dates. The DATE function can be used to create a date out of separate cells which contain the year, month and day.

Stretch 7

Mo wants to know how many days it has been since he issued an invoice.

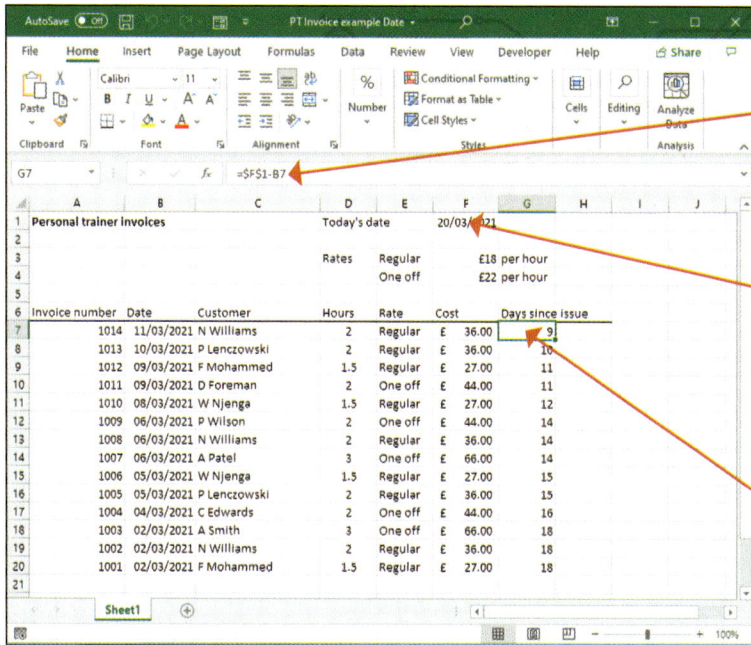

Absolute cell referencing has been used for the current date (F1) so it can be copied down the column

The formula in F1 is '=TODAY( )' so it always displays today's date

The formula in G7 subtracts the date the invoice was issued (in B7) from the current date in F1 and displays how many days have passed

Figure 2.19: Use of the TODAY function

Using your spreadsheet from Stretch 1, add a column C that displays a date. The date should use the number in column A and add this number of days to today's date. Don't forget to save your work.

SUBTOTAL

This function is really a combination of many different functions as it allows you to carry out different calculations on a range of cells. The first number corresponds to the calculation you want it to use.

Table 2.2: SUBTOTAL can be used with a number of different calculations

Number for SUBTOTAL	Function
1	Average
2	Count (counts only numbers)
3	COUNTA (counts only cells which are not empty)
4	MAX
5	MIN
9	SUM

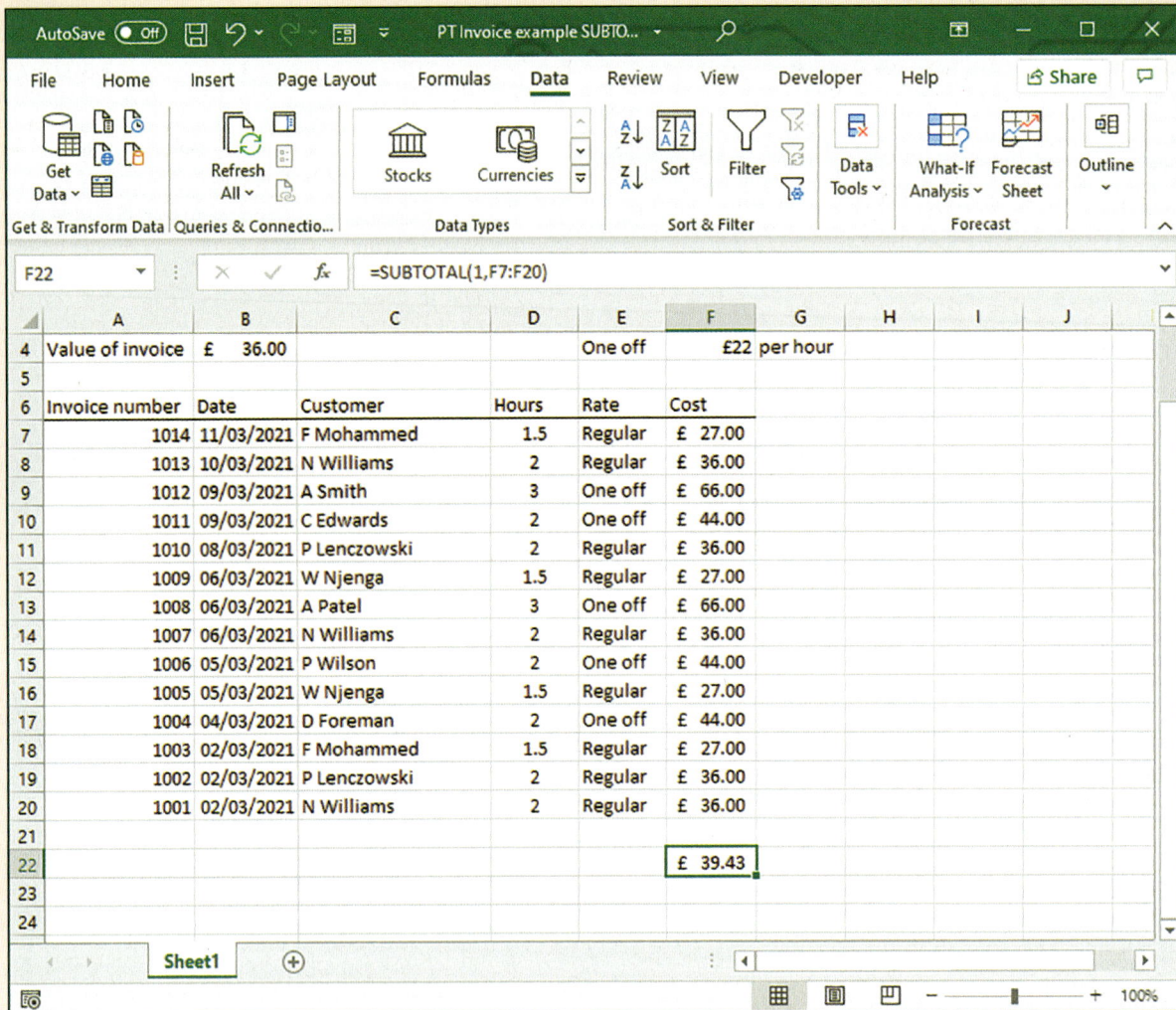

Figure 2.20: This example shows the use of the SUBTOTAL function in cell F22. The function is set to 1 so it shows an average of the values in F7:F20

This function is commonly used with a drop-down list or radio buttons to give the option of selecting a particular calculation. This is because otherwise it would be simpler to just use the original function. This is explained later in this section.

Naming cells

So far, we have always referred to a range of cells by their cell references such as D4:D17. You can also name a range of cells which, if you use a meaningful name, can make formulae easier to understand. To name a range you simply select it, then from the 'Formulas' menu click on the 'Define name' icon. This will display the 'New name' dialog box. Type a name for the range in the 'Name' box and click 'OK'.

In the example shown in Figure 2.21 the range D6:D19 has been given the name 'Hours'. This name rather than the cell reference has been used in the formula in D20.

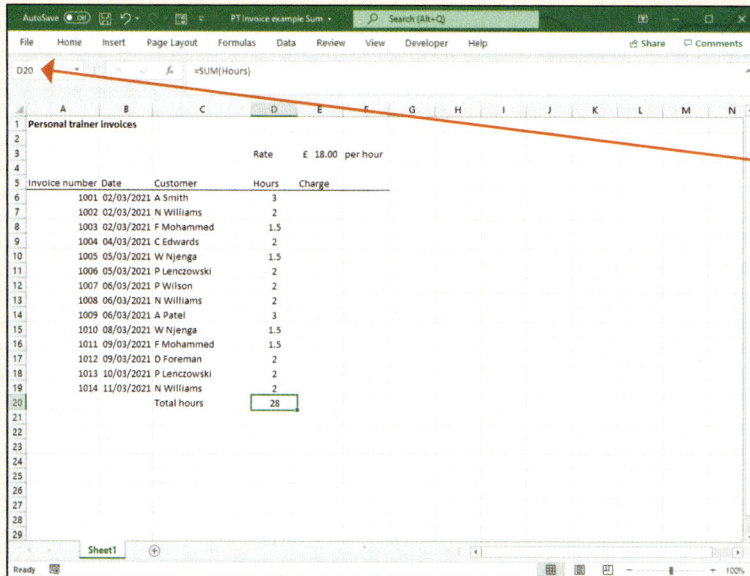

You can also select a range with your mouse and then add a name by typing in this box

Figure 2.21: Using a **named range** in a formula

Solving errors in formulae

Sometimes you might make errors in entering formulae. The most common error is probably forgetting to start the formula with an equals sign (=). There are also error messages that will appear in the cell if you have made a mistake.

Table 2.3: Error messages

Error message	What it means	How to correct it
#DIV/0	You have entered a formula which results in an attempt to divide a value by zero	Check that the cells referenced in the formula do contain values and they are greater than zero if used for division
#NAME?	You have typed the name of a function incorrectly, for example, =SUN rather than =SUM	Check that the function name is correctly spelt
#REF!	A formula references a cell that is not valid, often this happens because you have deleted some cells	Check that the cell references are correct

Let's get digital!   1

1   Collect some data that you can use to try out the HLOOKUP or VLOOKUP functions. For example, you could make a list of all your friends, their names, phone numbers, email addresses, etc.

2   Create the ability to extract specific information from the table of data using a VLOOKUP function. For example, you could have a cell where you enter a friend's name and the VLOOKUP function will return their email address.

3   If you have used numeric data such as age you could also use AVERAGE and MIN and MAX to find out the average, minimum and maximum age of your friends.

Cell formatting

You can use cell formatting to create a better looking and easier to understand worksheet. For example, you can highlight important cells using colours and bold formats. Each cell or group of cells can be formatted in a variety of different ways including:

The font options allow you to adjust the size, font style, colour, bold etc. of cell contents

You can change the number format of cells which contain numeric values here. Currency formatting, for example, adds a currency symbol (£) to the numbers. You can also increase or decrease the number of digits displayed after the decimal point

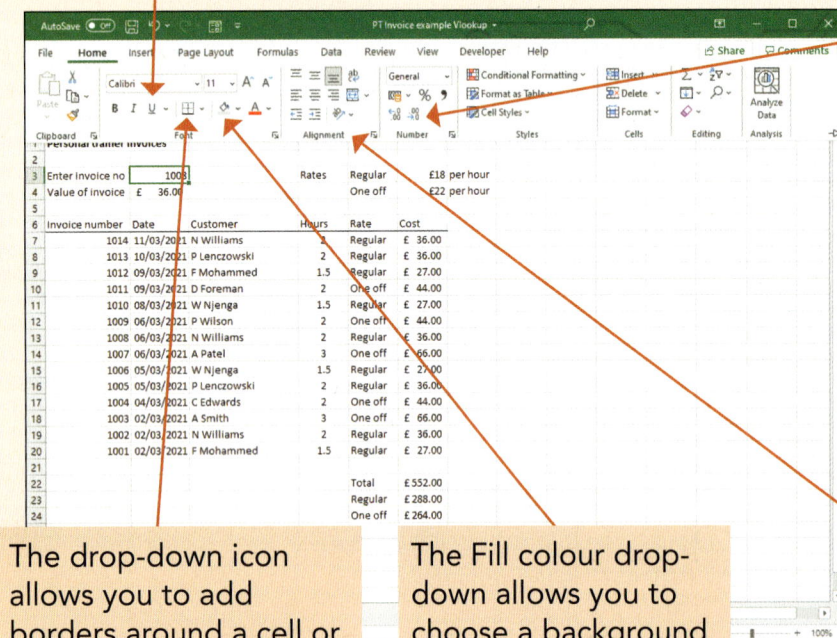

The drop-down icon allows you to add borders around a cell or selected group of cells

The Fill colour drop-down allows you to choose a background colour for cells

You can change the alignment of cell contents, both vertically and horizontally using these buttons. You can also allow text to wrap within a cell

Figure 2.22: The formatting options

Conditional formatting

This feature allows you to adjust the formatting of a cell based on its contents. This allows you to automatically highlight important values. To set up conditional formatting you need to decide:

- Which cell or range of cells you want to apply the formatting to

- What changes in the values in those cells will cause the formatting to change. For example, the formatting changes if the value in the cell goes above or below a certain value

- The change in the formatting you want to happen, such as a change in text or background colour.

Let's get digital! 2

Using your spreadsheet from Stretch 1, add conditional formatting to highlight the multiples that are greater than 100 in red. Use green to highlight the multiples that are less than 50.

Sorting

Figure 2.23: You might need to sort data

Spreadsheets have some useful tools for dealing with lists or tables of data.

You can sort a table of data based on any of the columns, either in alphabetical or numerical order. The simplest way to sort is to click anywhere in the column of data that you want to sort, then choose the 'Data' menu and click either the 'A–Z' or 'Z–A' buttons to sort the data. The 'A–Z' button will sort the data in alphabetical order if the data contains text or ascending order (smallest at the top) if it contains numerical data. The 'Z–A' button will sort the data in reverse alphabetical order or in descending order.

If you have a table with several columns, you can right-click anywhere within it and then click the 'Sort' button. This will open the 'Sort' dialog box where you can select which column you want the data sorted by and how you want it sorted. You can also sort by multiple columns if you need to.

Filters

These limit the display to only the rows within a table of data that match certain criteria. To use a filter first click within the table and then, from the 'Data' menu, choose 'Filter'. This will add drop-down arrows to each of the column headings in the table of data. Click on the drop-down arrow of the column you are filtering by and select the values you want to see.

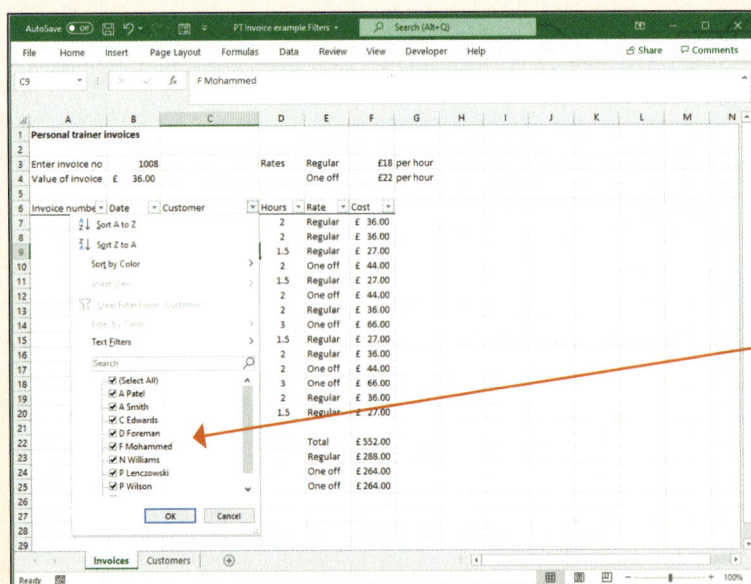

In this example, to display one customer's invoices, you would first click 'Select all' to deselect all the customer's names. Then you would click the check box next to the customer you want to list and click OK

Figure 2.24: Using filters

You can also use text and numeric filters. When you click on the drop-down arrow in the header for a numeric column you can click on 'Number filters'. (If the column contains text this option is replaced by 'Text filters'.) This will pop out a menu where you can choose the criterion you want to use such as 'Greater than'. Then another dialog box will open (see Figure 2.25) where you can enter the value that the rows must be greater than and click OK. Just matching rows will be displayed.

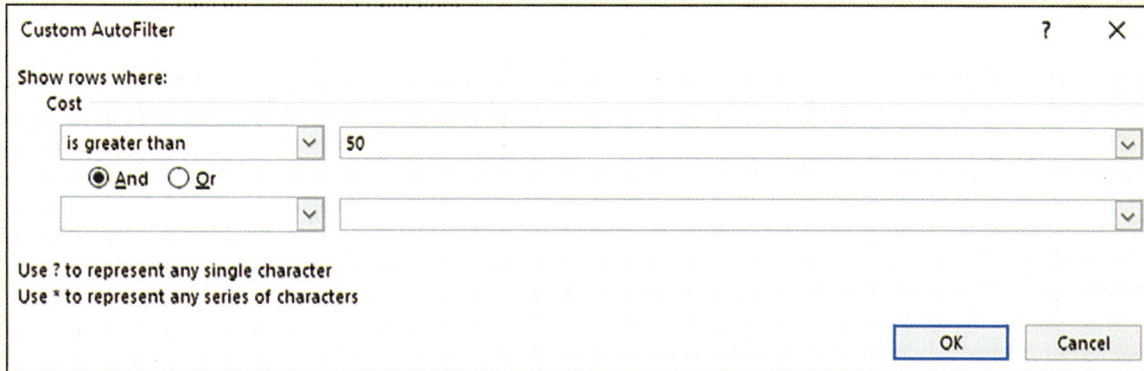

Figure 2.25: The custom AutoFilter dialog box

Whenever a filter is applied to a column you will see that the drop-down arrow changes to a filter symbol. When you click that symbol the menu that appears will have an option to clear the filter previously applied.

Data validation

Where possible, you should validate the data in your spreadsheet to ensure it is correct. Validation tools can help to check data as you input it. There are a number of different types of validation you can use – look for them in the Data tools section of the Data tab. Data validation is particularly useful if data from the spreadsheet will be sent to a **database**. Validation can help users to enter data that will not be rejected or cause errors.

Lookup validation

You can limit the user to only being able to select valid entries by using a list.

The data validation dialog box also has tabs for setting up input messages and error alerts. The input message appears when the cell that the validation is applied to is selected. The error alert sets up a dialog box which pops up if the validation rules are broken. You should define the text that appears for validation errors at the design stage.

Stretch   8

Mo has created another worksheet called 'Customers' in his spreadsheet and listed his customers' details in the range B3:B11. Mo enters the reference to the table of customers as the Source in the Data validation dialog box. This limits the input for column C to these values.

In Figure 2.26 a new invoice is being created with the customer name entered in C7. You can see the Data validation dialog box, with the List option selected in the Allow drop-down box.

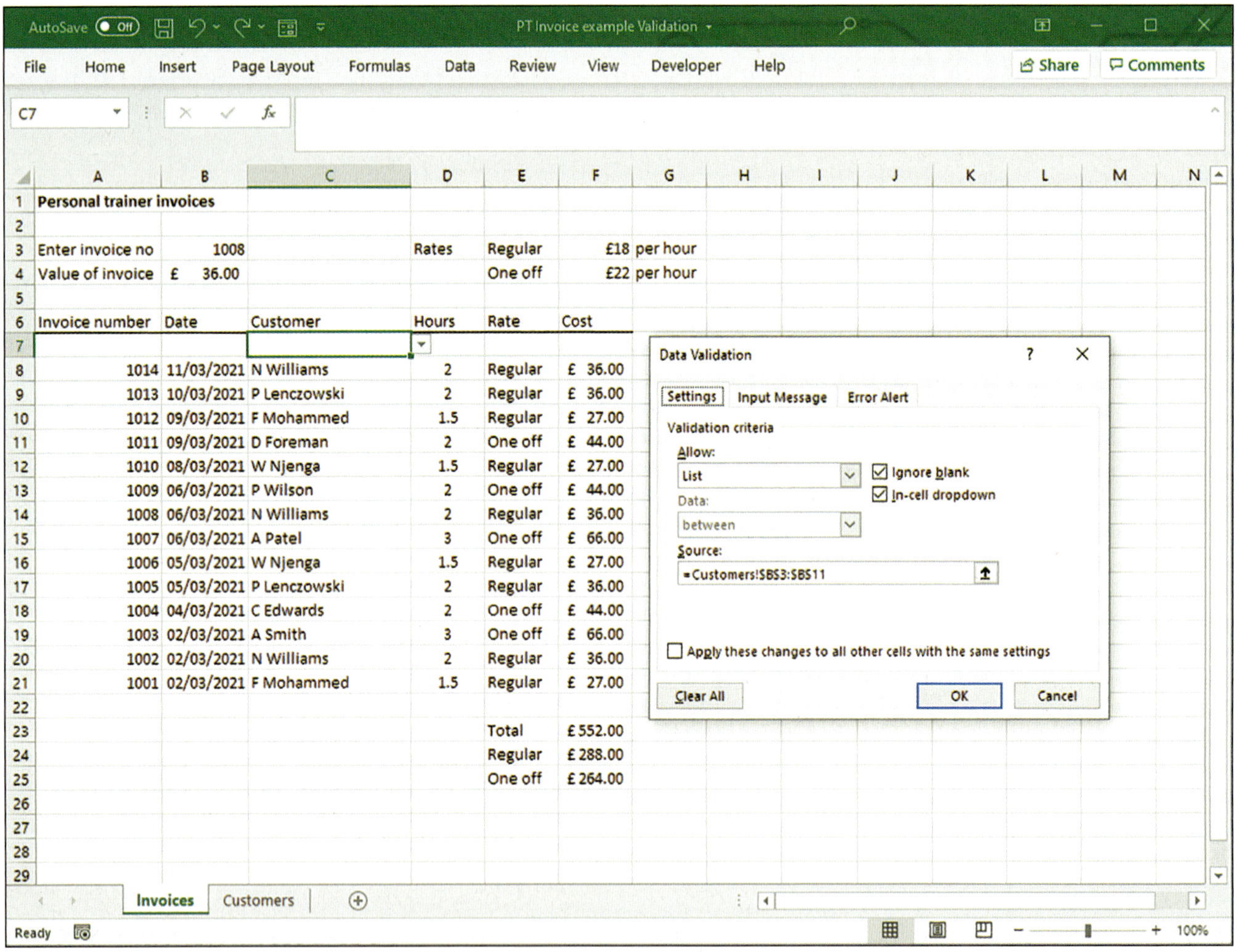

Figure 2.26: The data validation dialog box

Once validation is set up, a drop-down box will appear in C7 showing the list of customers. Only valid customers from the list can be selected.

Using your spreadsheet from Stretch 2, restrict the potential multiples listed in cell D1 to either 2, 10 or 20. Don't forget to save your work.

Range check

You can specify what values must be within a numeric range. This prevents values being input which are outside the range.

So, for example, imagine you wanted to keep a record of how much homework you do each day. You do at least half an hour each day, but never more than 4 hours. You could add validation to the column recording the number of hours to show this.

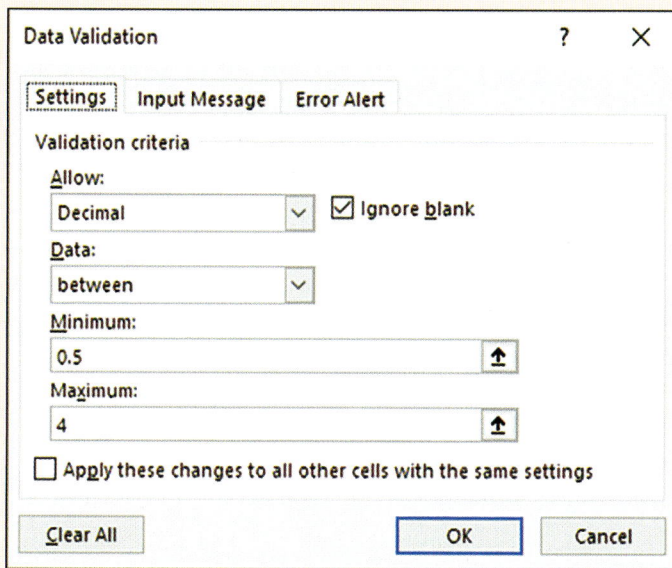

Figure 2.27: Validating the daily number of hours spent on homework

Text length

When inputting a text value, you can limit the length to a certain number of characters. To apply this kind of validation, use the 'Text length' option from the 'Allow' drop-down menu on the 'Data validation' dialog box. This allows you to choose either an exact length, greater than or less than a given length or between two lengths. Validating text length can be useful with some types of input such as National Insurance numbers, which are always nine characters long.

Limiting choices

Where the valid entries are limited, such a person's title, there are several different methods you can use.

Drop-down lists

This is like the lookup list but you can type the options into the Data validation dialog box rather than referring to a range of cells that contain the valid options. All you need to do is separate the items you want in the list with commas. Fig 2.28 shows the Data validation settings that Mo, the personal trainer, might use to validate an entry in the Rate column.

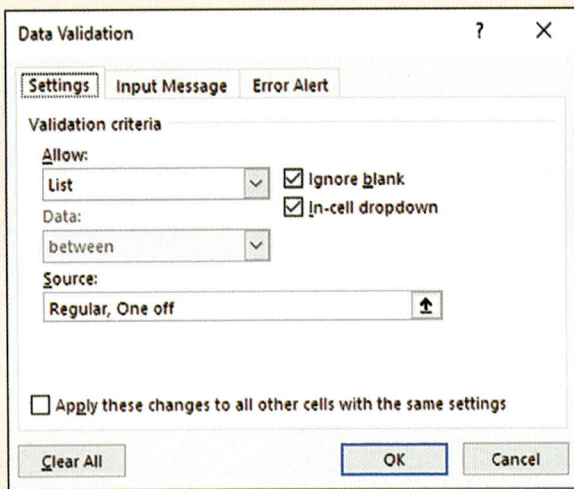

Figure 2.28: Data validation settings

Radio buttons and tick lists

Radio buttons allow selection of only one option from a range of options. So, for example, a person can only have one title (Mr, Mrs, and so on). Tick lists (or checkboxes) allow a combination of options to be selected, including several options within the same group.

In Excel, radio buttons and tick lists are a little more complicated to set up as you cannot use the Data validation features. Instead, you must use the developer tools. To access the developer tools menu you need to first go to the 'File' menu, choose 'Options' at the bottom then on the Options menu, choose 'Customise Ribbon' from the list on the left. In the Customise Ribbon menu click in the tick box next to Developer to add this to the Ribbon. Click 'OK' then the Developer menu is added to the Ribbon to the left of the Help menu.

To create a radio button set, first you need to create a Group box to put the buttons in. From the Developer menu click 'Insert' and then from the drop-down menu that appears, choose 'Group box' (in the 'Form Controls' section) and then drag out a Group box on the worksheet large enough to contain the buttons you will put in it. Once the group box is created you can name it and then you can add the options buttons and name these.

Having created the set of buttons we identify which one of the four options has been selected. As we have used a Group box this can be only one of the buttons. Right click on the first Option button and then choose 'Format control'. Make sure you have the 'Control' tab selected in the dialog box and then click in the 'Cell link' box and type in (or click on the worksheet) where you want the users' choices recorded. Then click 'OK'. You will see that what is displayed in the cell you have linked to the button is simply the number of the Option button that has been clicked (1, 2, 3 or 4). However, we really need the Title the user has selected, not the number of the button. To convert the number of the button to the title selected you need to add a list of the titles and then use an INDEX function to identify which actual title has been chosen.

The cell linked to the option buttons is J5

A list of the titles is in L5:L8

The INDEX function in J6 picks out the title selected from the list using the number of the option button selected

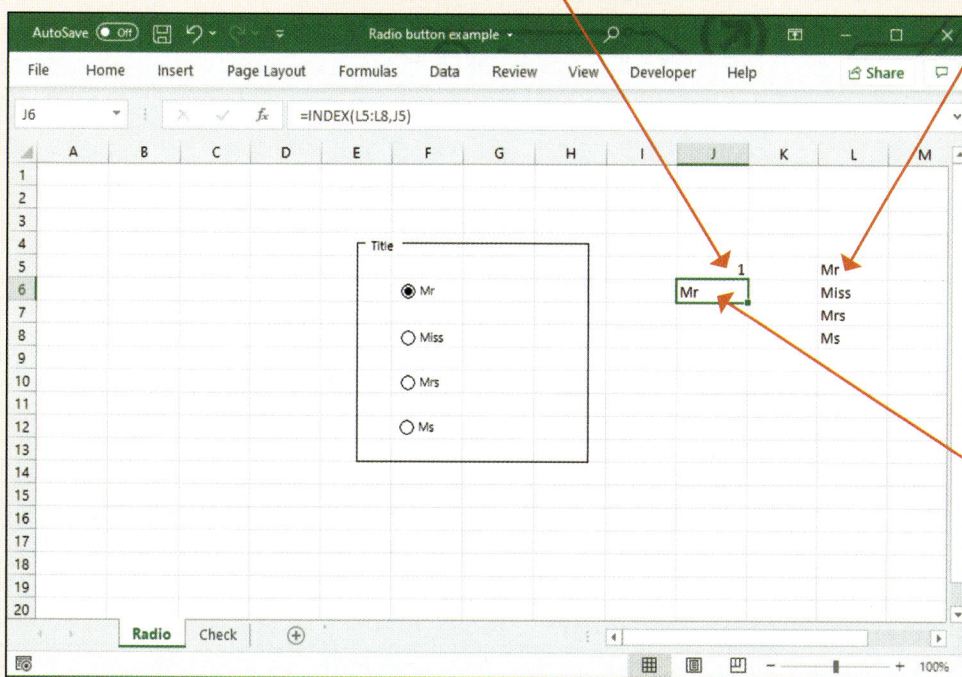

Figure 2.29: Using the INDEX function to identify the chosen option

Check boxes are created in a similar way except you don't need to use a group box. Also, when you link a cell to the check box it displays TRUE if the box is ticked and FALSE if it is not.

In Google Sheets there are no radio buttons. You must use check boxes and use code to limit the number of boxes that can be selected to one.

Let's get digital!   3

Create a data input form with validation to enter details of a student who wishes to enrol on a course. You should include the following:

a   A radio button group for the person's title

b   Input boxes for their first name and family name

c   A drop-down list for them to select the course. The list could include courses such as IT, Maths, English, Science, Sport and Languages

d   A set of tick boxes for them to choose their preferred method(s) of contact which should include email, text, phone and letter

e   An input box for students' age who must be between 16 and 28

f   An input box for their mobile number which must be exactly 11 digits long.

All the data from the form should be put into a different worksheet.

Data types

When you enter data into a worksheet cell it automatically gets set to a datatype that matches the entry. So, if you enter numbers, they are formatted as such. You can specify a particular number format using the 'Number' section of the 'Home' menu. There are a range of pre-set number formats, such as currency or you can set your own format by clicking on 'More number formats' at the bottom of the list.

Table 2.4: Entering different data types in a spreadsheet

Data type	Description
Boolean	A Boolean value is either true or false. We saw an example of this when using check boxes.
Dates	If you enter a valid date into a cell it is automatically formatted as a date data type.
Times	Like dates, times can be entered into a cell in the format hh:mm:ss (you can leave the seconds off).
Text	When you type text into a cell it is automatically formatted and left aligned in the cell. Sometimes you might find entering values such as phone numbers difficult as Excel assumes they are numbers that you want to do calculations with and so will remove a leading zero. You can force a number to be treated as text by starting it with a single quote. So, a mobile phone number can be entered as '07988 222333.

Table 2.4: Continued

Data type		Description
Numeric	Integers/real numbers and decimals	Integers are numbers without a decimal part (whole numbers). You can make any number an integer by reducing the number of digits displayed after the decimal point using the decrease decimal button in the Number section of the Home menu. Excel will round numbers so if a cell contains 16.6 and you click the Decrease decimal button it will change to 17. Note that using the increase and decrease decimal buttons does not change the number Excel stores, just how it is displayed. Numbers are right aligned.
	Currency	If you enter a numeric value with a currency symbol included (for example, £3.50) Excel will automatically format it as currency. You can use the drop-down in the Number section of the Home menu to apply the Accounting or Currency formats. The Accounting format can also be selected using the button. Note that the currency format and the accounting format display the numbers in a slightly different way.
	Percentages	If you enter a number followed by a percentage sign, then it is automatically formatted as a percentage, and the number is followed by a per cent symbol (%). The value in the cell is divided by 100, so if you enter 25%, the value in the cell is 0.25. This makes it easy to do percentage calculations. Simply multiply cell values by the percentage directly.

Importing different file types

There may be situations where you want to import data into a spreadsheet from an external source such as a webpage or a database.

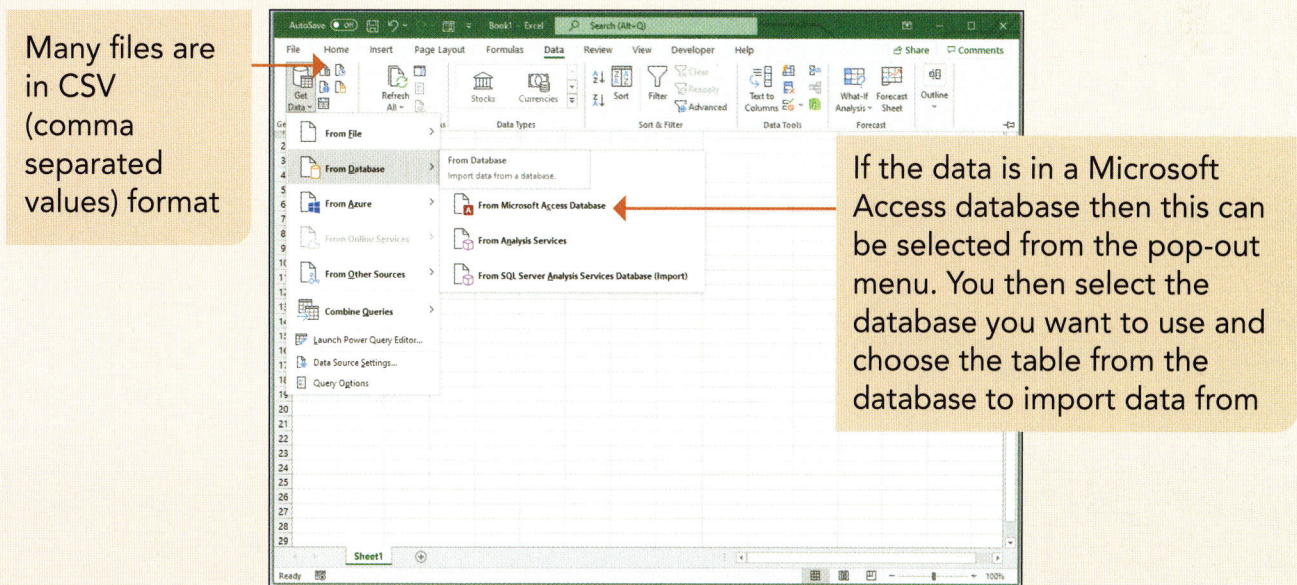

Many files are in CSV (comma separated values) format

If the data is in a Microsoft Access database then this can be selected from the pop-out menu. You then select the database you want to use and choose the table from the database to import data from

Figure 2.30: The way you import the data depends on the file format that the data is in

Security measures

When you create a spreadsheet solution for others to use you may well want to prevent users from changing formulae or other aspects of the solution as this may cause problems and prevent it from working. You can do this by first setting up those areas the user can access and then locking the worksheet (or the whole spreadsheet) to prevent them changing anything else.

Over to you!   2

Create the following worksheet used to input data into a spreadsheet solution.

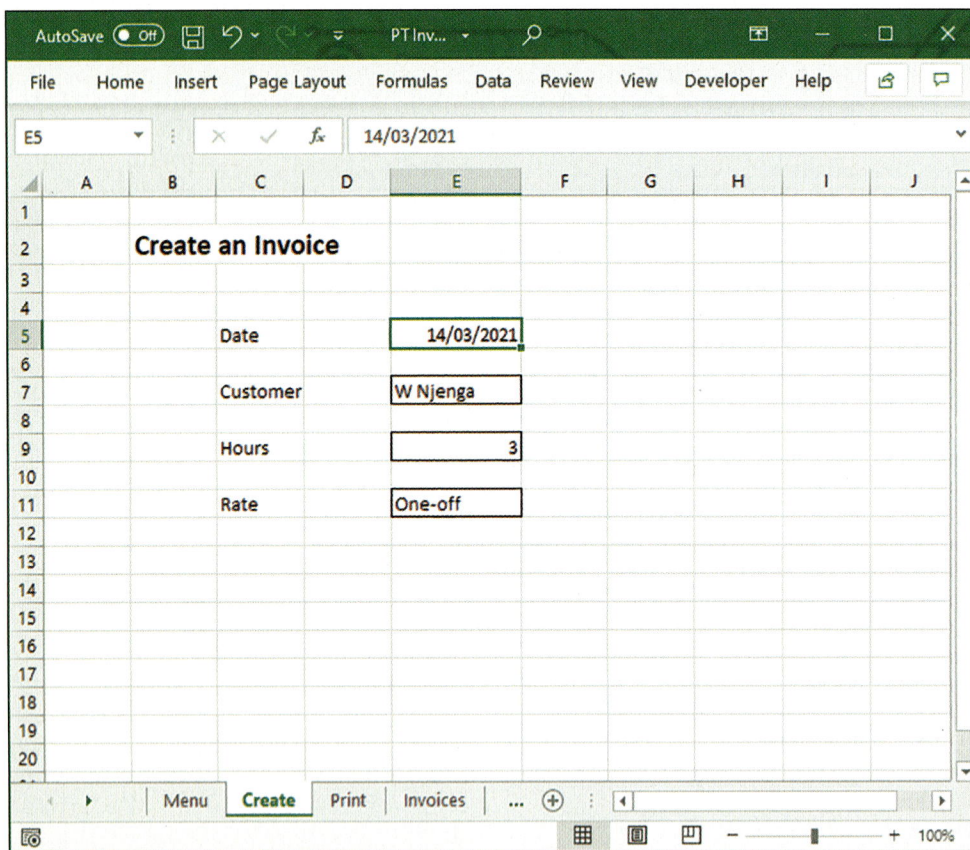

Figure 2.31: A data input worksheet

We only want the user to be able to access the four input cells (E5, E7, E9 and E11) so first, right click on these cells one at a time, choose 'Format cell' from the right click menu and then, on the dialog box that appears, click the 'Protection' tab (see Figure 2.32) and untick the 'Locked' check box.

Continued

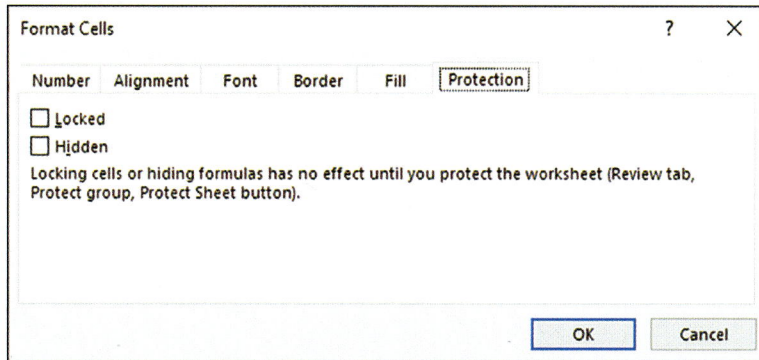

Figure 2.32: The Protection tab of the Format Cells dialog box

Once you have done this for the four input cells, protect the sheet by going to the 'Review' menu and clicking the 'Protect sheet' icon. Add a password if required to the 'Protect sheet' dialog box (don't forget it!) and untick the 'Select locked cells' tick box, then click 'OK'. Now the user can only select and input data to the four cells you previously unlocked.

Over to you!   3

Use the data input form you created earlier to enter student details on a course. Apply protection to the worksheet with the input form so that the user can only enter data in the input boxes you have created.

Modelling tools

Spreadsheets are often used by organisations to try to predict what might happen if there are changes to the business in the future. For example, what might happen if prices are lowered or how long would it take to recover the cost of developing a new product? This is often called 'What-if' analysis.

For example, suppose you wanted to save money to buy an expensive item like a car. You know how much money you need (for example £4,500) and you know you want to have the money for when you take you driving test in 2 years (24 months) time but how much do you have to save each month to have the £4,500? Fig 2.33 shows this in a spreadsheet with the months shown in B4 and an example amount to save (£100) in B5. B6 contains a formula which multiplies B5 by B4. We want to know what the value would need to be in B5 to achieve the target amount of £4,500.

Goal Seek can be used when you know the result you want from a formula. It will show the values you need to enter

This must contain the formula you are using in the calculation, which here is cell B6

This is the value you want in B6, which is the target savings amount of £4,500

This is the cell which Goal Seek will change to achieve the value you need. Here it is B5, the monthly amount to save

When you click OK, Goal Seek will work out the value needed in B5

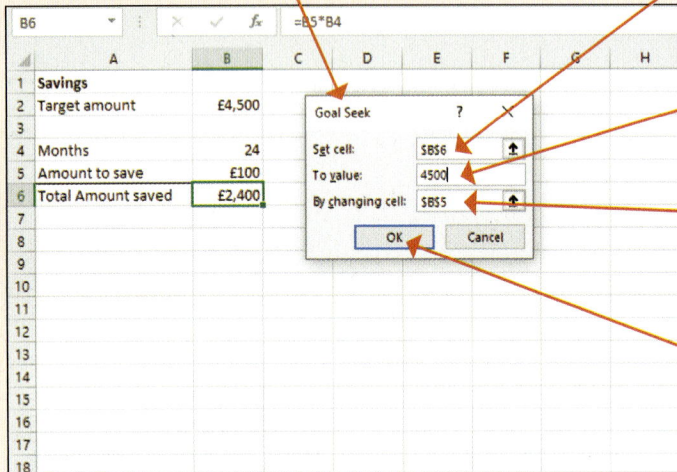

Figure 2.33: Using Goal Seek

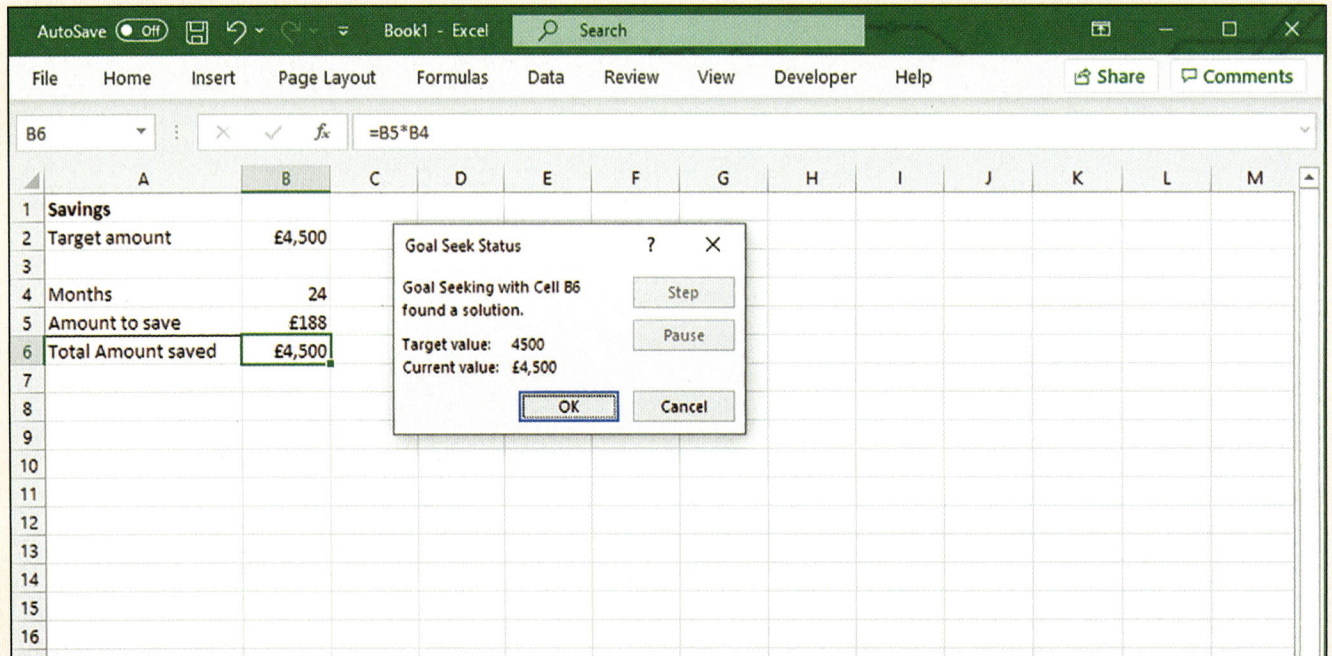

Figure 2.34: The Goal Seek result showing that you need to save £188/month to save £4,500 over two years

Pivot tables

Pivot tables allow you to rearrange data in a way that can make it easier to understand. They work best with data that is divided up by several criteria.

Stretch   9

Mo's customers appear several times in his invoice spreadsheet and they are classified by whether they pay for regular or one-off sessions. He wants to know how much income he makes from each customer and if he makes more from one-off or regular sessions.

He creates a pivot table from the invoice data to add up the values in the different categories.

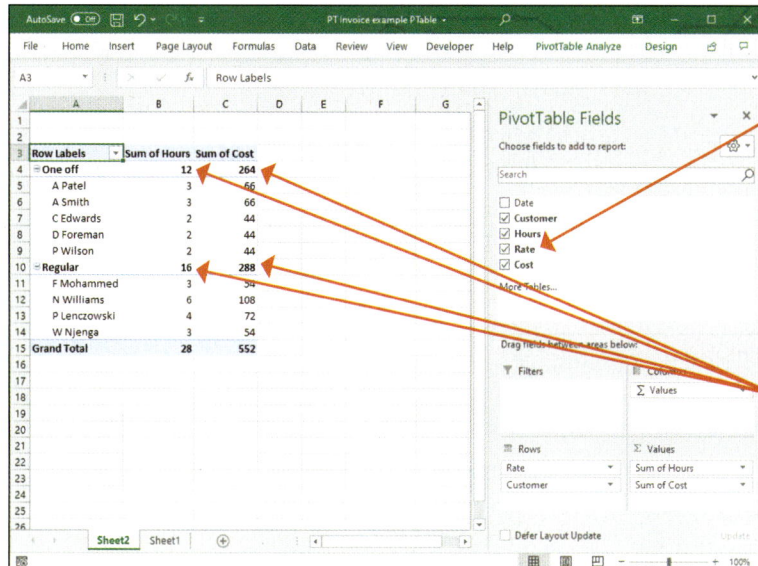

To create a pivot table, select the data to be used, then choose Pivot Table from the Insert menu. You then add the fields you want from the list on the right

The pivot table has added up the hours and the value of the invoices for each customer and grouped them into regular and one-off clients. Group subtotals have been added

Figure 2.35: Pivot table created using Mo's invoice data

Use the worksheet you created in Stretch 1. Add an additional column C containing 'yes' if the multiple is divisible by 5 and 'no' if it is not. Now create a pivot table that groups the data. Don't forget to save your work.

Techniques to generate the outputs

You will need to add features which display information in a clear format to your spreadsheet solution. Charts, graphs and tables are known as the outputs from data. These will follow the house style, if one is being used. You can use them to present the data in your spreadsheet clearly and in a way that makes it easy for end users to understand.

Charts and graphs

Charts and graphs are an effective way to visualise numerical data. They make trends, such as increases or decreases over time, easy to see.

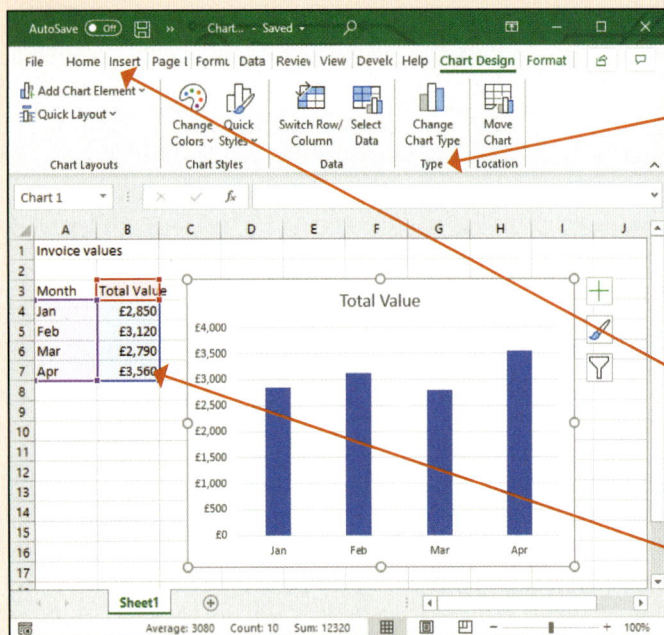

Once the chart is created the Chart Design menu is shown in the ribbon menu and you can modify the chart style

From the Insert menu choose the chart type; a 2D column chart is shown

Select the data in the cells first, A3:B7 here

Figure 2.36: An example of a chart drawn from the data in A3:B7

You can create a variety of different charts, as explained earlier. At the design stage you should have chosen the type and format of chart and the cells where the chart will get the data it uses from.

When you select a chart three icons appear to the right of it, see Figure 2.37.

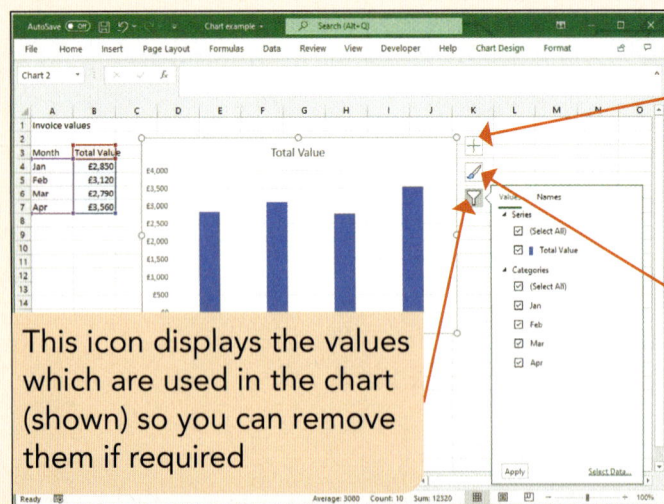

Click on this icon to select which chart elements (title, axis labels, etc.) you want on the chart

Click on this icon to select the style (colours and patterns) you want for the chart

This icon displays the values which are used in the chart (shown) so you can remove them if required

Figure 2.37: Changing the format of the chart

Page layout properties

To print out a worksheet, you can select the 'Print' option from the 'File' menu, which will display a preview of the printed sheet and the main settings you can choose. The page layout properties of any output will have been considered as part of the design.

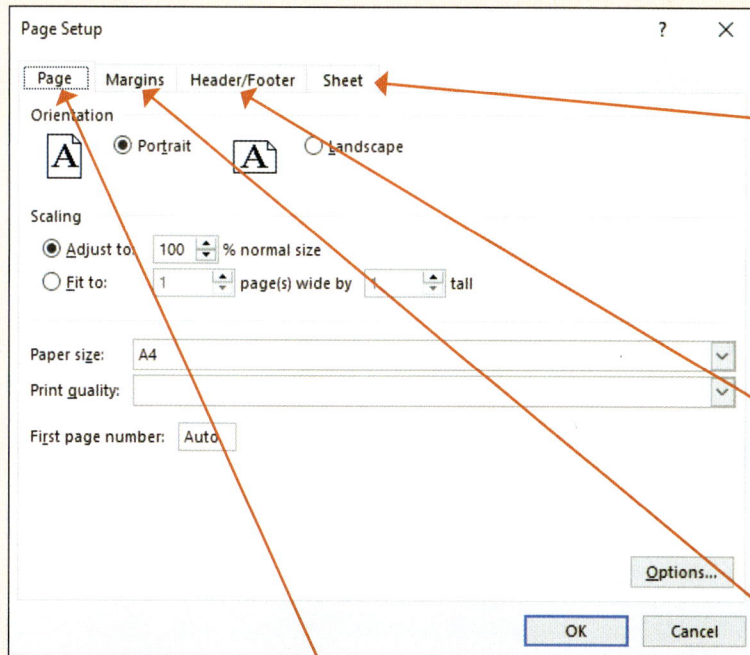

Sheet – this tab contains a number of different settings including allowing you to select the cell range you want to print, repeating titles from certain cells on each page and turning on the printing of the cell gridlines

Header/Footer – allows you to add text that prints at the top (header) and/or bottom (footer) of each page

Margins – here you can adjust the margins (gaps between the edge of the paper and where the printing starts)

Page – allows you to choose portrait or landscape orientation, scale the printout to a certain size or number of pages and choose the paper size and quality of the print

Figure 2.38: The page setup dialog box

Adjusting rows and columns

The standard row heights and column widths may not always be suitable and may prevent the display of all the information in a cell. There may also be situations where you want to hide the data or formulae in a row or column.

- Adjust the width of a column or height of a row by clicking the dividing line between the grey bars at the top of a column or left of a row. Then drag with your mouse.

- Select multiple rows or columns and then adjust the width so all the selected rows or columns are adjusted to the same size.

- Hide a column or row by right clicking in the grey bar at the top of the column (where the column letter is) or to the left of a row (where the row number is) and choosing Hide.

- Unhide a row or column you have previously hidden by dragging the grey bar across the rows or columns either side of the hidden one, then select multiple rows or columns including the hidden one, then right click and choose Unhide.

User interface

It is important that your spreadsheet solution is suitable for the users to complete the tasks they need to and that they can find the information they require. Sometimes user interface tools can help with this.

Buttons and macros

Clickable **buttons** that make the spreadsheet features work are a useful part of the user interface, but they need to be attached to a **macro** to work.

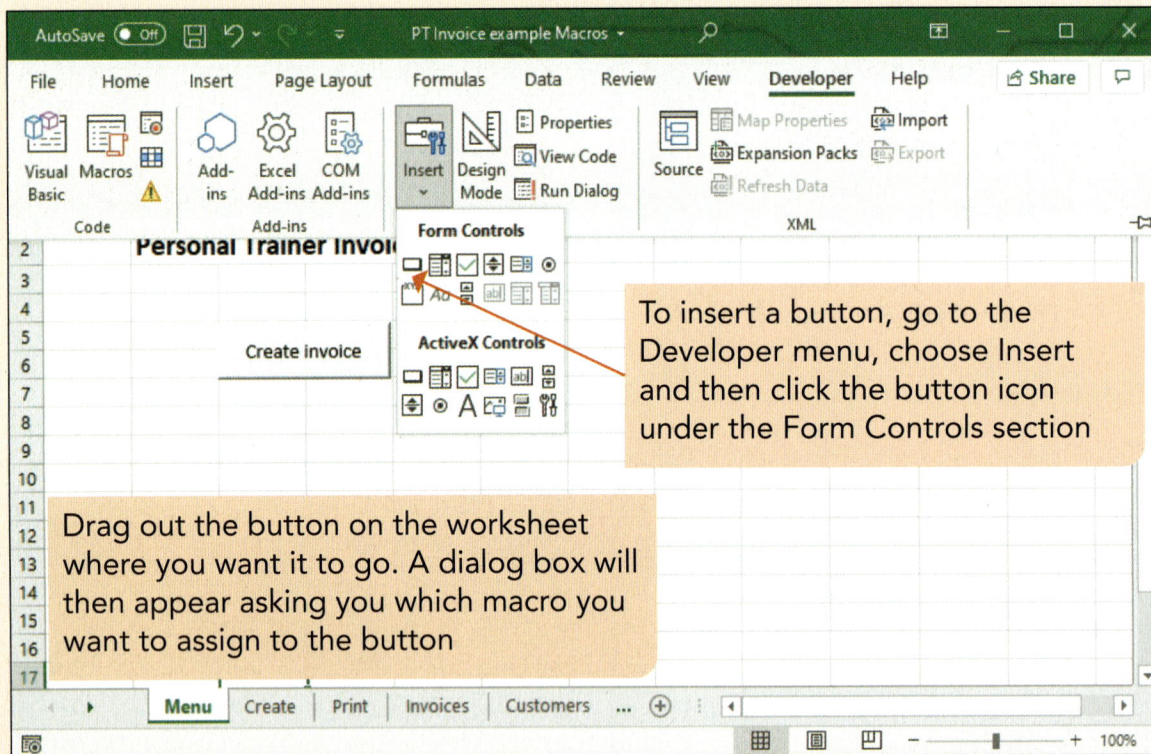

Figure 2.39: To add buttons to a worksheet you need to have the Developer menu visible, described earlier

Macros are used to automate actions you might carry out with a spreadsheet and therefore can be used to create a user-friendly solution. The use of macros may be restricted on your network.

Stretch   10

Mo wants to create and print out invoices from his spreadsheet.

Create a menu screen with a button for creating invoices and a button for printing them.

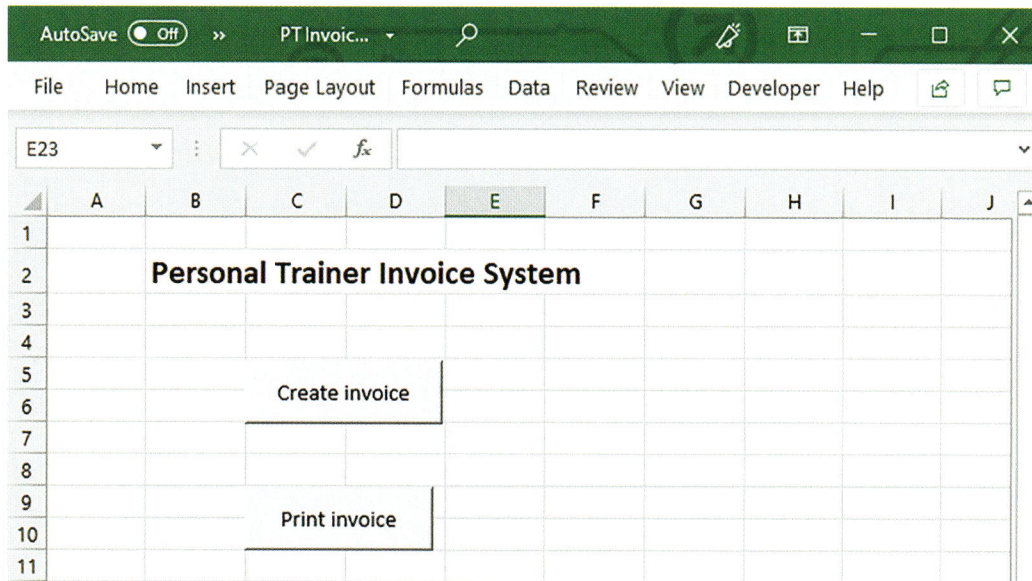

Figure 2.40: Creating and printing invoices

- On the worksheet 'Menu', go to the 'Developer' tab and click the 'Record macro' icon.

- In the Record Macro dialog box, give the macro a meaningful name, then click OK.

- From now on, take care to only do those actions that you want recorded in the macro.

- Click the worksheet tab to go to the Create worksheet menu to enter details of the invoice.

- Now return to the Developer menu and click the Stop macro button.

- Click the 'Create invoice' button on the 'Menu'. Choose 'Assign macro'. Follow the same procedure to create a 'Print macro'.

- Save the spreadsheet as a Macro enabled workbook as you cannot save macros in the standard Excel file.

Another potential use of macros is to ensure the correct menu is shown when the spreadsheet is opened, or to set up other information. To do this you can record a macro which changes the current worksheet to the menu worksheet. By saving the macro with the name Auto-Open, it will always run when the spreadsheet is open, ensuring that the menu worksheet is displayed.

Over to you!   4

1   Create a spreadsheet containing the worksheets 'Menu', 'Create', 'Print' and 'Invoices'.

2   Copy the screenshot to recreate the 'Create' worksheet in Over to you! 2.

3   Add the 'Save' button and record a macro that copies the date, customer, hours and rate from this worksheet to a new row on the 'Invoices' worksheet.

Hyperlinks

An alternative to using buttons to move between worksheets is to use hyperlinks. See Figure 2.41:

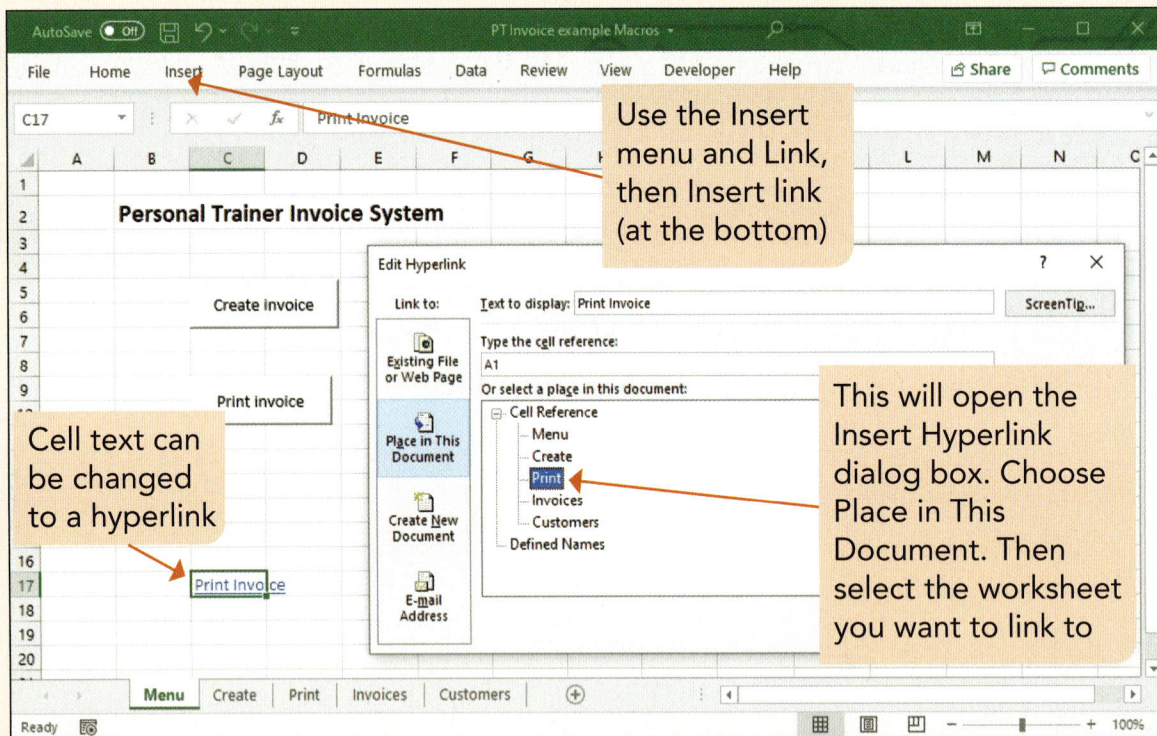

Figure 2.41: Adding a hyperlink

Forms

You can create a separate form to allow users to search for data in the spreadsheet solution. The form feature is not included on any of the standard menus. You need to add it to the Quick Access toolbar on the top left of the Excel window (which by default has the Save and undo/redo buttons on it already). To create an input form, first select the cells which contain both the column or row headings and the data. Then click the form button. See Figure 2.42.

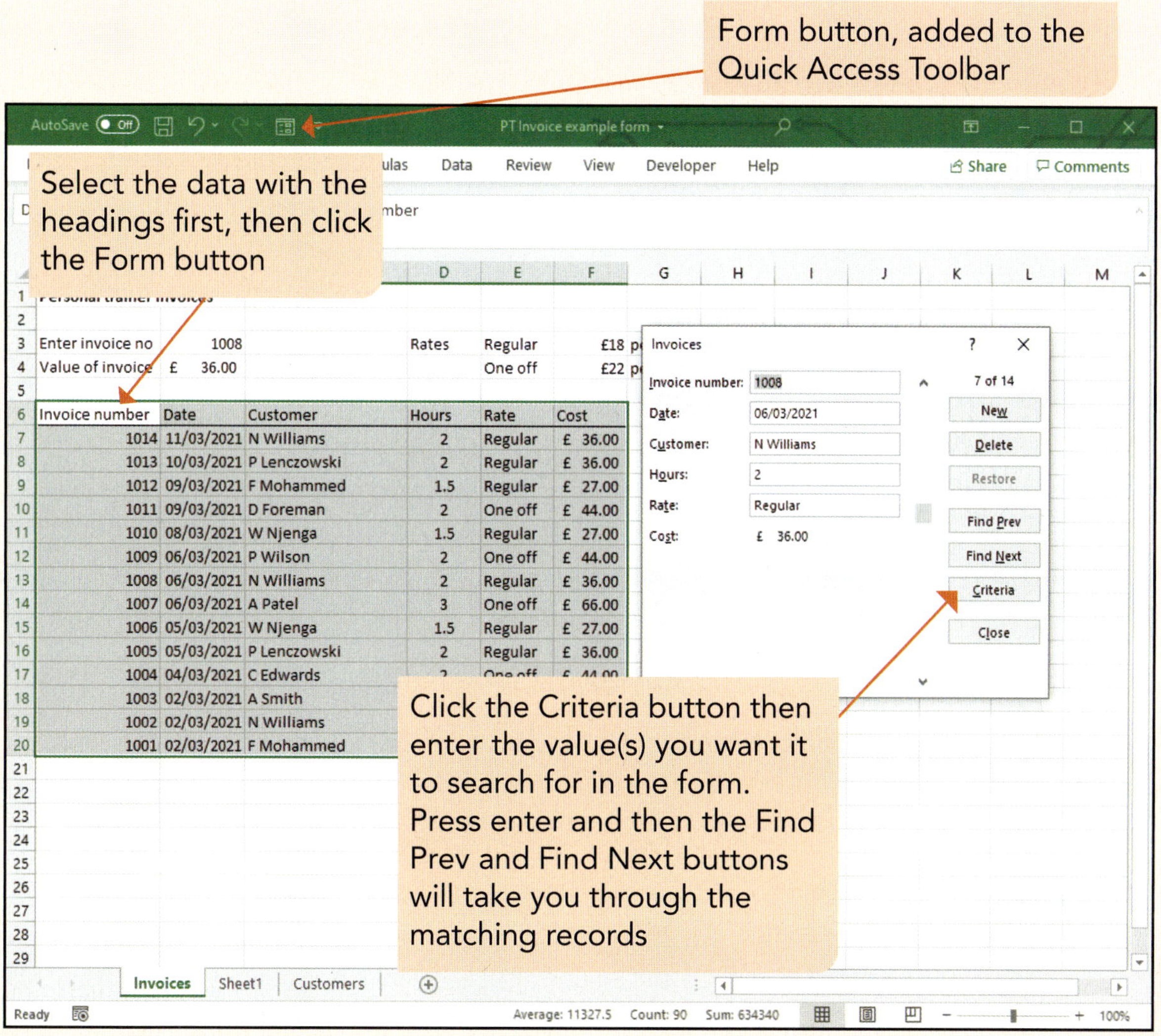

Form button, added to the Quick Access Toolbar

Select the data with the headings first, then click the Form button

Click the Criteria button then enter the value(s) you want it to search for in the form. Press enter and then the Find Prev and Find Next buttons will take you through the matching records

Figure 2.42: Adding a form

Over to you!　　5

1　Create a spreadsheet with a 'Menu' worksheet and three other sheets: 'Data input', 'Show graph' and 'Calculate totals'. Give each worksheet a title.

2　Create three buttons on the Menu worksheet and record and attach macros to each button which will swap to each of the worksheets when the button is clicked. If you are unable to use macros, create hyperlinks instead which link to each worksheet.

3　Add a hyperlink to a cell containing the text 'back to menu' to each of the three worksheets and link the hyperlinks so they return to the main menu worksheet.

Review your learning

Test your knowledge

1   What is the difference between a spreadsheet and a worksheet?

2   In a formula that has both subtraction and division in it, which is done first?

3   In this formula: =IF(A5>10, 'High', 'Low') what is displayed in the cell if A5 contains the value of 9?

4   If you get a #NAME error in a cell, what is the cause of this?

5   What's the difference between landscape and portrait orientation?

6   How can you unhide a previously hidden row or column?

7   Which menu do you use to create a graph?

8   What are margins and how can you adjust them?

9   What is needed to make a button do something?

10   How do buttons and hyperlinks differ?

11   Under which menu is the Record Macro icon found?

12   When you have finished recording a Macro what must you remember to do?

What have you learnt?

	See section
• Formulae and functions to carry out calculations.	2.1
• Formatting worksheets and set print options.	2.1
• Creating charts.	2.1
• Using buttons and macros to create menus.	2.1
• Using modelling tools such as goal seek and pivot table.	2.1
• Using input features (such as radio button and tick lists) and validation to check and accept input data.	2.1

Testing the spreadsheet solution

Let's get started

Have you ever used software or an app where you have discovered something that doesn't work correctly? What impression of the product did that leave you with? Did you find the experience annoying or frustrating?

What will you learn?

- **Testing** during and after development.
- Technical and **usability testing**.
- Creating a test plan.
- Test data.

3.1 Test the user interface and the technical aspects of the spreadsheet solution

Testing the spreadsheet solution is an important part of the development process. Testing is important to make sure the solution works as it should and produces correct results. It should also be able to handle user errors such as entering **invalid data**. This is known as **technical testing**. Technical testing should include checking that the navigation features such as menus and buttons work and take the user to the correct worksheet or cell in the solution. The spreadsheet calculations included in the formulae should be checked that they produce the correct result. The output should also include correct data. For example, are charts correct? Has the record uploaded to the database?

Unlike technical testing, usability testing needs to be carried out with the help of the users. The purpose of usability testing is to make sure that the users of the solution find it easy to use. Does it make it easy for the users to do the tasks they need to do using the solution (is it intuitive)? You may want to include some invalid data so the users can comment on how the solution deals with it. For example, are the error messages clear?

Testing during development

While developing each part of the solution you should carry out some technical testing to ensure what you have developed works before moving on to the next step of the development. This is sometimes called module testing. You may also do some usability testing during development of the solution, for example, making sure that screen text and error messages are clear and the use of text fonts, colours and other formatting is consistent. You may also want to show the user interface you are developing to others to check if they think it is clear how the solution should be used.

Testing after development

Once the solution is complete it should be tested, with both technical and usability testing. It is common for the developer of the solution to do the technical testing, but usability testing needs to be done by someone who is going to use the solution.

Testing spreadsheet solutions is usually either simple or part of the wider testing of an overall solution. Testing is discussed in more detail in R050, Section 3.5.

Test plan documentation

You would not normally create a test plan for usability testing of spreadsheet solutions. Instead, you would provide the user with some scenarios or tasks to complete. You will need to provide test data to be used when completing the tasks.

Table 2.5: A test plan uses a table which has these columns

Table column in test plan	Description
Test number	A sequential number identifying each test
Test description	A brief description of what the test involves
Test data	Lists the data (if there is any) that will be input to the solution as part of the test. If the test is simply clicking a button to check navigation features then test data may not be required
Expected result	This is what should happen if the solution is working correctly
Actual result	This what actually happens when the test is carried out. If the expected result and the actual result are the same, then the test is passed. If not, then the test is failed
Remedial action	If the test fails then enter the changes you made so it works correctly in this column
Retesting	Here you confirm that, after remedial action and retesting, the test passes

Technical testing is more formal than usability testing and a test plan is used. This is a document created before the actual testing is started. It lists the tests to be done and what the expected outcomes will be (in other words what the correct results for the test are).

In a situation where a test fails, you must take some remedial action to correct the issue. Then repeat to make sure the test is now passed. If the remedial action involves major changes or if a lot of tests fail, you should retest the whole solution.

Let's get digital!

1   Create a test plan template using a **word processing** program.

2   Use a table with the test plan headings listed in Table 2.5 (use landscape page orientation so you can fit in all the columns).

3   Include general details at the top of the plan such as the solution being tested, the date of the tests and who is carrying out the tests.

Case study

Lost results

In the Coronavirus pandemic of 2020 Public Health England lost the details of more than 16,000 positive test results because of an error in an Excel spreadsheet. This data included people's names, addresses, date of birth, postcodes, and so on. The mistake meant that contact tracing was not carried out for the people whose data was lost. The error was caused by using an old Excel spreadsheet format that could only handle around 65,000 rows and 256 columns (when it actually needed around 1 million rows and 16,384 columns).

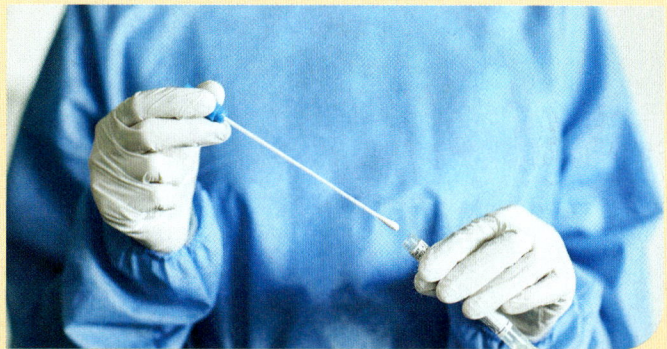

Figure 2.43: Doctor with a Coronavirus swab

Check your understanding

Create a test plan which includes:

- A test to check the maximum size of the spreadsheet has not been reached

- Extreme test data for the date of birth field

- Invalid test data for the postcode field.

Test data

When testing input data, particularly if it will be validated, you need to test if correct entries are accepted and incorrect ones are rejected. To fully test the input in the spreadsheet solution you should choose data that falls into each of these categories:

- **Extreme data**: which usually comes in sets of four, two at the lower boundary (accepted value and rejected value) and two at the upper boundary (accepted and rejected values). Extreme data is discussed in R050.

- Invalid (**erroneous**) data: which is data that is incorrect. An example is a text input to a numeric field. The data is used to check that invalid data is rejected and does not cause any problems. For example, if a text value is used in a formula, it will cause a #VALUE error to be displayed in that cell. Useful error messages should be displayed.

- Valid: You should include some **valid data** to make sure this is not rejected.

Figure 2.44: It is important to ensure that invalid data is rejected

Over to you!

Suppose you had an input worksheet for a company that sells cars with these fields and validation rules:

a Car make – text must be between 2 and 25 characters long

b Car model – text must be between 2 and 25 characters long

c Number of doors – must be numeric and between 2 and 5

d Price – must be numeric and between £1000 and £30,000.

Create a test plan for these four fields including (where appropriate) valid, extreme and invalid (erroneous) test data.

Review your learning

Test your knowledge

1   What are the columns of a test plan?

2   What is the difference between technical and usability testing?

3   What is extreme test data?

4   What is invalid test data?

What have you learnt?

	See section
• What to test in technical testing.	3.1
• Creating and using a test plan.	3.1
• Creating extreme and invalid test data.	3.1
• When retesting needs to be done.	3.1

Evaluating the spreadsheet solution

Let's get started

How do you evaluate a spreadsheet? Have you ever used a badly designed spreadsheet? Products like cars or mobile phones have specifications and features that you can use to evaluate them and compare them with other similar products. What makes a good or not so good spreadsheet solution?

What will you learn?

- Evaluating how well the **client requirements** have been met.

- Evaluating the design and HCI of the solution.

4.1 Methods used to evaluate the success of the spreadsheet solution

Client requirements

When you create a spreadsheet solution you might be provided with the requirements, including the functionality. You must follow these carefully. You will need to evaluate your spreadsheet solution against how well it meets these requirements.

You could list each of the client requirements in a table and then describe how well your solution meets them. Can users navigate the system easily? Are there data errors? Is a graph displayed?

When completing the table, you should describe how you met the particular requirement. For example, you might describe the data input validation you have used. You might also add any alternative methods you could have used and why you rejected them and chose the ones you did.

Another aspect of the spreadsheet solution you should evaluate is how well the eventual solution you produced matches the design you originally created. In this part of the evaluation, you need to compare the design with the product and explain any differences.

Let's get digital!   1

Throughout this unit we have used an example spreadsheet for Mo, the personal trainer. Mo will want certain features in the spreadsheet such as being able to see how many hours he spends with each client. An evaluation of the spreadsheet would need to consider how well these requirements are met.

HCI design principles and conventions

When your spreadsheet solution is complete you might be required to include an evaluation of the HCI you have designed and created. For this part of the evaluation, you need to consider how easy to use the solution is. In the first section of this unit HCI design principles and conventions were explained so an evaluation might look at how well the completed solution meets these principles and conventions. Your evaluation of the HCI needs to answer the question:

How effective is the visual style?

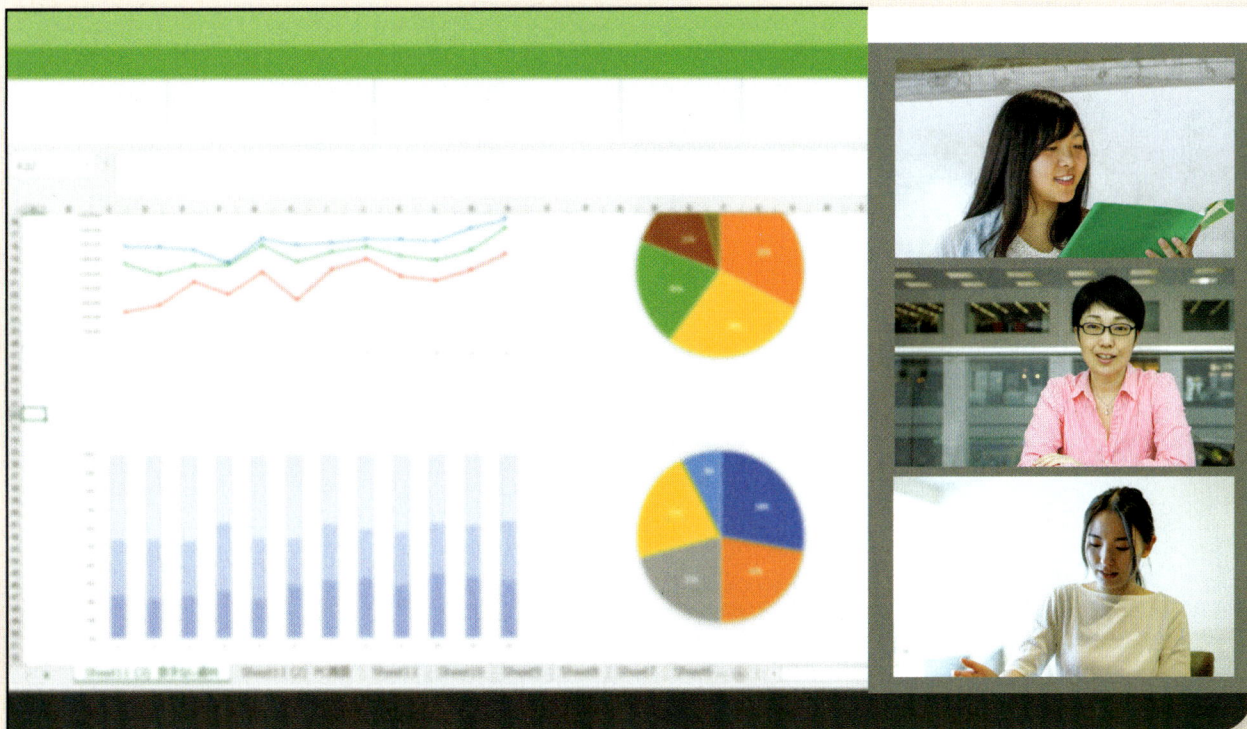

Figure 2.45: The screen must show effective visual images

An evaluation of the visual style of a spreadsheet solution can be difficult because style can be a personal choice. The evaluation needs to consider what is good and what is bad about the visual style. It's not very helpful just to say that something is good or bad, you need to give reasons why you think they're good or bad. Remember the purpose of an evaluation is to help improve something or do a better job next time. If you don't identify why something is good or bad you may not be able to repeat the good aspects and improve or avoid the bad aspects.

Let's get digital!   2

Working in small groups, carry out an evaluation of the HCI of one of the spreadsheets solutions you have created. Before you start looking at the solution, make a checklist of the aspects of the HCI you will look at, such as the house style and the navigation.

Review your learning

Test your knowledge

1 What is a house style?

2 What do you need to consider in terms of the visual style of your solution?

3 What aspect of the design of the solution can be evaluated?

4 What do you need to include in your evaluation of the HCI?

5 What aspects of the navigation system can be evaluated?

What have you learnt?

	See section
• Completing an evaluation of how a solution meets client requirements.	4.1
• Completing an evaluation of a solution's HCI.	4.1

Let's get started

Do you know what Augmented Reality is?
Do you think reality needs improving?
What parts of our lives would be better
with more information?

What will you learn in this unit?

Just as smartphones and tablets have radically changed the way we access information and communicate, Augmented Reality (AR) has changed the way we see information and use it. The first sixty years of creating applications has been focused on making the information on a computer monitor appear as human friendly as possible, but now with AR we can display information and details about our surroundings in the real world. You're going to learn how different industries can use AR to make the digital world easier to access and how to make your own AR app.

In this unit you will learn about:

- Augmented Reality (AR) **TA1**
- Designing an AR model prototype **TA2**
- Creating an AR model prototype **TA3**
- Testing and reviewing **TA4**.

How you will be assessed

This unit will be assessed through a series of coursework tasks that show your understanding of each topic area. You will complete the assignment independently in class with teacher supervision. The assignment will be marked by your teacher. The assignment contains between three and five tasks, which will cover:

- planning and designing an AR prototype for the brief in the assignment
- creating your prototype for the brief using an AR software development kit (SDK)
- testing and reviewing the prototype against the brief.

Augmented Reality (AR)

Let's get started

Have you tried any **AR** applications? What are the different businesses that use **Augmented Reality**?

How could AR be used in education? Could children interact with nature inside their own homes, for example?

Figure 3.1: A child viewing a 3D tree through an AR app

What will you learn?

- What AR is used for.
- Who uses AR and how they use it.
- The types of AR.
- The ways in which users interact with AR.
- The different types of devices that support AR.

1.1 Purposes and uses of Augmented Reality (AR)

What is AR?

If something is **augmented**, it means that it's had something added to what was already there to make it better. So, how does that work with reality? It means adding extra **information** or details to the real world, that a user can access with an electronic device.

The creation of the **internet** means that people with access can find all the information they could ever search for. However, a web browser doesn't understand your exact circumstances or surroundings.

This is where Augmented Reality or AR takes interaction with information a step further and makes it relevant to you. It is a method of laying extra, digital information on top of the real world. This is usually using a device with a camera on it. The camera shows the user the real world and then the application adds more information to the images. This information is mostly visual but can also be sounds, physical feelings or even smells!

The purpose of AR

The main purpose of AR is to add something extra to your world. It can be informative, fun or educational.

Since the first experiments in **smartphone** AR in the 2000s there has been a huge increase in the amount of Augmented Reality applications that we use. Although relatively new, many people use AR every day to play games, design their homes or learn how to do a new job. It's a very exciting part of the IT industry and a skill that has many different career opportunities.

Let's get digital!   1

- Spend some time looking at different AR products which only have one purpose: fun!
- Compare and discuss with friends, family or classmates.
- Consider why the product is more fun because of AR.

The sectors where AR is used

Different areas of business use AR in many ways. Sometimes AR is used to promote other products or services, such as a clothing brand or new model of car. However, AR is also used in apps that are products in their own right. Star maps are examples of this, allowing people to see the names of the constellations in the sky above them using their phones or other devices.

Figure 3.2: Augmented reality apps can be used for town planning

Table 3.1: Examples of how different sectors use AR

Sector	How AR is used
Architecture	AR can help architects explain space in a way that is difficult to do on paper. Their customers can see a whole floor plan mapped out onto a muddy building site. Or it could give technical information that the builders need such as where electricity cables should be installed.
Education	Museums and textbooks have been creative in using AR. Instead of just reading about something you can see animated 3D models of how it would move or hear audio of what it would sound like. AR allows students to access even more information about what they can see in front of them.
Entertainment	The entertainment sector has really pushed AR forward through social media apps and video games. Pokémon Go is probably the most famous AR app ever. You can walk around real places scanning a map for virtual creatures that can then be captured using your phone camera.
Lifestyle	You can improve your lifestyle with various AR fitness apps. One unique approach uses audio AR (more of that later) to get you up and running as zombies chase you. Another lets you work out the best way to approach a difficult hole on the golf course.
Retail	You can see what clothes look like without actually trying them on, using Augmented Reality. Some shops have **augmented** mirrors that show you in real time, wearing different clothes. Other shops such as IKEA let you use an app to test out furniture inside your house.

Over to you!   1

1   Pick one of the **sectors** listed in Table 3.1.

2   Think of a business from the sector and who their customers are.

3   Make a list of all the different types of information that those customers would need.

4   Decide whether AR would be beneficial for the business.

Stretch

5   Find out if any businesses in this sector have used AR to share information with their customers.

How AR is used

New ways of using AR capabilities are being created all the time. You can add information to what the camera sees through text, video, images and sound. For example, a label might appear to float over a food product in the supermarket that tells you if it's allergy safe. This creates a huge amount of variety for what you can use it for. When you also consider where AR is being used, the possibilities expand even more. Here are some examples.

Training

It costs a lot of money to train people to do certain jobs. It could be that there are safety precautions or expensive equipment that you wouldn't want people to use before they have been trained. But how does someone get experience if they aren't allowed to use the equipment? This is where AR becomes very useful. It can save companies money by making sure that people know what they need to do before trying it for real. It can even save lives.

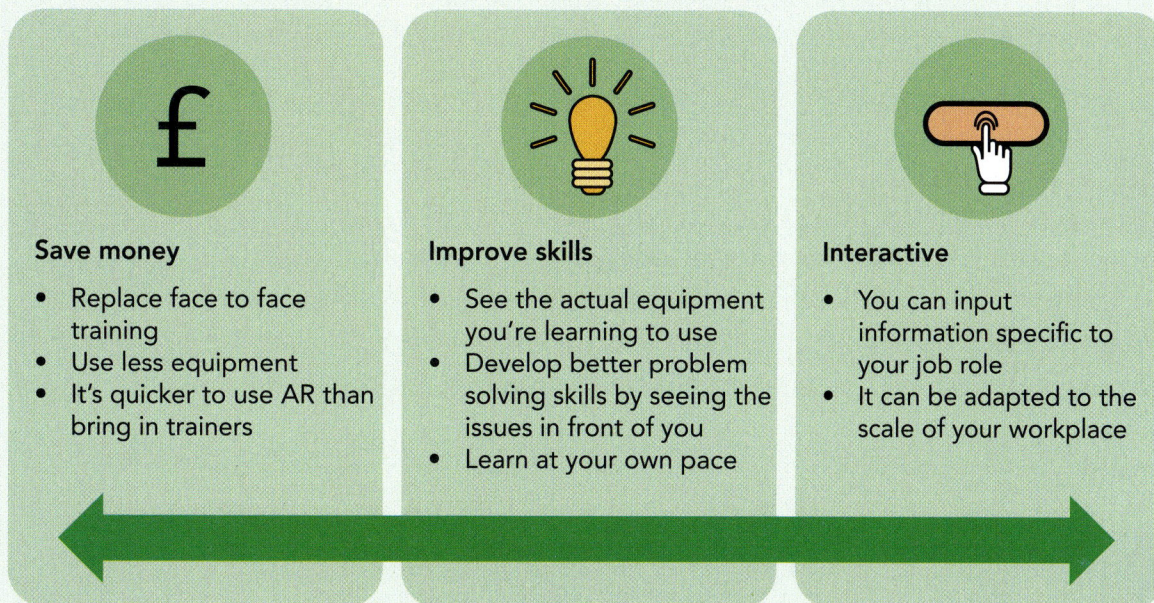

Save money
- Replace face to face training
- Use less equipment
- It's quicker to use AR than bring in trainers

Improve skills
- See the actual equipment you're learning to use
- Develop better problem solving skills by seeing the issues in front of you
- Learn at your own pace

Interactive
- You can input information specific to your job role
- It can be adapted to the scale of your workplace

Figure 3.3: The advantages of using AR to train staff

Marketing

The marketing industry has also been quick to use AR. It can be a cheap way to let customers try things before they buy them when shopping from home. This could be clothes, shoes or even make-up. There are lots of AR make-up apps, which as well as being fun to use, help companies to sell more products. Customers might feel more confident in buying a new product if they have tried it on, even if it's just a digital experience. We'll see more examples of marketing AR later in the unit.

Visualisation of designs, interiors and concepts

We've considered how architects can use AR to show what their designs would look like. This happens in lots of other useful ways. For example:

- Interior designers can show clients what rooms would look like in a different colour

- New furniture can be tested out to see if it fits

- Product designs can be shown next to existing products

- Town planners can show the public where they might build new houses

- You can see what different colours of a jacket you want to buy look like.

Virtual tours

Map technology and satellite **navigation** on mobile phones have made it easier for people to get around. Satellite navigation is a technology that uses chips in your phone or car to get to places that you haven't been to before. Once you arrive though, things might not be that simple. AR can help by allowing you to see more information about the world in front of you. This can be achieved with apps like Google Maps Live View.

Figure 3.4: Google Maps Live View allows people to navigate on foot with all the information they need

Museums have also embraced AR. Around the world there are now museums with AR virtual tours. You look through your phone camera and see more information and detail about the exhibits than could ever be shown.

Case study

The Donuimun Gate – Showing us what was there before

The city of Seoul in South Korea once boasted four great gates that allowed people into the city. One of these was the Donuimun gate. It was destroyed in 1914 and for many years the government wanted to rebuild it. Unfortunately, the gate was in a part of the city that had become very busy with traffic in modern times. AR came to the rescue and created a detailed 3D model of the gate building. Through a phone app or kiosk, visitors can stand safely near where the gate was and see it from different angles. It also reacts to different light levels throughout the day. Something that was impossible to recreate in the real world has been achieved through Augmented Reality.

Figure 3.5: A street scene at the Donuimun Gate

Check your understanding

1   What are the benefits to visitors of the Donuimun Gate project?

2   What is the advantage of this being phone-based AR?

3   Research other cultural monuments around the world that are damaged or have been demolished and consider whether they could be brought back with AR.

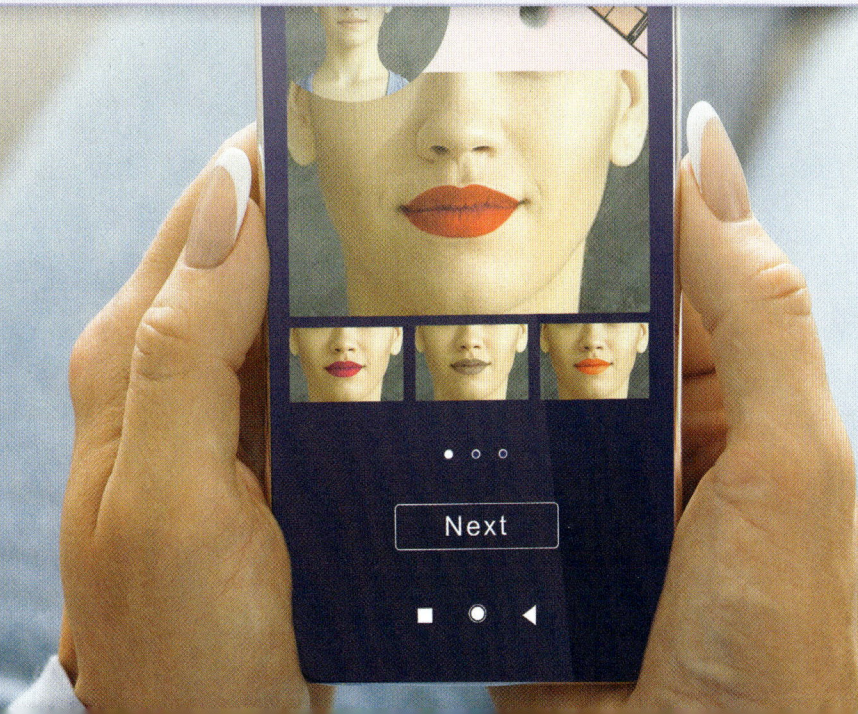

1.2 Types of Augmented Reality (AR) and user interaction

Types of AR

It's time to start learning more about how AR works and how we can create our own. AR can be created using several different approaches.

Marker led

The first method is marker led. This works when your camera can see a unique pattern. The first experiments in AR worked this way as it was the most efficient way to get digital content to appear in a specific place. The user places a card on a flat surface and the camera **scans** it. Barcodes and **QR codes** are often used because they are an easy way of creating a unique code that the AR application can recognise through the camera.

Another advantage of using flat, easy to understand patterns, is that the camera can read them from different angles. This removes any problems caused by users holding their phones at funny angles or wobbling around.

Once the code, or marker, has been scanned, the AR application will then project an image in 2D or 3D that appears to be floating above that space.

An early example of **Marker Led AR** was the AR Games package that came with the Nintendo 3DS handheld. In the box Nintendo included some cards with different characters from their games. Players scanned the cards using the built-in camera and a range of different games loaded which used the markers to **spawn** small game **assets** like archery targets, fishing rods and Italian plumbers!

Figure 3.6: A user scans a unique code from an AR application using the camera

Object recognition

Sometimes it's not convenient to use cards with codes or markers on. It can be a lot more fun to play an AR game or use an AR application without having to find or print out cards. This is where **object recognition** or object tracking AR comes in handy.

The AR application will use its camera to scan the room in front of it and work out what objects need to be included in the scene that it creates. For example, if you want to see what a new chair would look like, the AR application must be able to scan the existing furniture. The chair can then be placed in an empty space.

AR apps that use object recognition will also detect **planes**. A plane is a 3-dimensional flat surface. If you are playing a game that needs to create and display 3D characters or objects in the room with you, the game will know that it has a flat surface to spawn them on.

Figure 3.7: A space recognised on a flat surface can be used to spawn assets

Over to you!   2

1   An AR application using plane detection will be looking for a flat surface that has four corners or points. Look around to see how many flat surfaces there are around you.

2   Think about your surroundings as if you are an AR camera. Can you detect any planes big enough to be used to spawn a 3D model?

3   Why do you think bumpy surfaces wouldn't work as well?

Stretch

4   Phones are carried around by people and don't always have a lot of processing power. Why would a phone AR product that uses a lot of plane detection cause problems?

Another good example of object recognition is a face filter on a social media app. The camera is programmed to recognise eyes, ears, nose and mouth. Once it has done this, it can then apply different effects such as a dog's nose and ears where your nose and ears should be.

Object recognition is a more advanced form of AR. It can be harder to create apps using object recognition, because of the complicated **algorithms** that are needed.

Location based/markerless AR

The next type of AR is **location based AR**. This is where the user's position and location affect the information that is shown. Mostly used with smartphones, location based AR needs to know where you are. Smartphones are often able to access the **Global Positioning System**, a series of satellites in orbit which let you find your position on Earth.

It does this using **GPS coordinates** that can measure your location to within five metres. An AR application can use this **data** to show you different information based on where you are.

Location-specific information is very useful. Tourist boards use it to show visitors information about the exact place that they are in. Location based information can be placed on top of a map, or it can be linked to a camera. A clever app can even use your phone's compass and work out what direction you are looking towards. If it knows where you are and which way you are looking, it can show you specific information about things in front of you.

Pokémon Go uses location based AR to spawn animated 3D Pokémon onto the world map. As you walk you can see a simplified map of where you are and what Pokémon are around you. The game then switches to an AR camera feed when you get to that location so you can catch the Pokémon.

Location based AR is sometimes known as '**markerless**'. It doesn't use any specific codes or visual cues to load information onto the screen. It simply uses your location. Object recognition AR can also be markerless because instead of using a marker to choose a place to spawn something, it scans the scene and calculates where there is space.

Figure 3.8: Rare Pokémon are restricted to certain GPS coordinates and people travel great distances to 'capture' them

Superimposed

The last type of AR is **superimposed**. When we superimpose an image, we are laying it over another image but still showing both. Superimposition in AR uses object recognition to work out what an object is, and then it overlays it with something else.

A successful example of this is AR navigation in modern cars. The navigation app runs from a screen on the driver's dashboard. When the camera in the car detects a junction or a roundabout, it superimposes an image onto the map showing what direction or lane to use. This is more sophisticated that just putting images on the screen because it must understand the size and shape of the road and place the direction image in the exact spot.

Car displays are also becoming more impressive. Information can be projected onto the windscreen at an angle that only the driver can see. This information can then track other cars on the road and superimpose them with information such as their speed or distance away. This is also how self-driving cars work, but without showing the information.

Figure 3.9: A head-up display (HUD) superimposes information on the windscreen

A third example of cars using superimposition AR is the Nissan Leaf electric car. Nissan launched an app where the camera recognised a Nissan Leaf in a showroom and superimposed the image with animated 3D graphics showing the technology inside when the car was moving.

Superimposition is used a lot as a training aid in different industry sectors. For example, in engineering and manufacturing, superimposition can be used to show where damaged or missing components need to be placed. This can then be completed by inexperienced employees.

Figure 3.10: An engineer uses smart glasses and superimposition techniques to see where new parts should be installed

Industry training apps work in the same way, showing users things that they can't see about the objects directly in front of them.

Let's get digital!   2

Thinking about the types of AR, match the examples to one of the types in the table.

Marker led	A QR code outside a shop shows you where to find the department you need
Object recognition	A koi pond is projected onto your desk in front of you
Location based	Holding your camera up to a famous landmark shows you information about when it was constructed
Superimposition	Holding your camera up to a demolished landmark shows you what the missing sections looked like

User interaction and layers

The information we see and control on our electronic devices is known as the **User Interface (UI)**. UI design has become a fascinating study known as the **human computer interface (HCI)** (See page 143). Businesses are also really interested in designing applications with the best possible interfaces so that people keep using them. If you struggle when interacting with an app, you're unlikely to recommend it to a friend.

Augmented Reality has been a significant factor in UI design because it helps show us what we want to know based on what we're looking at. This makes applications much simpler to use and so people will feel confident using them.

Table 3.2: The UI used in AR can be either **static** or **interactive**

UI type	Description	Sectors that often use it
Static	The information on the screen is designed to be 'read only'. It is displayed as text, 2D images, 3D images, animations or sound. The user views or listens to it.	Architecture – showing plans Education – information in different locations Lifestyle – showing distance to hole on a golf course
Interactive	The information on the screen can be affected by the user. It can be text, 2D images, 3D images, animations or sound. The user may be able to control it with on-screen buttons or gestures. They may be able to influence what happens on screen through certain movements or actions.	Entertainment – AR games where the player controls characters Retail – trying on clothes virtually and changing the colours

This isn't a complete list of examples, but it gives you an idea that some sectors want the user to be able to control the augmented content. Others just want to show you useful information.

Layers

Layers are virtual overlays that go on top of images on a screen. They are used in image editing software to allow designers to position separate images individually. In AR the layers are positioned over what the camera sees. Information is then put on top of the layers.

You can have just one layer, but then you won't be able to have any images behind or in front of each other. If you wanted to use AR to make someone look like they were in space for a selfie, for example, you would use one black layer as the background and then maybe another layer for stars in front of it. A third layer could have planets in front of the stars.

Layers make a scene in AR look deeper than it really is. AR can't make images projected onto the camera image look very real. Layers allow the developers to position 2D and 3D images in a way that overlaps and makes them look more natural. For example, you could add a shadow layer underneath an image layer so that it looks like it is really there. Layers can also be used to make sure that menu options are always on the top so that users can't get lost within the app's menus.

1.3 Devices used with Augmented Reality (AR)

Types of devices that AR can be used on

We know what types of AR we can make and the different types of industry sectors that use them. But what can we use them with?

Mobile devices

Mobile devices such as smartphones, tablets and handheld games consoles have been the main platforms for AR since the beginning. A camera is essential for making AR work, so smartphones and handheld games consoles are ideal because they almost always have a built-in camera.

Smartphones can:

- Support marker led AR with their cameras

- Support location based AR with their **GPS** receivers

- Support superimposition with increasingly powerful processors.

The main advantage though, is that you always have your device with you when out and about. AR can help you explore the world and see more information.

Over to you!   3

Find three different smartphones available for sale and look up the technical specifications. Try to choose a budget model, a mid-range model and an expensive one.

Find out:

a   What kind of GPS they have.

b   What kind of cameras they have (front, back or both).

c   How powerful they are, and how much memory they have.

Smart devices

As AR has developed, new types of hardware have been created just for AR. There have been major developments in AR glasses. These glasses project images onto the lens directly in front of your eyes. This allows you to see all the same content that you would on your phone, but without having to look at a screen in your hand.

Smart mirrors are another type of smart device that can use AR. These are computer displays built into a mirrored surface which project extra information onto your reflection. As well as for fashion and entertainment these mirrors can be used for health benefits through fitness classes and body fat analysis.

Figure 3.11: Smart glasses can use all the different types of AR

Laptops/PCs

Laptops and desktop PCs are all capable of using AR as long as a camera is attached. It can be more restrictive if the camera cannot be moved, but any AR that uses a 'selfie camera' approach will work just as well. For example, a social media camera can generate masks or decorations on your face. Location based AR cannot be used on a desktop PC as it doesn't go anywhere. A laptop can be used if it has a GPS receiver.

A more interesting approach to AR is where it can potentially replace desktop computers. If a user has a pair of smart glasses that makes a computer screen float in front of their face, then they don't need a traditional computer. All their programs and documents can be accessed through the glasses.

Figure 3.12: AR mirrors use superimposition to project images onto your reflection and object recognition to identify what you're wearing

Case study

The Eye of Judgement

An earlier game created using AR was The Eye of Judgement. Released in 2007 for the PlayStation 3, this was an example of how a traditional board game could be brought to life on a TV games console with AR. In the game, the players used a classic board with card decks featuring different characters. In the middle of the board, on a stand, a PlayStation camera scanned the codes on whatever cards had been placed down and the characters on the cards would appear in animated 3D form on a nearby TV screen.

A review from gamers.temple.com said:

'As you play, the game projects the image of the playing surface onto the screen and it overlays this with animated images when actions take place. Whether you are playing against the AI or another player, the game acts as referee and rule monitor, keeping track of the current phase, informing you of when it is time to draw a card, and other similar things.'

Check your understanding

1   What are the benefits to players of mixing AR with a traditional board game?

2   What marker led features could you add to other traditional games?

3   How could you use **geolocation** or superimposition AR with a board game?

Review your learning

Test your knowledge

1 Why is a camera needed for an AR application?

2 What is the difference between marker led and markerless AR?

3 What is superimposition?

4 What system of satellites does Geolocation AR use?

5 Give an example of when layers might be used.

What have you learnt?

	See section
• What AR is.	1.1
• The purpose of AR.	1.1
• Different sectors that use AR.	1.1
• Different types of AR.	1.2
• What kind of devices use AR.	1.3

Designing an Augmented Reality (AR) model prototype

Let's get started

What is a **prototype**? Is it something unique to designing Augmented Reality applications or is it a term used whenever software is created?

Look at Figure 3.13 for a prototype urban transportation system. Why do you think it's important to test the **functionality** of this on a small scale before installing it in a large city?

Figure 3.13: A man testing a prototype transportation system

What will you learn?

- The purpose and user requirements of an **AR** application.
- Who the target audience is for an AR prototype.
- What content will be needed.
- What types of assets can be used.
- How the AR prototype's functionality will be triggered.
- How the user will interact with the AR prototype.
- What design tools are used to plan an AR prototype.

2.1 Planning and design considerations

In all software development it is important to know what the purpose and audience of your product is before you start developing it. Therefore, planning and designing your AR product must be done clearly and carefully. A manager of a development team will have a set deadline and budget to work with. If the planning is not completed properly then costs could rise, and deadlines could be missed.

The purpose and user requirements of an AR product

Every AR product needs to have a specific purpose. This is the driving force for the design and defines what it is going to do. In Figure 3.14 you can see a shopping app that helps customers check if a product will fit in their home. The purpose of this app means that the designers must consider the size of the products and scale them accurately to what the camera sees.

Figure 3.14: An Amazon shopping tool which lets customers visualise where a smart device could fit in their home

The designers can also plan for what the user requires the app to do.

User requirements for a shopping tool:

- Access the smartphone camera
- Allow user to choose a product
- Allow user to change products
- Prevent user from changing size of product.

The target audience for an AR product

The people who will use the product are as important a consideration as its purpose. Your target audience are the people who you intend to be the users of the AR application. If they are children, then you can't assume that they will have their own AR device. If they are elderly then you can't assume that they're going to know how to use an AR device. You must consider the needs of your audience as soon as you start planning, as your app might need different assets such as larger fonts and clearer images for people with visual impairments.

Let's get digital!   1

Think about your nearest corner shop or convenience store.

1   Come up with an idea for an AR smartphone app that they could offer to customers.

2   With you in mind as their target audience for this app, what considerations would they need to bear in mind?

Stretch

Your teacher will be in a demographic group of Over 21 year olds with an interest in IT and Education. What demographic groups are you part of? How would this affect the app's design?

Content

The next step in designing an AR product is to list the **content** that will be needed to create the product. AR products are created using many different assets. Assets are all the different elements that go into the application and they are usually grouped by their type. Assets can be images, sound or text.

The content of the product is the information that is unique to that product and the assets are the format of the content.

Designers must plan what content they need and then it will be clear what kinds of assets will best communicate this content to the user.

Assets

Audio

Audio assets are important to AR products because they can communicate a lot of information without cluttering up the screen. For example, if you are using an AR map navigation on your phone, an audio beep can make you look at your phone and see that there is a turning ahead. AR product designers know that audio notifications can bring their users' attention back to the screen when they might have stopped looking. When planning which audio assets are needed, the designers must think about who will be listening to these notifications and what sounds they would respond to.

Charts and graphs

We use **charts** and **graphs** to take complicated numerical information and display it in a user-friendly way. As most AR apps are on phones, designers are aware that they must plan their apps for small screens. Too much text and information will block the camera image and make the use of AR pointless. It will just look like a normal app without the real world and information blended together. Charts allow a lot of information to be shown in a small space.

Over to you!   1

1   Pick a building that you know well and either take a photo or make a drawing of it. It could be your home, school or a leisure centre.

2   Make a list of all the rooms and facilities inside it, and how many people use it. It could be four residents, three bedrooms, one kitchen, or it could be one swimming pool, two dance studios, four changing rooms, for example.

3   On your photo or drawing, add a graph that shows the information you have worked out.

Stretch

4   Create this digitally, making the graph in a **spreadsheet** and copying it across.

Hyperlink/Weblink

AR products are designed to help people find out more information about the world around them and hyperlinks and weblinks are a great way of doing this. A hyperlink is a link to a page or document that is stored within the app or online, and a weblink is a link to a specific website. Using these links, you can allow people to point their cameras at something and be given the opportunity to connect to a website that shows them as much information about the product as they need.

Consider an AR product that is intended to show people historical buildings. Only so much information can be shown on the screen without blocking the image of the building from the camera. Using links means that the user can find out information about the lives of the people that lived there using the internet. When designing AR, all the different websites must be checked to make sure that they are all still working and kept up to date. Usually, these websites will be managed by the same company that the AR product is being made for, otherwise there is a risk that a blank website would load.

Photograph(s) / image(s)

Some of the most important assets used in AR products are visual. We understand so much more from a photograph or drawing than we can from text or sound. An image can show us detail. It can help us understand complicated information or someone's character.

AR products use images in different ways. Photographs and drawings are 2D assets.

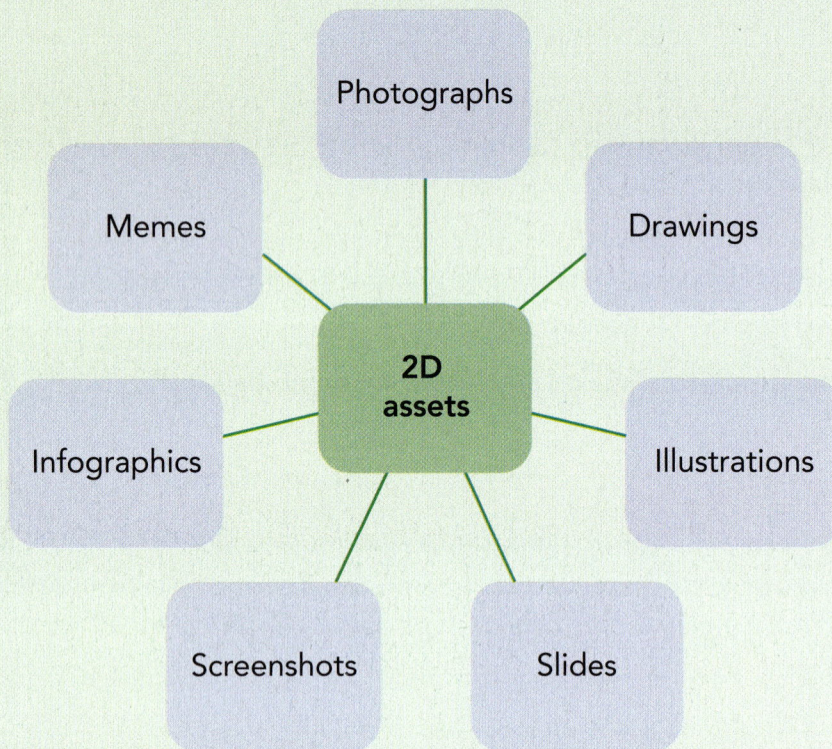

Figure 3.15: Different types of 2D assets that are used in AR products

Designers must be careful with the detail and sizes of the images that they use. If images are scaled down in size, then they will be easier to display on a device with a small screen such as a smartphone. Each device that uses the AR product will be able to choose the right size.

Text

Text is an important component of AR products as it is one of the easiest ways to communicate information. Designers tend to keep the amount of text they use to a minimum because it can be distracting for the user, especially on a small screen. Text is an incredibly useful asset though because modern devices can translate into different languages. This allows the AR product to be used all over the world.

Designers will have to consider the font, size and colour of the text they use. They should also consider that people have different reading abilities and the right fonts can be an important aid to making this easier. A font is a file that controls the text displayed.

FONT
ABCDEFGHIJKLMNOPQRSTUVWXYZ
0123456789 abcdefghijklmnopqrstuvwxyz

Figure 3.16: This text uses a font called Times New Roman

Video

The last type of asset that might be used in an AR product is video. Video files are large sequences of images that are compressed together and played as an animation. When planning an AR product that uses video, it is important to consider that film crews and video editors may be needed to get video content that doesn't already exist.

Quality of assets in an AR product

Issues can arise in terms of the quality of the assets used. AR products use a lot of a device's **processing power** because the images sent from the camera are constantly updating. The AR product then layers this with different assets and the position and size of these assets must be constantly changed and amended as the camera moves and updates.

This means that all the assets must be saved in files that aren't too large or detailed to slow down the AR product when it is running. Issues can arise like visual assets flickering or not being displayed properly.

All designers want their products to look professional and unique so that their audience enjoys using them. They must look good.

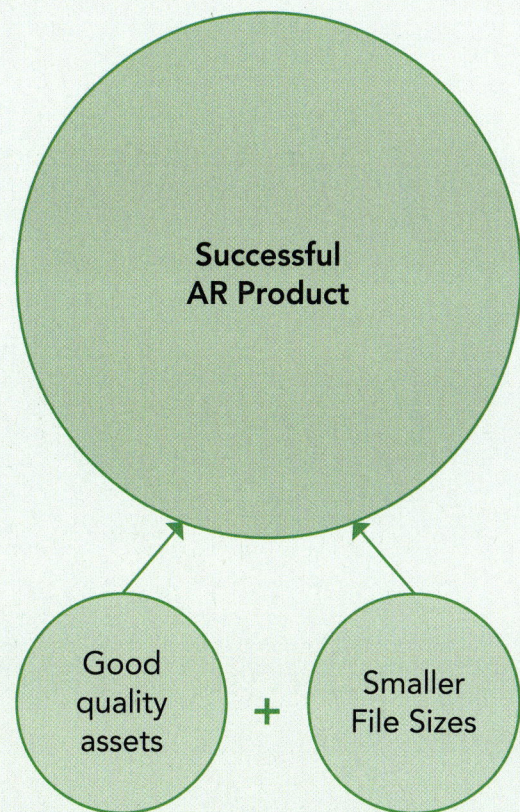

Figure 3.17: Successful AR products have good quality assets with small file sizes

Triggers

When designing an AR product, the purpose and audience will drive the functionality of the app. The user interacts with the functionality using **triggers** and planning these is the next step in the design stage. A trigger is an event that takes place while the application is running and AR products use a variety of different types, causing assets to appear or play. One of the strengths of AR products is how easy to understand they are for any user. AR products use a variety of different triggers that cause different assets to appear on the screen or play through the app.

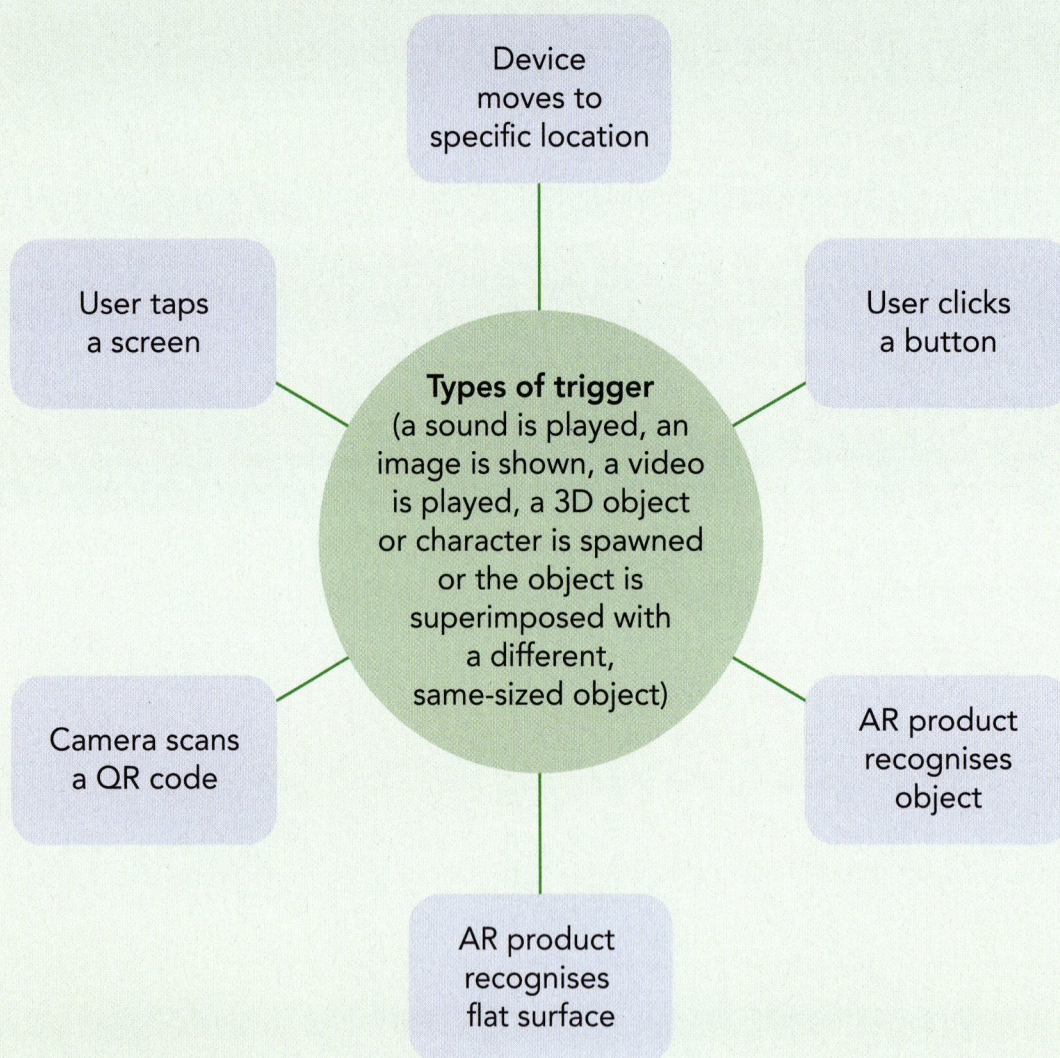

Figure 3.18: Types of triggers

Marker led triggers

These are the most straightforward AR assets to spawn as the trigger is very specific. When the camera recognises a QR code or a barcode it knows exactly which asset to spawn on screen. Fewer commercial AR products use marker led triggers because they rely on the users having copies of the code. However, where an AR product is fixed in place, such as in a kiosk, these triggers work really well.

Figure 3.19: AR markers can be images as well as codes

Object recognition

AR products that use object recognition have a bank of objects that they will be able to identify in the real world. The camera on the AR device will scan objects and translate their shapes into a series of points in 3D space. The points are then compared to the objects that the AR product has listed in its file system or **database**. If a match is found, then this is a trigger for the AR product to spawn one of its assets.

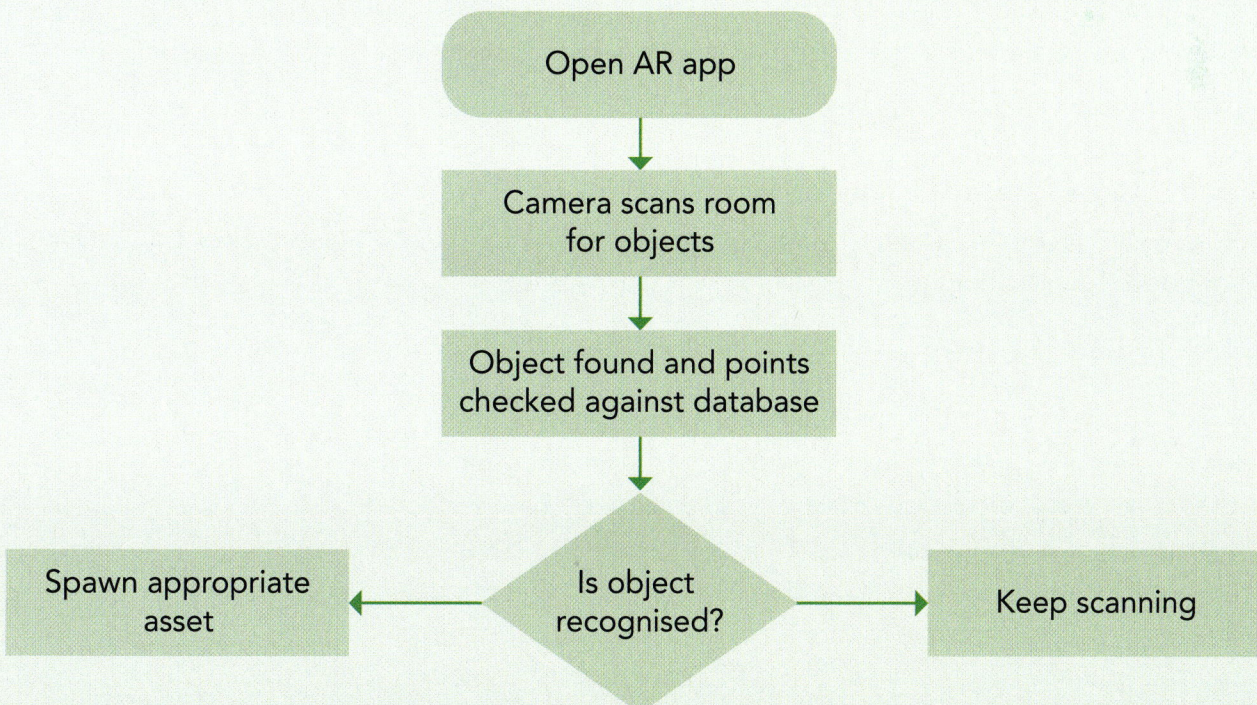

Figure 3.20: A flow chart showing how object recognition works

Markerless

AR products that don't use markers will trigger the different assets depending on how they are designed. The user interface (UI) will be more important in these situations because there will be no visible QR code that the camera can see. It will then be up to the product or the user as to how the assets will be used.

Over to you!   2

Search for the basic rules of the game of chess on the internet.

Imagine that you have been asked to create an AR chess product that is designed to be used on a smartphone.

The game will always involve the same pieces used in the same way, so it can use markerless AR.

Create a short presentation to sell your idea of an AR chess product. You can name it whatever you want and decide the following:

- What unique features would it have?

- What would it be called?

- How many people could play it?

- How would AR make it more fun than a normal chess game?

What assets would it use? Make a list of all the different assets that would be needed.

Next draw a plan which shows how the product might look on a smartphone screen. It doesn't have to be neat or to scale but think about where the different pieces would be spawned on the screen in relation to the real world.

Would it need a flat surface? How much space would be needed for the assets to spawn on?

Location (GPS) triggers

If a trigger in an AR product is led by the GPS location, it is a simple process to decide when the trigger should take place. An AR product that uses this approach will keep a constant track of the location of the device. The app will have a list of locations where certain assets need to be spawned. When the location of the user matches one of the locations in the app's list or database, the asset linked to that location is spawned. Pokémon Go is a great example of this. It has a list of which Pokémon can be found in different locations around the world. Within these locations, the position you are in is a trigger for the 3D Pokémon character to appear on screen.

Superimposition

Superimposition is a partial or entire replacement of an object that the AR product identifies. Making sure that the object to be recognised is fully understood is an important part in designing an AR product that uses superimposition to present information. If the product scans an environment and recognises objects incorrectly it might fail to superimpose information onto it or superimpose information wrongly.

Over to you!   3

Let's think about an AR product designed for a pair of smart glasses. The product is designed to recognise windmills in the landscape and superimpose animated 3D assets which show the inside mechanics of the windmill.

Figure 3.21: A 3D view of a windmill

The AR product uses the camera for object recognition. It compares the shapes found in the camera image to reference shapes it has stored.

On paper, draw the shapes you think the camera would need to recognise to superimpose information onto a windmill from the front, the side and the back. Use the internet to find more images of windmills from different angles.

Layers and user interaction

One of the final stages for the planning of an AR product is the design of the layers that can be used and how users will interact with them.

Users can interact with AR products in the same way they interact with normal software applications.

Table 3.3: User interaction methods

Device type	User interaction methods
Smartphone or tablet	Swipe, tap, double tap, multi-tap, voice control, pinch/spread
PC or laptop	Mouse click, mouse move, keyboard input
Smart glasses	Physical button press, hand gesture, voice control

Action flow

The designers will plan what the user will do, often thinking about the **action flow**. This is the steps taken to complete a specific action.

If we think about using a social media AR product that superimposes bunny ears onto the head of the user, the action flow may look as shown in Figure 3.22.

When considering the different layers required by the product, it's important to understand the difference between static and interactive layers.

Static

These layers are fixed and cannot move. They won't receive any input from the user and usually won't change during the use of the AR product. The images sent from the camera will be on a static layer. It's often the layer that the user won't interact with directly. It just displays the image that the camera can see at that time.

Other static layers could contain text or images that don't change during use of the product. This could be icons, logos or text.

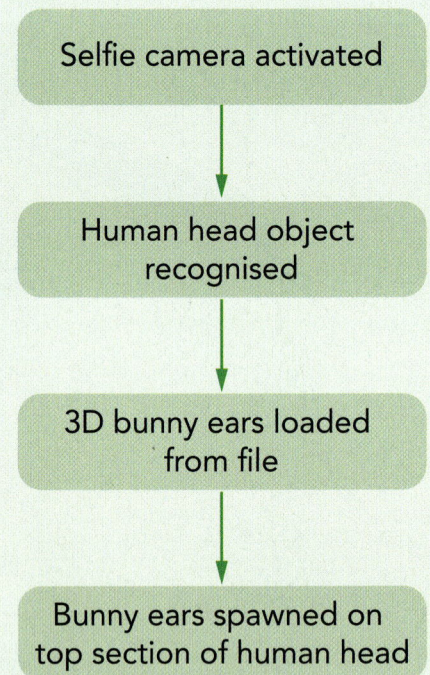

Selfie camera activated

↓

Human head object recognised

↓

3D bunny ears loaded from file

↓

Bunny ears spawned on top section of human head

Figure 3.22: An action flow showing a selfie camera AR product

Interactive

Whenever user input is received it will be through an interactive layer. Any input which is received through a click or a touch will be recognised by an element on an interactive layer. When planning interactive assets, the designers have to think about the users being able to see the interactive features but also make sure that these features don't block the rest of the AR product content.

Figure 3.23: An AR app with icons and text which would be displayed on a static layer. The distances would be updated depending on the position of the phone so they would be on a separate layer

2.2 Design tools

Tools used to design the content and action flow for an AR product

Like most software development, the creation of AR products is undertaken by teams of people rather than individuals. This means that the function of the product and what it should look like will need to be communicated to different people in the team at different times. The best way to do this is to use design tools that everyone understands.

Three areas of design are covered by these tools to ensure the AR product meets its purpose. They are:

- **Content Design** – the design of the information contained within the AR product
- **Action Design** – the design of how the AR product functions
- **House Style** – the choice of colour, fonts and image styles favoured by a company.

Flow charts

Flow charts are used to show the options that are available to users as they navigate a software application. They work in exactly the same way for AR.

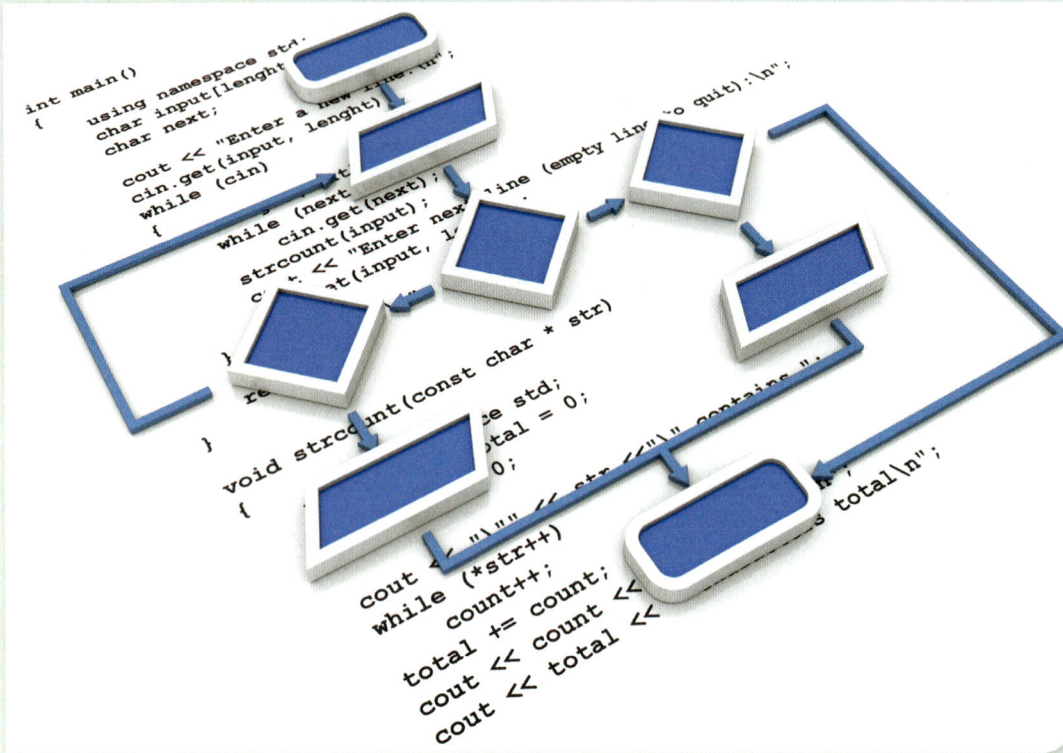

Figure 3.24: Flow charts can even be converted into programming code

A flow chart uses specific shapes to show which action the software is taking, depending on the user's actions. It's a really important design tool which lets all of the development team see how many options are available to the user and what the result of their actions will be. Being able to see a program's functionality helps the team make sure that the app will work correctly and avoid problems. Another useful feature of flow charts is that they allow the designers to plan which user interaction elements are needed.

Let's get digital!   2

1   Find out which shapes are used in flow charts. Looking back at Unit R050 IT in the digital world might be useful here.

2   Create a flow chart that shows how you spend your time and which choices you have depending on the day of the week.

Mind maps

Mind maps are diagrams that can be used to picture ideas and see the connections between things. When used for software design such as for an AR product they allow the designers to plan the hierarchy of assets. A hierarchy is an arrangement of items, ordered from top to bottom, and in software this can be used to show what assets the user sees and in what order. Mind maps are a simple way to show this hierarchy very effectively.

Figure 3.25: A mind map doesn't have to be neat and many people can contribute to it

Unlike flow charts, mind maps don't need to use specific shapes. They are informal diagrams that can be made using software, on paper or even with sticky notes. Mind maps can be made quickly and shared easily so they're very popular in development teams. They let people understand each other's ideas, and also the order in which assets for an AR product need to be created.

Over to you!   4

a   Make a mind map that shows all the features of your favourite social media platform. Looking back at Unit R050 IT in the digital world might be useful here.

b   Link the different features that connect to each other, such as messaging, posting images, comments, etc.

c   Then add a section of features that you would like to see added.

Mood boards

When creating a new software product, it is important that everyone in the development team understands the purpose of the product and its audience. This can be explained in meetings or documentation, but most people benefit from a visual input, so a **mood board** is a great design tool for showing everyone what kind of product is being made and who it is for.

A mood board is a collection of images, grouped together with something that links them. It could be images showing a set of colours, styles, types of people who might use your AR product or even places where it might be used. Sometimes a mood board will show similar apps, games or websites which have helped inspire the designers.

Once a team sees the mood board, they should have an instant understanding of what the designer is trying to achieve so that they make their individual content or assets fit with the overall style.

Figure 3.26: A mood board can include a mixture of drawings, photographs and textures to communicate a theme

Let's get digital!   3

1   Choose your favourite film, game, book or TV show.

2   Without using any images of that product, create a mood board to help others understand what it's all about.

3   Use photos, drawings, colours and textures.

4   See how many people can guess what your chosen product is.

Storyboards

Originally a design tool used by the film industry, a **storyboard** is a series of ordered drawings showing what people are doing and interacting with. In a film they show the crew what is taking place so that they can plan all the shots and positions. In an AR product they are used in a very similar way.

A software design storyboard shows the development team what the user is doing when they are using the product. This isn't always needed if it's traditional software for a PC, but when designing AR, you are combining the real world and the digital world and a storyboard can show this very clearly.

Figure 3.27: A storyboard uses different drawn scenes to show what the user is doing, with notes to add detail

Visualisation diagrams

We know that the content of an AR product is communicated through different types of assets. A **visualisation diagram** is a useful tool that shows the development team what the product will look like.
Think of it as a way of showing people screenshots of the product before it's been made so that they understand what it should look like.

These diagrams could be rough sketches or they could be made from a collage of images. They will have notes to show what different features or assets are. They will provide an idea of what the final product should look like. If you have ever designed a product then any planning diagrams you have made are visualisation diagrams.

Wireframes

The final type of design tool that we will use is a **wireframe**. These diagrams are like visualisation diagrams in that they show the user what the final product will look like. They are made using simple lines and are often only in black and white. The wireframe will show the developer the size and shape of different assets and elements without containing any detail as to what the content includes.

Wireframes allow the developers to accurately create the **layout** of the AR product when the designs have been approved. The developer will have the technical skills to put the assets where they need to be, but the designer might not. Wireframes can therefore be made using simple office software or specific wireframe tools.

Review your learning

Test your knowledge

1   Why is it important to understand the purpose of an AR product?

2   Why does the audience change the content that you would use?

3   What is a trigger?

4   Why do AR product designers need to consider what type of AR is being used?

5   Which types of design tools best match the different purposes? Match the numbers with their correct letters.

1	Flow chart	A	To plan the theme and style
2	Mind map	B	To plan the decisions the user makes
3	Mood board	C	To show what the app looks like
4	Storyboard	D	To show the size and location of the assets
5	Visualisation diagram	E	To show what the user is doing
6	Wireframe	F	To plan the order in which things happen

What have you learnt?

	See section
• What AR products have been designed to do and who for.	2.1
• The difference between content and assets.	2.1
• Six different types of assets.	2.1
• What triggers are.	2.1
• How layers can be used and how users interact with them.	2.1
• AR design tools.	2.2

Creating an Augmented Reality (AR) model prototype

Let's get started

Have you ever made an AR product?

Find a software development kit (SDK) that lets you create AR products such as Arloopa Studio and see if you can follow a simple tutorial. When you log into the dashboard for Arloopa, it provides four easy to follow videos.

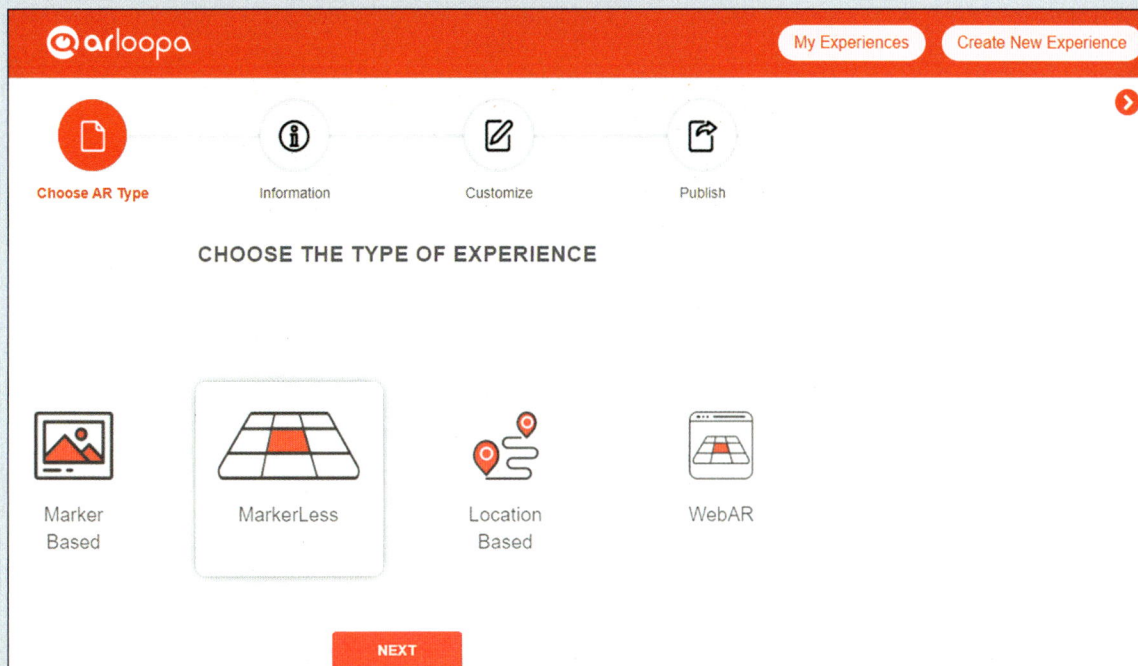

Figure 3.28: The Arloopa Studio online AR creator

What will you learn?

- The characteristics of a prototype.
- The characteristics of triggers.
- How triggers are selected based on the purpose of the product.
- When to use single and multiple layers.
- How to access layers.
- How information is output.

A prototype is a sample that shows off some of the features of the main AR product that is being designed. Augmented Reality works with a combination of software and real-world objects or locations. This means that lots of things have the potential to go wrong. Having a prototype of the main features makes development easier in the long term as problems can be solved in the prototype stage. AR products and prototypes are created using an Augmented Reality **software development kit** or **SDK**.

3.1 Augmented Reality (AR) model prototype

Characteristics

Partial product

It's important to remember that a prototype is not the full product. The team are at the beginning of their development process and creating a prototype allows them to check that their designs are realistic.

> **Over to you!   1**
>
> 1   Find out what the term 'Early Access' means and think about if you have ever used a software product that is in early access.
>
> 2   If you haven't, find one on a digital store (such as Google Play or Steam) and try it out.
>
> 3   What functionality is missing?
>
> 4   Can you figure out what the developers have prioritised?

Confirming functionality

The prototype must confirm the functionality that has been agreed in the design documentation. Sometimes all the functionalities would be created in the same prototype and sometimes a prototype will just focus on one individual function.

Imagine an AR product that was designed to show local points of interest and allow you to rate them. You could create a prototype which confirmed that the location based AR was able to find a list of local points of interest and load them on the screen. This functionality would be tested on a smartphone so that different locations could confirm that the code works as it should.

Someone else in the team could be creating a prototype to confirm that the user rating system worked and created a record in an online database. Once this functionality was confirmed, the two prototypes could be brought together to create the final product.

Confirming aesthetics

It's also important for the developers to check the product's **aesthetics**. What should it look like? What font should be used? How many different colours, logos or line styles should there be? These are all aesthetic choices that designers make to ensure that their product is stylish and fits what their audience would like. The designers look at their visualisation diagrams and wireframes to ensure that the developed product matches their original plans.

Real world data

The prototype needs to use real information and content that is accurate and appropriate, rather than pretend information that's made up for **testing** purposes. In **desktop publishing** and graphic design, sample text is used to check layout and aesthetics. In AR product development this isn't the best approach because the developers need to know exactly how much space the information is going to take up. Most AR works on phone screens that are very small and the wrong data

Figure 3.29: Some AR products must ensure that their information does not distract the viewer and cause dangerous situations

can clutter up the screen. Other AR products such as in-car HUDs and smart glasses must make sure that they are not reducing the users' vision and creating risks for their safety.

3.2 Triggers

Triggers provide the interactivity of the AR products. They are the reason information is displayed, 3D models spawned or sounds played. It's really important that the triggers are behaving exactly as they should otherwise the user's experience will be unsatisfactory and the product will not be well received. Imagine an AR game where there was a delay in how quickly your characters moved or an AR navigation app that didn't show you the next turning until you had passed it. The types of triggers required for the needs of the product will have been selected in the design stage.

It's important that triggers use as many graphical elements as possible so the user can see that something has happened. It's important to avoid repeating the same styles and shapes for different triggers so that each unique response is easily identified.

In the prototype stage of development, the triggers' exact behaviours and set ups are put into action. The types of trigger that are chosen depend on what the AR product needs to do and how it achieves this.

Trigger characteristics

Table 3.4: Characteristics triggers should have

Trigger characteristics	Effects of characteristic
Must be unique	Whatever causes the trigger must be unique otherwise it could happen too often. If you used geolocation and set the trigger to 'Planet Earth' then it would always be triggered. If you set it to your GPS location within 5 metres then it would be more useful.
Should not contain blurred images	If your prototype uses marker led AR then the camera needs to be able to recognise a marker. If you're using a QR code then it should have crisp lines and if it's an image marker then it should not be blurry otherwise the camera won't recognise it.
Should not contain too much text	Text can be scanned and read as a trigger. This is very useful for translating AR or retail AR. The text should be as simple as possible. The more text the camera needs to read, the slower the app will become.
Should not contain too much blank space	If there are large blank spaces in an image, a QR code or an object that should be recognised, then the camera might disregard it and not activate the trigger.

Figure 3.30: This AR marker has been designed for spawning a 'camera droid' game character

Object recognition triggers

One of the easiest triggers to design for is not necessarily the easiest trigger to develop. Object recognition AR needs to understand the size, colours and shape of very specific objects. This means that the object needs to have easily recognisable standard features for the camera to scan.

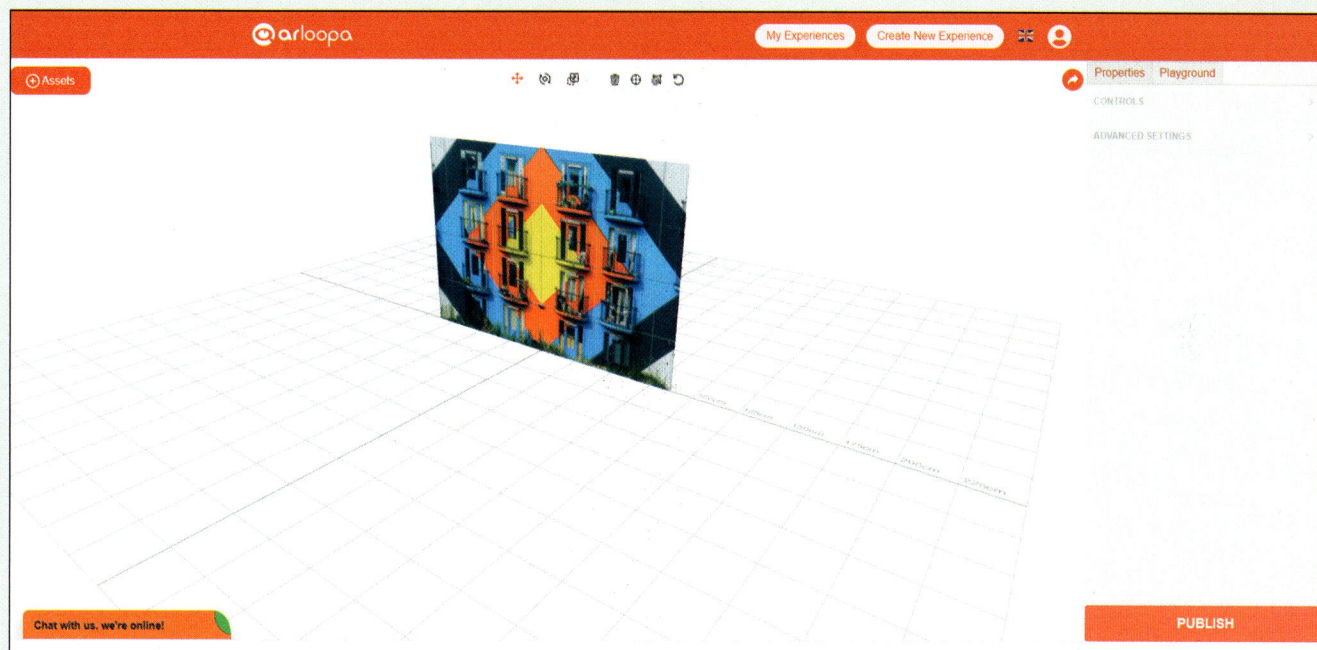

Figure 3.31: Arloopa is an AR studio that runs in a web browser for easy access to AR projects

One of the most common types of object recognition used in AR is face recognition. There are so many great examples of this on social media apps and because of their popularity, developers have become very good experts at creating products that can recognise a human head. Just try using one of these apps on your family pet, the camera knows the difference!

Marker led triggers

Another well-established trigger is the marker led approach to AR. Since this was the first way that AR was developed, marker led AR has become more sophisticated with time. Instead of simple barcodes, AR products are now able to recognise complex images as markers and use them to present information on the screen. Markers work well when used on tourist attractions, noticeboards or in shops. Less processing power is needed for marker led AR so it is very useful in creating AR websites.

1   Using a simple paint application, design a marker that could be used in your favourite place to eat. In Paint 3D on Windows create a new document.

Select 2D shapes from the top ribbon and create a design using the different shape tools. Change the fill colour, line type and thickness to make them unique.

Finish it off by using the Text tool to add the name of your chosen food location.

When you have made it go to the website: 'Ar.js marker training'.

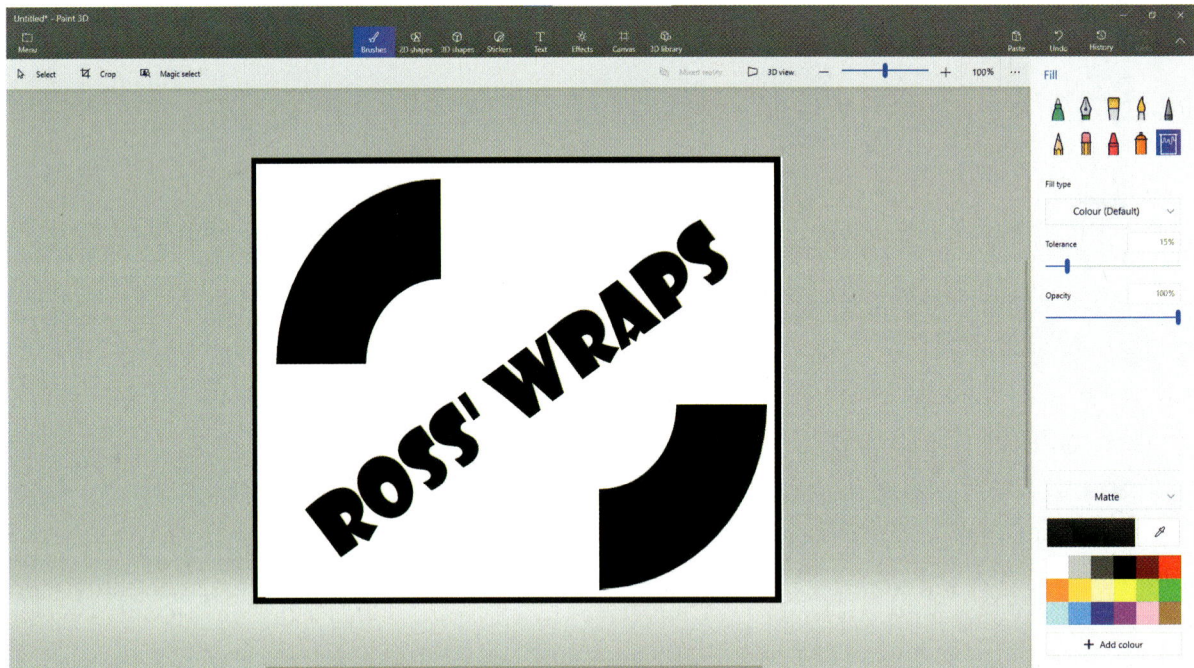

Figure 3.32: Creating a simple AR Marker in Paint 3D, a free image editor

2   Using this online tool for creating AR markers, upload your design and see how it looks.

Stretch

3   Test your marker in an AR SDK. Check that it works on an actual device.

Location based and markerless triggers

When a marker is not required for a product it requires a more specific user interaction to trigger an action. This could be a button press or voice command for AR products that spawn assets on flat surfaces.

Where the app uses location based triggers it is much easier to decide what information is triggered based on where the user is.

Superimposition

Creating a prototype that uses superimposition is more of a challenge to developers. To superimpose information over an object, the AR product must first recognise the object and then work out the exact position on which to spawn the asset. Every time that the AR device moves or the lighting changes, the AR product must respawn the asset to make sure that it's in the right place. It's because of this that superimposition works best on devices with more powerful processors or additional **memory**.

Over to you!   2

The oldest form of superimposition is paper characters with cut out clothes. Think about this in three dimensions. It's going to be a lot more complicated!

a   Choose a simple, curved, real world, object such as a pencil case, a clock or a computer mouse.

b   Using paper or acetate craft a 'superimposed' image of what is inside the object and place it on top. This simulates an asset used for superimposition.

c   Next, rotate and move the object to see if your asset still fits.

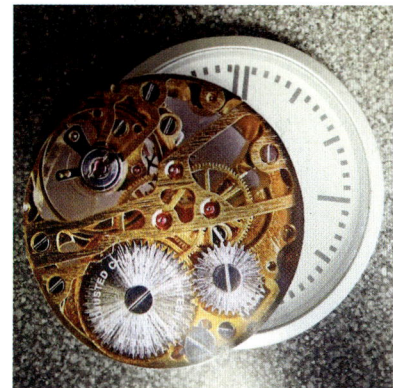

Figure 3.33: A superimposed image of inside a wrist watch overlayed onto the watch face

---

3.3 Layers and user interaction

The prototype that you create will need to demonstrate the same layers that are required in the final product. There might be no need to create aesthetic layers when checking the functionality of a product, but it is important to do so. This is because it will also check that the target device is able to run the product satisfactorily. Layers need to be kept simple. The more complicated the arrangement of the layers, the more likely the user could get confused and be unable to access the AR product's features.

Single and multiple layers

A very simple AR product might use a single layer that presents an image or some text on top of an image sent from the camera. As soon as more information is needed, we must start using multiple layers.

In fact, it would be impossible to have any kind of user interaction on a single layer because so much information is needed.

Once multiple layers are in use, they need to be organised with names indicating what they are used for. The layer groups should be merged where they contain similar assets that are displayed together.

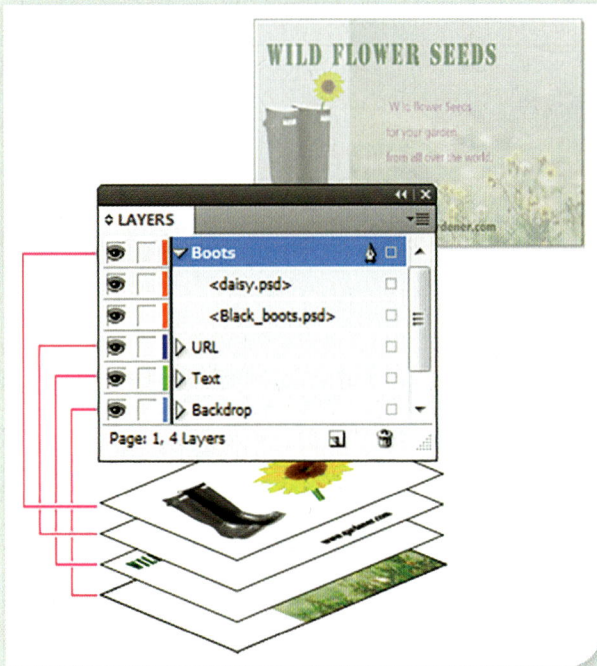

Figure 3.34: An example of layers being used to create a button asset which sits over the camera image. Here the software being used has the highest layer at the top of the list and the lowest at the bottom

Over to you!　　3

Layers are important when it comes to the user interface and ensuring a consistent design.

a Using an image editing program such as Photoshop, Paint.net, or similar, create a background shape, saving it as a PNG to maintain any transparency.

b Next, create a slightly larger, black or grey version of the same shape and save it as a PNG.

c Finally, make a third version of the original shape but remove any borders and change the fill to a gradient of the original colour going from full colour to clear.

d Put each of these image assets on top of each other in your AR SDK. The black/grey shadow image should be at the base, then the block colour shape, then the gradient.

Access to layers

Static

Static layers are interacted with directly by the user. They are displayed by the code in the product and they use less processing power because the user doesn't have any control over them.

Layers should be kept simple so that the AR product does not use too much processing power and so that they don't get confused. Layers are used in graphic design to make flat images seem more three dimensional. Where information is being presented over reality it is important to try to keep things as simple as possible.

Interactive

Whenever interaction is needed, multiple layers must be used. Layers will be grouped together, or merged, to ensure that the developer is able to activate them all at once. Interactive layers will need to be accessed via the code so it is important that they are named suitably to make it clear which layer is dealing with which asset.

Table 3.5: Examples of interactions used in AR products

Interaction	How it is used
Swipe	The user will move their fingers across a touchscreen to manipulate something in the scene. This is useful for rotating objects or dismissing assets.
Click/select/tap	The user will use a mouse, controller or their finger to click on an asset on the product.
Voice	The user will use a pre-determined command word to make something happen without having to touch anything.

In the Adobe Aero program screenshot in Figure 3.35, a single layer is being used to show three different animal models at the same time. Each of these 3D assets has its own trigger and action to provide interactivity for the user. The horse asset has a bounce action which makes the asset bounce several times when the user taps it.

The developer of the AR product is responsible for setting up the required layers and deciding how and when they use the triggers. For example, if you had a location based trigger which showed information as soon as you arrived at a particular location, it would be set to the topmost layer so that it got the user's attention immediately.

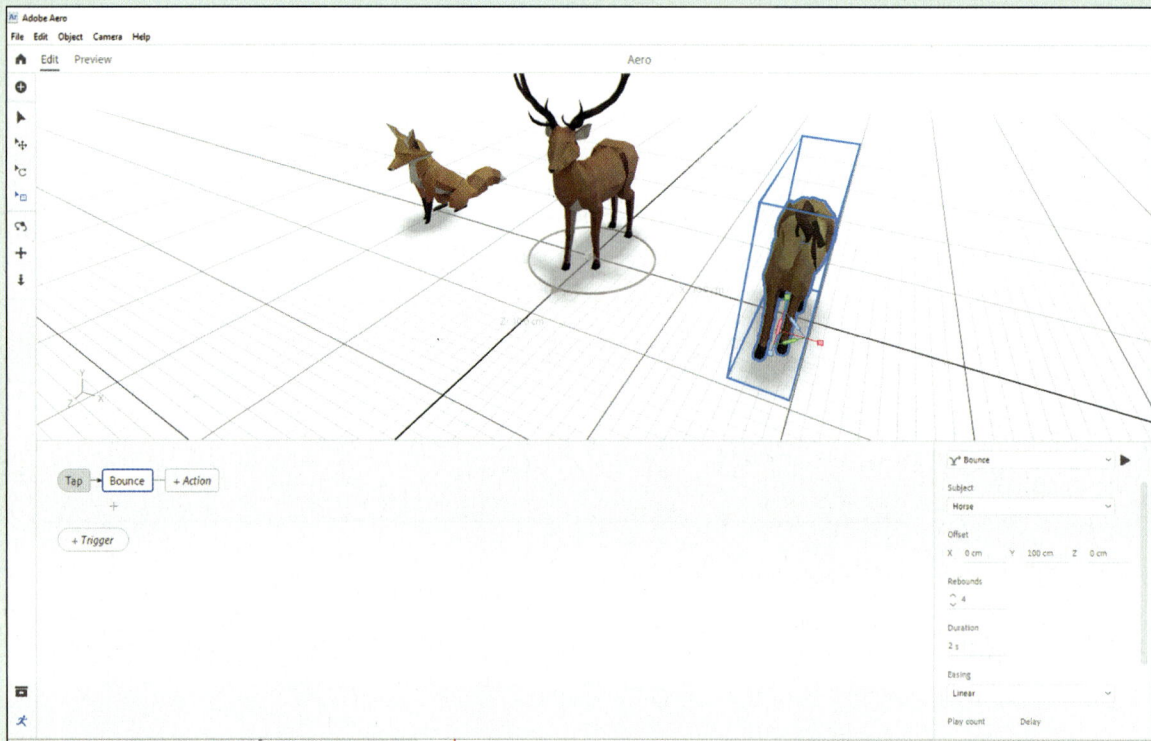

Figure 3.35: The Adobe Aero program lets users easily add interactions

3.4 Information output

The main purpose of an Augmented Reality product is to present useful information to the user in ways that add to the real world. When making a prototype, the information is output because of a trigger. It might be as simple as opening the app or it could be based on a specific object being in a specific place. Either way, the information that is output must be in the format required by the product.

Audio

As humans, we respond to audio constantly in our lives. We use our voices to communicate, and we listen to audio cues around us to receive information. Most software uses sound effects to communicate information. In video games, various sounds will let the player know if they have collected something useful or taken damage. AR can use audio in the same way to communicate with the user. Some products will use audio as an optional extra and others will be more reliant on it. However, it is important to remember that when designing AR products, not everybody is able to hear. So, if you are using audio, then you should always include the option to turn it off so that the product is not exclusively dependent on it.

Case study

Zombies Run

The fitness app, Zombies Run has been using audio based Augmented Reality since 2013. The technology is quite straightforward and only requires a smartphone with either a step counter or GPS receiver. Users will decide if they want to run for a set distance or a set time and during that run the story of a zombie apocalypse is played through their headphones.

Figure 3.36: Angry walking zombies

The idea behind the app is to make people want to run further and stay in shape by listening to an exciting story.

The game doesn't use location based AR or marker led AR but instead, it calculates how much of the story can be told based on the runner's pace. Any gaps are filled by letting the phone's normal music player continue in the background. Additional zombie chases can be included in runs to make them more exciting but also because changing the speeds at which we run has more health benefits.

Check your understanding

1　Why would AR help to motivate people to exercise?

2　How could this product be adapted to work with location based AR?

3　How could you enhance the functionality of the app to work for people with hearing impairments?

Charts and graphs

If an AR product is going to present numerical information in the form of a chart or graph, then the developer needs to decide if the information is going to be stored statically or dynamically. Static numbers won't change so the charts or graphs could be stored as image files. If the numbers change, then the app will need to be developed so it can create graphs that are different every time.

Hyperlinks and weblinks

The **World Wide Web** is a huge source of information that has been formatted so it can be displayed easily in web browsers. This means that if an AR product needs to access extra information, then instead of storing it within the app, it can be downloaded from the internet. AR products will often contain a button which will link to more information on a website. In the development stage, the programmers will have to check that they are using the exact web address to make sure that the links work. However, because they are connecting to an external source there is always a risk that the website could be taken down after the prototype has been made.

Let's get digital!   2

Think about a museum or historical attraction that you've visited.

1   Create a list of all the informative websites that would be useful to anyone wanting more information. The list should be saved as an image that can appear in AR.

2   Create a prototype AR product that uses location based AR to display the list of websites that you've gathered. For example, using Arloopa you would create a new experience, choose "location based" and then upload the image that displays the list of informative websites.

Stretch

3   Adapt your product so that the list appears as soon as you are close to the attraction.

Photographs and images

Using images in AR is one of the best ways to create useful content that the user will benefit from. 3D content is useful for showing users the shapes and scales of objects, but it requires larger image files and more technical experience for its creation. A 2D image is a relatively small file and can be quickly displayed on a screen. The added advantage is that it only has two dimensions so there are fewer issues with flickering or loading times.

Developers must make several considerations when using images:

- They must not be too high **resolution** or they will take too long to load

- They mustn't be too low resolution or they won't show enough detail

- They should include hidden captions for visually impaired users

- Whether they have **transparency** that might cause issues when used on top of a camera feed

- Whether the image width and height will be set manually in the code or whether the image size will be specific.

A final thought is that not all images are used as content. Images are used as backgrounds, buttons, sliders, and so forth. These images must be clear and consistent so that they make it clear to the user what their purpose is.

Text

Text might seem to be one of the more straightforward asset types that you will use in your AR prototype. It's easy to display text on a plain screen or menu system. However, when the text must float over the images from the camera, it becomes more challenging to make sure that the text is readable. Choosing the right font plays an important role and developers must assume that their users have a wide range of reading abilities. The most successful software products use icons and simple text instead of long sentences or paragraphs.

Text can be 2D or 3D. If you use the simpler 2D text then you still must decide if it is going to be laid over the camera images, text that is flat on the screen and facing the user, or if it is going to exist in the scene.

Over to you!   4

1 In the Arloopa Studio software, add a "new experience" and create a new project using marker led AR.

2 From the Add Asset menu, create a new Text Model.

3 Change the colours, font, curve segments and bevel offset values to see what happens.

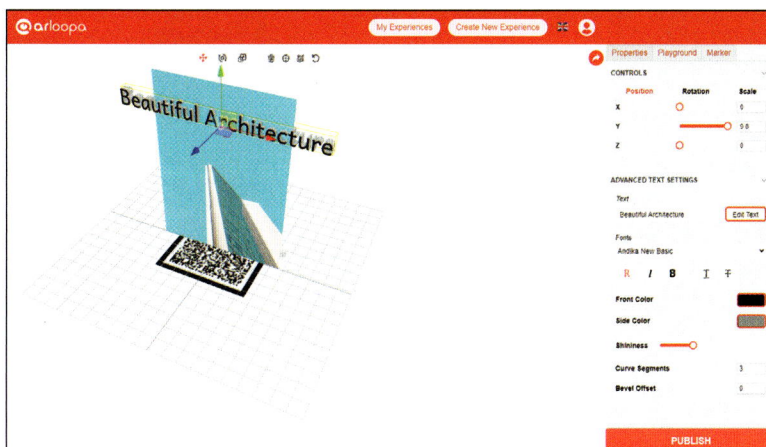

Figure 3.37: Text assets can have a variety of properties such as font, size and colour

Video

Video is a very useful asset for sharing information with users. A video can communicate very complex ideas through animations or recorded camera footage. Video files are always very large so video clips that are used must be very short. The developer must also decide whether the video will play automatically when it is spawned in the scene, or if the user will have access to playback controls. Many companies have video files that they use in advertising or training. It makes sense to use these assets in an AR product where the location can add even more understanding for users. Think about a training video that explains how part of a factory assembly line works. If it can be spawned on location through an AR product then the users will get a much better appreciation of how the machinery works.

Review your learning

Test your knowledge

1　What is the difference between a prototype and a full product?

2　What does the term aesthetics mean?

3　What does the developer need to consider when choosing a marker?

4　How is superimposition triggered?

5　Name three types of interaction.

6　Why is it useful to use charts in AR?

What have you learnt?

	See section
• The characteristics of a prototype.	3.1
• Trigger choice with the appropriate characteristics.	3.2
• Trigger choice based on the purpose of the product.	3.2
• When to use single and multiple layers.	3.3
• How to access layers.	3.3
• How to output information in different formats.	3.4

Testing and reviewing

Let's get started

Do you know what testing is? What happens if we release software that hasn't been tested? Can we learn from our mistakes?

What will you learn?

- How to carry out testing.

- How to create a test plan and record the results.

- How to review the effectiveness of the processes, tools and techniques that you've followed.

- How to reflect on your success and lessons that you have learnt.

4.1 Testing

You have created prototypes to make sure that the AR product you have designed works the way it should. To make sure that the prototype works as it was intended to, it must be tested.

How to carry out testing of an AR model prototype

When creating software, it is crucial to test all prototypes and the final products. If this doesn't take place, then there is a chance that there will be issues with the products and the users will not be able to use them properly. Poorly tested software gains a lot more attention than software that is error free. Nobody wants to spend money on something that is broken.

Testing is often broken up into two categories: **technical testing** and **user testing**.

Technical testing

Technical testing is the testing that takes place as the prototype is being developed. Depending on the size of the development team it can be undertaken by the developers themselves or by software testers.

This stage of testing requires an understanding of the code that has been used to create the prototype. The testers will check all the functionality of the prototype and make sure that it works. The testers will check that the prototype works with:

- Normal input – the expected clicks, swipes, and so on, that the prototype has been designed for

- **Erroneous** input – incorrect inputs that should receive an error message. The test here is whether the user can crash the prototype. Anything that the user does wrong should be handled by the product with a clear error message and a chance to try again

- Extreme input – testing the product by pushing it as much as possible. This could involve using fast button clicks or long text for user input.

Let's get digital!   1

Trying to break something can be a fun way to test an app!

1   Download an AR product onto a smartphone or tablet.

2   See if you can find any software bugs.

User testing

It's important for programmers and testing specialists to go through all the prototype's functionality. However, they might not be able to produce all the issues that normal users would. This is where user testing is crucial. The development team will find normal users who form part of the product's audience. If a medical AR product is being developed then it makes sense for medically trained staff to test it before it's released. They will be able to find issues and problems specific to their industry sector; issues that the development team might have overlooked.

User testing normally takes place after the technical testing and in a supervised environment. User testers might be asked to sign a contract to agree that they won't reveal what they have been asked to test. This makes sure that if an AR product is being developed, rival companies won't find out about it until it is released.

Over to you!   1

Test your AR prototypes on the people you live with.

Make notes about:

a   Anything they struggled with.

b   Any features you had to explain.

c   If they managed to break the product!

Using a test plan

Testing is a very detailed process. It's important to make sure that all the code is tested and no aspect of the prototype's functionality is missed. To ensure this, a test plan is created. A test plan is a simple table with set headings. Each test should be performed quickly but there might be many different tests and the plan can run to many pages.

Table 3.6: Headings used in a test plan

Heading examples	Description
Test number	A way to log all the tests that need to be undertaken in a sensible order
What is being tested	A description of the type of functionality that is being tested
Expected result	What the developer thinks should happen
Actual result	What the tester observes happening
Remedial action	What action needs to be taken to fix it

Table 3.7: An example of a test plan for a simple marker led AR prototype

Test #	What is being tested	Expected result	Actual result	Remedial action
1	Marker identified	Camera correctly identifies marker	Marker is not identified	Ensure correct marker image loaded in code

The remedial action will be completed after the test plan has been used. The developers will look at the issues and create a fix. A new version of the code is then released and it will be tested again. This cycle should keep happening until the prototype is free of errors. However, deadlines and budgets mean that prototypes can sometimes be released to the public when the testing hasn't finished.

4.2 Reviewing the process of creating the Augmented Reality (AR) model prototype

Testing isn't the final stage of the development process. Once the prototype is completed then it is important for the team to review its success. There are several important approaches to this.

Ways to review the effectiveness of the processes followed

The development team will have selected the most appropriate design processes to follow at the start of the project. However, the prototype could draw attention to flaws or issues in the design that might need revisiting.

Think about an AR prototype game. The designers might have wanted to create a multiplayer battle game but then found after the prototype was made that there were too many buttons on the screen. Had they created a wireframe for the game then this would have been clear sooner. It's important for the team to look back at the processes they used to understand where they might need to review the approaches used. This is why creating prototypes is useful. If the development had continued through to the full product without taking any time to reflect on the success of the designs, it would result in a product with more issues and less time to fix them.

Another issue that could arise at the review stage is how well the designs were followed.

Over to you!   2

Pair up with someone who is studying this unit.

You will both create a set of design documents for one of the following client briefs. This could include a wireframe, moodboards or even a flow chart.

Brief 1 – Portal posters

A new marketing company is specialising in Augmented Reality posters. Using marker led AR they offer a service to customers which includes poster designs that contain AR markers. The markers can be scanned in AR and will reveal more information about the poster contents. They would like you to create a sample AR poster for a product or an event of your choosing.

Continued

Brief 2 – Magic maps

A new publishing company is specialising in Augmented Reality maps. Using marker led AR they offer a service to customers which includes creating maps for towns, parks or festivals that contain AR markers. The markers can be scanned in AR and will reveal more information about the map contents. They would like you to create a sample AR map for a place of your choosing.

You should pick one of these briefs and your partner should pick the other.

1   Create the design documentation for your chosen brief.

2   Once your designs are complete, swap them with your partner.

3   Create the AR prototype that your partner has designed.

4   Present your prototype to your partner.

5   Compare and discuss how well the prototypes matched the designs.

Ways to review the effectiveness of the tools and techniques used

As we have explored, there are many different tools and techniques that can be used to create AR products and prototypes. These must be reviewed to ensure that the correct ones have been used.

The development team need to ensure that the SDk that they selected was appropriate and that it allowed for the development of the features that the user needs.

Some of the issues identified when looking at the effectiveness of the tools used could have expensive consequences. If your prototype has been developed for a popular development platform like Android Smartphones, then switching the target device to a Microsoft Hololens 2 would mean a lot of new development tools had to be purchased. Changing the SDK might be a cheaper decision as all the assets could be reused.

Measuring the success of an AR model prototype

Augmented Reality is designed to improve upon the real world. It should present information in a way that helps or entertains users in a specific situation. When a team reviews the success of a prototype, the purpose of the prototype should be one of the first things they consider.

The development team might not have access to the same audience information as the designers and as a result might not fully understand the purpose of the prototype. It is crucial then that the whole team reviews the prototype to ensure that it has been made with the original purpose in mind.

The user and their needs must be at the forefront of the experience. AR products are often quite short experiences that address a specific need. AR used in industry however might be used for extended periods and the developers must take this into consideration and ensure that the products are well designed and deemed to be truly useful by the user.

Lessons learnt

For a development team to be successful they need to make a record of lessons that have been learnt throughout the prototype development process. Software developers often work together in studios, for larger companies or individually. Every project that they work on will give them some insight into how the next project could go better. The software industry is subject to so much change and evolution that nobody is ever an expert in one area for long. New platforms and sectors soon come along and replace it. Self-reflection is an important skill for a software developer to have.

The Augmented Reality industry is very young when compared to other parts of the IT industry. Due to this there are no clear 'right or wrong' ways to make an AR product. Everyone needs to be conscious of things that have gone well or poorly in their previous projects.

Bluetooth technology, there is generally no interference from other devices and it has a low power consumption.)

Bot: This is a piece of software that does a specific task. (Context: A botnet is a group of internet-connected devices that are running a bot.)

Button: An object on the screen you can click on to do something. (Context: Clickable buttons that make the spreadsheet features work are a useful part of the user interface.)

Cell reference: A grid reference way of referring to one square of a spreadsheet using the column letter followed by the row number. (Context: At the design stage calculations do not need to include actual spreadsheet cell references.)

Charts: A visual way to display data in a spreadsheet. (Context: Charts can be every effective in summarising large amounts of information.)

Chat room: A place on the internet where people can talk, often in real time, on a specific topic. For example, there are chat rooms available to discuss popular soap operas or films. (Context: They met in the chat room to discuss their favourite TV shows.)

Client requirements: The client requirements are the original description of the problem or functional need that the solution was designed to resolve. (Context: A description of what the person or organisation paying for the solution development (the client) actually wants the final product to do, in other words the required features of the product.)

Closed questions: Questions that have a limited number of options to choose from. (Context: The interviewer asked closed questions.)

Content: The information contained in an AR product. (Context: The next step in designing an AR product is to list the content that will be needed to create the product.)

Cyber-security: The combination of policies, procedures and technology to keep our devices secure. (Context: Cyber-security is the combination of using policies, procedures and technology to keep our devices secure from internal and external threats to data and information.)

Data: Raw, unprocessed facts and figures. (Context: In its basic form, data is just facts and figures that have no meaning or links.)

Data entry messages: These are text labels on a spreadsheet which indicate to the user what data they are expected to enter. (Context: Data entry messages should be included on the wireframe design.)

Data sanitisation: This masks data as a user enters it. (Context: Some systems add extra *s when a password is entered as data sanitisation.)

Database: Software that helps data that has been collected to be stored in an organised way. (Context: A database is an organised collection of data that is easy to search and sort.)

Decrypt: A method used to unscramble secret information. (Context: If you try to decrypt the files without paying the ransom you risk losing them.)

Desktop publishing/DTP: Desktop publishing software is useful when designing digital communications. (Context: DTP is beneficial in its adaptability for your audience, as it is simple to change a publication, based on their needs.)

Distribution channel: The method whereby the communication is delivered to the intended audience. (Context: Leaflets were the most effective distribution channel for the takeaway.)

Embedded system: A computer system that is built into a bigger system for a specific purpose. (Context: An embedded system is not usually programmable and so cannot be easily updated.)

Encrypt: A method used to make information secret. (Context: A unique piece of malware that encrypts all the files on a device.)

Erroneous: Data that can be entered into a product, knowing that it should be rejected. (Context: This is data that is specfically incorrect.)

Extreme data: Data that is on the boundary of being invalid. (Context: The maximum value allowed was entered as an example of extreme data.)

Filtering: Filtering removes the results in the data that do not match certain criteria. (Context: Click on the drop-down arrow of the column you are filtering by and select the values you want to see.)

Firewall: Software that helps protect a computer from attackers. It does this by controlling what data can and cannot pass through it. (Context: To prevent a DoS attack, a firewall can be used to prevent large amounts of traffic.)

Flow chart: A logical, step-by-step diagram that shows the different actions in the order in which they happen. (Context: A flow chart is a visual illustration that shows the order of something taking place.)

Formatting: Changes you can make to the visual appearance of an object such as a cell, row, column, worksheet, chart or table. (Context: Design decisions about how a document looks, for example underlining titles or putting key terms in bold.)

Formula(e): A formula uses functions and/or arithmetic operators to perform a task in a spreadsheet cell. (Context: When you copy this type of formula, you don't want the cell reference of the fixed value to change.)

Forum: A webpage used to discuss a particular topic. (Context: The topic being discussed in the forum was ICT.)

Function: A function is used within a spreadsheet formula to carry out a mathematical task. (Context: There are also a wide range of spreadsheet functions that carry out more complex mathematical tasks.)

Functionality: A term used to describe what software does. (Context: Why do you think it's important to test the functionality of this on a small scale before installing it in a large city?)

Geolocation: This is the same as Location based AR and refers to the identification of the geographic location of a user or AR device. (Context: Pokemon Go uses your device's geolocation to show you spawn locations.)

Global Positioning System: A system of satellites in orbit and computer chips that can communicate with the satellites to find locations. (Context: Smartphones are often able to access the Global Positioning System: a series of satellites in orbit which let you find your position on Earth.)

GPS: This stands for Global Positioning System. (Context: Other features also include a digital camera, typically with video capability, and GPS.)

GPS coordinates: Location specific measurements that are understood by the GPS system. (Context: It does this using GPS coordinates that can measure your location to within five metres.)

Graphs: A graphical representation of numerical data that shows its mathematical relationship. (Context: Charts, graphs and tables are known as the outputs from data.)

Hacking: Where an individual looks for the weakness in a computer system and tries to exploit it. (Context: Whilst hacking in general is illegal as it breaches the Computer Misuse Act, there are different types.)

HCI/Human Computer Interface: The different ways in which people interact with computers. (Context: A Human Computer Interface (HCI) is about how a person uses or interacts with a computer in order to exchange information and instructions.)

Hotspot: This is a small mobile device that allows you to access the internet when you are out and about. (Context: You can also use your smartphone as a hotspot.)

House style: Formatting that is consistently applied across all of the documents used by an organisation. (Context: You might need to think of using a company or organisation house style across all parts of the spreadsheet solution.)

Identity theft: This is when someone uses your identity without your knowledge, usually to create debt. (Context: The user was a victim of identity theft.)

Infographic: This is a collection of images, charts and minimal text that gives an easy to view understanding of a topic. (Context: Not all infographics are easily accessible to their intended audience.)

Information: Data that has been given meaning and structure. (Context: The relationship between information and data is that information has been given meaning.)

Inputs: Values that are fed into a process. These can be manual inputs by the user or could be data that is drawn from other places such as tables of information. (In some cases this could even be data drawn from other files.) (Context: This is what is entered into a system.)

Interactive UI: Elements of the UI that respond to the user-like buttons, menus, taps, and the like. (Context: The UI used in AR can be either static or interactive.)

Internet: This is an ever-growing network of devices that are connected using standard protocols (communication rules). (Context: The IoE uses the internet to share data between devices, such as requesting a light to be switched on.)

Internet of Everything: Using people, processes, data and the Internet of Things together. (Context: The Internet of Everything builds on the Internet of Things to use people, processes and data to make everyone's lives better.)

Internet of Things: A collection of devices that are connected globally, sharing data. (Context: The Internet of Things is a general term that refers to devices being connected to the internet and therefore sharing data.)

Interviewee: The person who is answering the questions during an interview. (Context: The interviewer asked the interviewee if they had any questions.)

Interviewer: The person who asks the questions during an interview. (Context: An interviewer can adapt their questions to the answers or ask further questions to clarify responses.)

Invalid data: Data that can be entered into a product, knowing that it should be rejected. (Context: The users were asked to enter invalid data during testing.)

Keylogger: An example of spyware that keeps track of every key that is pressed on a device. (Context: An example of spyware is a keylogger.)

Layers: Virtual overlays placed on a screen to position image elements separately. (Context: Layers are virtual overlays that go on top of images on a screen.)

Layout: Where items are placed on the screen or on paper. (Context: There are several things to consider about the layout of the interface.)

LCD: Stands for Liquid Crystal Display. (Context: Display screens commonly found with HCIs can be light and thin. They are usually either LED or LCD.)

LED: Stands for Light Emitting Diode. (Context: Display screens commonly found with HCIs can be light and thin. They are usually either LED or LCD.)

Live-streamed: This is a live event that is shown on the internet. Common examples include sporting events or music events. (Context: Location can be limiting unless a presentation is recorded or live-streamed.)

Location based AR: An AR process that loads images, sounds and text based on where you are in the world. (Context: Location based AR is sometimes known as 'markerless'.)

Macro: These are used to automate actions you might carry out with a spreadsheet and therefore can be used to create a user-friendly solution. (Context: They need to be attached to a macro to work.)

Malware: Software that has been designed to cause a security risk on a device or computer network. (Context: There is a wide variety of malware that can be used, each with its own purpose.)

Marker led AR: A process in which scanning an image or a code triggers some AR assets. (Context: An early example of marker led AR was the AR Games package that came with the Nintendo 3DS handheld.)

Markerless AR: A process where an image or code is not needed to trigger AR assets. (Context: Location based AR is sometimes known as 'markerless'.)

Memory: A computer stores information in its memory. (Context: The number of tasks an HCI needs to perform will determine the memory and processing power it needs.)

Mind map: A visual way of organising information, focusing on the relationship between the different elements. (Context: A mind map is a way of visually organising information that also shows the different relationships between the elements.)

Mood board: A collage of images that can be used to show the style of an AR product. (Context: A mood board is a great design tool for showing everyone what kind of product is being made and who it is for.)

Named range: A series of adjacent cells that are grouped together and given a collective name rather than being referred to with their row numbers and column letters. (Context: A spreadsheet cell range which is given a name to make its use within formulas easier, so for example if you name the range of cells B2:B24 'sales' you can use this name in a formulas such as =SUM(sales) rather than =SUM(B2:B24).)

Navigation: How you move around a website or the internet through the use of links. (Context: A wireframe focuses on the structure of the product, such as layout and navigation rather than any other design features.)

Object recognition: An AR process that scans an object with a camera, recognises what it is and displays additional information about it. (Context: AR apps that use object recognition will also detect planes.)

Open questions: Questions where the person can answer in as much detail as they wish; there are no restrictions or limits. (Context: The interviewer finished by asking an open question.)

Open source: Software where anyone can modify and distribute the code. (Context: This is because the OS is open source.)

Operating system: The software that controls the computer and its basic functions. (Context: Different interfaces (ways to interact with software) are provided by the operating system.)

Outputs: A digital document that is produced by a software program. (Context: Designing outputs for the solution such as charts and reports.)

Parenthesis: Brackets can be used to control the order in which calculations are done; anything in parenthesis is done first. (Context: Brackets are sometimes called parentheses (this is the plural of parenthesis) and can be used to modify calculations.)

Peripheral device: This is an item that can be attached to a device and receives data from it. Key examples include a printer, scanner and speakers. (Context: You can connect a range of peripheral devices, including adding additional displays.)

Phishing: Contacting a user on behalf of a legitimate business or organisation using a fake email or website. (Context: Phishing is using a copy of a website that looks real.)

Pivot table: A way to group and display data in a spreadsheet by criteria. (Context: Pivot tables allow you to rearrange data in a way that can make it easier to understand.)

Plane: A flat two-dimensional shape with four corners. (Context: AR apps that use object recognition will also detect planes.)

Podcast: These are digital audio files that are available to be downloaded or streamed; they usually focus on a topic that is discussed by the narrator. (Context: Podcasts are an effective method of communication as they are easily copied.)

Portable: A characteristic of an item that shows that it can be easily moved or carried. (Context: It enables wider choice and quick, portable access to content.)

Pretexting: This is where someone tries to convince someone to give them information or access to a service or system by pretending they need to confirm the individual's identity. (Context: Always check who you are speaking to in case they are attempting pretexting.)

Processing power: The ability of a computer to process information. (Context: The number of tasks an HCI needs to perform will determine the memory and processing power it needs.)

Prototype: A sample version of a software product that tests features. (Context: A man testing a prototype transportation system.)

QR Code: A QR, or quick response, code, is a pattern that can be read by a machine. It usually contains information about the item it is attached to but with AR it contains information about the asset that needs to be projected. (Context: When the camera recognises a QR code or a barcode it knows exactly which asset to spawn on screen.)

Quid pro quo: This is used by individuals to call random numbers pretending to offer help, usually IT support. (Context: Quid pro quo means something for something.)

Range: A group of cells referenced by a starting cell then a colon and then a finishing cell. Ranges can be given names. (Context: COUNTIF counts the number of times a test is passed within a range.)

Range check: Where input values are checked to ensure they are between two chosen values (the chosen values are the upper and lower limits in the range). (Context: This is where you are checking that the data fits within a specified range e.g. is the date between 1st Jan 2023 and 30th June 2023.)

Ranking questions: Questions where the person is asked to put a list of items in order of preference. (Context: The interviewer asked some ranking questions.)

Ransomware: Encrypts the files on a device and only lets a user into them once they have paid the ransom. (Context: Hackers have been using ransomware as their main way to gain money.)

Relational operators: These are the symbols that are used in solutions for making decisions and they include: = (is equal to), < (is less than), > (is greater than), <= (is less than or equal to), >= (is greater than or equal to), <> (is not equal to). (Context: these are comparison operators used in a spreadsheet formula such as > (greater than), < (less than) and >= (greater than or equal to).)

Relative referencing: Cell references in a formula that change relative to where the formula is copied. (Context: This is called relative referencing (as the cell reference changes relative to where it is copied).)

Resolution: How many pixels are used in an image. The higher the resolution, the more detailed the image can be. (Context: They must not be too high resolution or they will take too long to load.)

Router: This is what accepts the data from an internet provider and sends it to any connected device. (Context: A device can access the internet without the need for a Wi-Fi router.)

Scan (using the camera): Where software is programmed to read images captured by a camera to identify particular things. (Context: The user places a card on a flat surface and the camera scans it.)

Scareware: This builds on the user's worry about malware and convinces them to download or buy malicious software. (Context: Never download software from an unknown source in case it is scareware.)

SDK: A software development kit is an application that lets you create, code and design software, usually for a specific platform or type of software. (Context: AR products and prototypes are created using an augmented reality software development kit or SDK.)

Sectors: Different areas of industry and business defined by their primary customer or product type. (Context: The different types of industry sectors.)

Sensor: A device that detects something measurable, for example, speed. (Context: Many of the HCIs we use when keeping fit are touchscreens or use sensors to track our progress.)

Shoulder surfing: Shoulder surfing is a type of social engineering that involves an individual looking over your shoulder as you are using a device in public. (Context: Always cover your PIN at a cash machine to prevent shoulder surfing.)

Smart TV: Like a smartphone, a smart TV has a connection to the internet which gives access to additional services when compared to a traditional TV. (Context: They downloaded the episodes on their smart TV.)

Smartboard: An internet connected whiteboard, commonly used in the classroom. (Context: A smartboard has plenty of features that enhance a presentation.)

Smartphone: A smartphone has an instant connection to the internet, often through a mobile browser. (Context: To keep a smartphone simple, it has a touchscreen and a software-based on-screen keyboard.)

Social engineering: The art of manipulating people to reveal confidential information. (Context: Social engineering can take many forms, and usually looks very innocent.)

Spawn: When an asset appears on the screen and can be seen by the user. (Context: Markers or triggers in an AR product are what cause additional assets to be spawned.)

Spreadsheet: This is a collection of cells used to organise and manipulate data. (Context: An IT professional will often create the spreadsheet solution to meet the requirements of a user.)

Spyware: Software that is used to monitor what the user does on a device. (Context: The downloaded software contained spyware.)

Static UI: Information displayed for the user that cannot be interacted with. (Context: The UI used in AR can be either static or interactive.)

Storyboard: A series of drawings showing what people do and in what order. (Context: Originally a design tool used by the film industry, a storyboard is a series of ordered drawings showing what people are doing and interacting with.)

Superimposed: An image placed on top of another image. (Context: Superimposition is the process of placing one image on top of another.)

Tablet: This kind of device is often seen as a happy medium between having a smartphone and having a laptop, and as such it shares similar features. (Context: A tablet will have a larger touchscreen than a smartphone.)

Technical testing: Where a product is tested to ensure it works without errors. (Context: Technical testing also has some disadvantages.)

Testing: A formal, planned process that ensures that software is free of issues. (Context: Information that's made up for testing purposes.)

Transparency: When parts of a picture are see-through. (Context: Do they have transparency, which would cause issues when used on top of a camera feed?)

Trigger: An event that occurs in an AR product that causes something to happen. (Context: The user interacts with the functionality using triggers and planning these is the next step in the design stage.)

Trojan Horse: A piece of software that looks normal but infects the device so that it can be controlled by another device. (Context: A Trojan Horse is hidden within a piece of useful software.)

UI/User interface: The elements of a computer application that humans interact with, like buttons and menus. (Context: The information we see and control on our electronic devices is known as the User Interface (UI).)

Usability testing: This is the process of testing the solution with users, testing how long it takes to complete tasks and how easy the solution is to use. (Context: testing that is completed on the user interface of a solution to ensure it is easy to use.)

User testing: Where a product is tested from the point of view of the user. (Context: User testing focuses on the quality of the product more than technical errors.)

Valid data: Data that can be entered into a product and is accepted. (Context: The test checks if the data is valid data.)

Validation: Checking that data being entered is sensible and reasonable. (Context: All validation does is return an error if the data entered fails the check.)

Verification: Checking that the data being entered matches the original data. (Context: Verification does not check that the data is correct.)

Virus: A simple computer program that attaches itself to another program with the aim of using the device's reserves as well as changing or destroying files. (Context: The virus can easily spread to other devices.)

Visualisation diagram: A rough drawing or diagram of what a finished product might look like. (Context: A visualisation diagram is a rough drawing or diagram of what a finished product might look like. It helps plan the visual layout.)

VoIP (Voice-over Internet Protocol): This is a set of rules that makes it possible to use the internet for telephone or video conferencing. (Context: The meeting was over VoIP.)

Wired: A wired connection allows internet access directly from an access point to a device via an ethernet cable. (Context: In using a wired connection, the data is transferred much more quickly than using a wireless connection, and without any interference.)

Wireframe: A plan for what something will look like and how the elements will work together. (Context: When planning a website, a wireframe will show the style of the page as well as the planned interactivity.)

Word processing: This is software used to create digital communications. Whilst similar to DTP in that it has a range of templates that you can use, you are more limited in how you can arrange your information. (Context: Word processing is of benefit when you need more control over the format, such as typographical details.)

World Wide Web: A collection of webpages and other documents that are connected together. (Context: My website pages are part of the World Wide Web.)

Worm: A simple program that self-replicates with the aim of using the device's reserves as well as changing or destroying files. (Context: A worm can do all sorts of damage to a device.)

Index